577

E. Ken Borthwick

£2.40.

D1356966

The Leaping Hare

books by George Ewart Evans

★

WHERE BEARDS WAG ALL:
The Relevance of the Oral Tradition

THE PATTERN UNDER THE PLOUGH:
Aspects of the Folk-Life of East Anglia

ASK THE FELLOWS WHO CUT THE HAY

THE HORSE IN THE FURROW

THE FARM AND THE VILLAGE

(edited by)
WELSH SHORT STORIES

★

books by David Thomson
published by Barrie & Rockliff
THE PEOPLE OF THE SEA:
A Journey in Search of the Seal Legend

DANIEL

BREAK IN THE SUN

(for children)
published by Penguin Books
DANNY FOX
DANNY FOX MEETS A STRANGER

The Leaping Hare

by
GEORGE EWART EVANS
and
DAVID THOMSON

FABER AND FABER LIMITED
3 Queen Square, London

First published in 1972
by Faber and Faber Limited
3 Queen Square London WC1
Printed in Great Britain by
Latimer Trend & Co Ltd Plymouth
All rights reserved

ISBN 0 571 09559 3

© 1972, George Ewart Evans
and David Thomson

Contents

Acknowledgements   *page* 11

1. WHY THE HARE?   13
2. NATURAL HISTORY: ANCIENT AND MODERN   18
3. THE MOUNTAIN HARE   33
4. THE IRISH HARE   41
5. THE COMMON HARE   50
6. HUNTING THE HARE   59
7. ANCIENT WAYS OF TAKING THE HARE   80
8. THE HARE AS FOOD   91
9. THE HARE IN MYTHOLOGY   103
10. THE HARE AND THE MOON   111
11. THE HARE AND FIRE   121
12. THE HARE: A SYMBOL OF INCREASE   127
13. THE HARE AS WITCH   142
14. THE HARE AS TRICKSTER   178
15. THE NAMES OF THE HARE   200
16. OTHER BELIEFS AND CUSTOMS   213
17. AND NOW GOOD DAY TO YOU, SIR HARE   237
  Appendix One   242
  Appendix Two   248
  Glossary to the Poems   253
  Index   255

Illustrations

PLATES

1. The Irish Hare: summer and winter pelage   *facing page*   48
2. The Mountain Hare: winter and summer pelage   48
3. The Common Hare   49
4. Two hares; a late eighteenth-century design by William Blake   49
5. Return from the hunt (detail) Egypt. New Kingdom. About 1500 B.C. (*British Museum*)   64
6. Hare hunt, Ancient Greece. From a phial, showing four hounds chasing a hare which flees towards a net and a crouching hunter (*British Museum*)   64
7. Hare and Hound. The handle of a Roman knife   64
8. From the Metz Pontifical: The Frightened Hare, The Mother Hare and the Tailor, Hares Investing a Castle and The Hare as a Soldier   65
9. Japanese myth of the giant boy dancing with his companions; the hare, the monkey, and the bear. Woodcut by K. Hokusai (1760–1849)   112
10. The Moon Palace showing the Hare of the Moon with three children. Detail from a Japanese woodcut by Totoya Hokkei (1780–1850)   113
11. Hieroglyphs from the coffin of Djedhoriufankh, Thebes, twenty-first dynasty (*British Museum*)   128
12. Hare depicted on a bell crater, Ancient Greece (*British Museum*)   129
13. A cupid catching a hare, from an Ancient Greek vase (*British Museum*)   176
14. Tail side of florin with cross, 1921 and a Scottish silver groat of David II, son of Robert the Bruce   176

Illustrations

15. Luxuria. Drawing by Pisanello, now in the Albertina, Vienna *facing page* 177

16. Hare with watermark beneath it. Hieroglyph from an inner coffin, Middle Kingdom (about 2000 B.C.) (*British Museum*) 192

17. A cupid with a hare seated on his left hand, from an Ancient Greek vase (*British Museum*) 192

18. The Holy Family with three hares. Woodcut by Albrecht Dürer (1471–1528) 193

19. Hare and frog wrestling and hare thrown by frog. From the twelfth-century scrolls of frolicking animals, Kozanji, Kyoto 224

20. Hare-headed divinity of Ancient Egypt. From the coffin of Bakenmut, divine father of Amum. Thebes, twenty-first dynasty (*British Museum*) 225

21. Graffito from Lacock Abbey, Wiltshire 240

22. Graffito from Cathedral and Abbey Church of St. Alban 240

23. The stag of the cabbages, the cropper of herbage (from Hoffman's *Atlas*, 'The Common Hare') 241

24. Tracks of Scottish mountain hares in the snow 241

TEXT FIGURES

1. Wall engraving of a hare at Le Gabillou *page* 59

2. Magdalanian mobile engraving on stone from Isturitz 104

3. The Idol of the Moon 119

4. The hieroglyph depicting a hare with a ripple of water below means 'to exist' 127

5. Lapp Shaman's drumhead with 150 symbols 151

6. The Great Hare brought down from a god to a trickster 181

7. From the copybook of a Suffolk schoolboy: 'Master William Aldous, *Eius Liber*, A.D. 1805' 219

8. The Tinners' Rabbits as they appear on Widecombe church roof 225

Acknowledgements

Most of the people who helped us to compile this book are mentioned in the text. But there are many whose exact words are not quoted and who gave a lot of their time and care in answering our questions and in giving us advice. Of these we wish especially to thank: Dr. Mary Douglas, Department of Anthropology, University of London; Ives Goddard, visiting lecturer in Linguistics, Harvard University; H. G. Lloyd, without whose many letters the chapters on natural history could not have been written; Walter Flesher, naturalist, broadcaster and gamekeeper; Professor J. H. Delargy, former Director, Seán Ó Súilleabháin, Archivist, J. G. Delaney, and Dr. Tom Wall, Librarian, of the Irish Folklore Department, University College, Dublin; Dr. Iorwerth C. Peate, former Curator of the Welsh Folk Museum, St. Fagans, Cardiff, and his staff, especially Robin Gwyndaf Jones, and Lynn Davies; Fergus O' Gorman, Forestry and Wildlife Service, Department of Lands, Dublin; Professor Tomás de Bhaldraithe, University College, Dublin; Dr. Jonathan Miller; Professor A. S. C. Ross; Dr. P. J. Ucko, Department of Anthropology, University of London; Dr. Andrée Rosenfeld, Department of Prehistory of Roman Britain, British Museum; Dr. C. F. Voegelin, International Journal of American Linguistics, Indiana University; L. S. V. Venables, naturalist and author; and K. C. Walton, Bangor, and D. A. White, Cardiff, both of the Nature Conservancy in Wales.

We also wish to thank the following publishers and authors for giving us permission to quote: Hortors, Johannesburg, *Bantu Heritage*, by H. P. Junod; Charles Peirson Lyman, Curator in Mammology, Museum of Comparative Zoology, Cambridge,

Acknowledgements

Mass., for a quotation from *Control of Coat Color in the Varying Hare*; Macmillan, *The Life of a South African Tribe*, by H. A. Junod; Oliver and Boyd, *A History of British Mammals*, G. E. H. Barrett-Hamilton; The Board of Foreign Missions of the United Presbyterian Church of N.A., and Dietrich Reimer (Ernst Vohsen), Berlin, *The Shilluk People*, by Diedrych Westerman; Faber and Faber, *The Lady of the Hare* by John Layard; Merthyr Tudful Press, *Hanes Plwyf Llanwynno*, by Glanffrwd, English translation, *The History of Llanwynno*, by Thomas Evans; and the Royal Anthropological Institute, the Editor of *Man* and Miss M. M. Howard. We are also grateful to Dr. D. Aubrey Thomas, Douglas Miller, Lionel Reynolds, Helen Hackman, Elizabeth Harland, Gwen Yorath, Tony Martin, Geoffrey Weaver and Charles Priestley for providing and suggesting additional material.

In respect of the illustrations we acknowledge the following sources: Plates 1, 2, and 3 from drawings by Archibald Thorburn in *Mammals of Great Britain and Ireland*, by J. G. Millais, London, 1906; Plate 4, the City of Birmingham Museum and Art Gallery; Plates 5 and 16, photographs by Peter Clayton; Plates 8, 9, 10 and 18 are included by permission of the Trustees of the Fitzwilliam Museum, Cambridge; Plates 11 and 20, photographs by C. M. Dixon; Plate 15, photograph Giraudon, Paris; Plate 24, photograph by Alex Tewnion; Plates 7, 21, and 22 are from Mrs. V. Pritchard's *English Medieval Graffiti* (Cambridge University Press) which she and her publishers kindly allowed us to use.

Finally, we wish to thank our publishers and their staff, especially Elizabeth Gordon and Michael Wright, for the care and attention they have given to the book at all stages of its production.

1
Why the Hare?

Why study the hare? The brief answer is that we agree with a Suffolk gamekeeper[1] who said: 'We don't know the hare because we haven't observed it enough.' He said this in spite of his having handled thousands of hares himself and of being familiar with them over a period of forty years as a keeper, an occupation which his family had followed for at least three generations before him. No creature in the British countryside is the focus of so many different points of view as the hare; and it is probable that no other creature has raised so many unanswered questions or differing attempts at answers.

Why at some periods of the year, notably the spring, is the countryside—in East Anglia, for instance—teeming with hares while at other periods, for long weeks at a stretch, there is not a hare to be seen? Where do the hares go? Do they all take cover in woods? A hare squatting on its form, or immobile in the stubble, is as nearly indistinguishable from its background as it is possible to be. Yet why on occasions is it so reckless and so forgetful of itself and all its marvellous equipment for making itself part of the field or the hedgerow? The hare is traditionally timid, but is it as fearful as story suggests? Is it really timid? If so, how do we square this fear with the obvious delight it takes in collecting in huge colonies on aerodromes? A hare is a curious creature: like a child it wants to know what is going on. Is it the force of this curiosity that enables it to overcome its natural fear? How do we explain its apparent madness in leaping out on to the road in front of a motor car, and running for a quarter of a mile or so on the

[1] Archibald Tebble, head gamekeeper to the Helmingham Estate, Suffolk.

crown of the road, then turning suddenly to dart off as if it were playing some dangerous childish game like 'last across the road'? What are the hares up to when they collect together and squat in groups during the mating season? Why do they box with one another? Why indulge in the curious drumming with their paws on the ground? Some animals that are forced to feed in a hurry regurgitate their food and chew it again later. But the hare does not do this: it eats its evacuated food and digests it once more. Is there a specific reason for this? And why has there been a traditional doubt about the sex of the hare, and disagreement about much of the doe's behaviour while she is giving birth and during her rearing of the young?

In an attempt to get satisfactory answers for these questions, and for many more, we have gone to the countryman in many parts of the British Isles: to gamekeepers, farmers, farm-workers, poachers; and also to natural historians, zoologists and scientists. We have collated their answers, and suggested some reasons why long-standing disagreements about various aspects of the hare's behaviour have arisen. But in the present book we have also—and chiefly—posed questions other than those which grow directly out of the hare's unusual and fascinating habits and behaviour. Anyone who reads the literature about the hare or listens to the countryman's stories is bound to be struck by a further question, perhaps the most interesting of all: why is it that the hare has such a place in myth and story all over the world?[1] We don't propose to attempt an answer to this, here at the beginning of the book, but at least we can indicate the range of reference to the hare in world myths.

The hare was built into early Chinese mythology. In China they referred not to 'the man in the moon' but 'the hare in the Moon'; and the hare was a resurrection symbol, the creature that was translated to the moon where it pounded the herb of immortality. In India, too, the hare figured in a similar legend, and also as a sacrificial animal that willingly offered itself to be burnt in order to provide food for a Brahman. In Ancient Egypt the hare was used

---

[1] In an attempt to answer this question we have relied a great deal on John Layard's outstanding study, *The Lady of the Hare*, London, 1944.

as a hieroglyph for the word denoting existence; and it was also an important creature in both Greek and Roman mythology. Among the North American Indians the Great Hare of the Algonquins had many of the attributes of its Old World counterparts. In Europe there are widespread remnants of a cult of a hare-goddess. Even if we had no direct evidence of this, we could justifiably infer that the hare was once worshipped, had *numen*, chiefly because of its association with witches. For it is the usual pattern, once a later and stronger religion has become dominant, for the deities of the former cult to be demoted to lay figures, to giants or devils and their adherents to lesser devils or *witches*; and eventually for those figures to be de-mythologized completely and to become harmless characters in traditional stories or the games of children. There are numerous examples of this pattern in the *Mabinogi*, the early Welsh tales, especially in the *Four Branches* the most ancient cycle in the collection. Further examples are Magog, the Earth Goddess and her follower, Gog (Helioth or Baal)[1] becoming Gog Magog; Flora,[2] the classical goddess becoming the May-queen in the may-pole and May-day games; and various pre-Christian ritual figures becoming Hob, Robin Hood, Puck and the Bogeyman.

But a reading of the literature of the hare also brings up another question: why is it that the hare figures in so many divergent cultures in particular myths—for example, those linking the hare with fire or the Moon—that recur with remarkable identity of form in each culture? It may well be that the explanation is a commonplace one. The hare is simply one of that phalanx of creatures like the horse, the cow, the ox, the cat, the seal, and the wren, that have either been domesticated by man or associated with him in the long process of his evolution. This being so, it is natural that man, just as with other creatures, has tended to anthropomorphize the hare and to project on to it some of the qualities he is dimly aware of in himself.

Yet even if there were nothing more to the myths than this, an

[1] T. C. Lethbridge, *Folk-Lore*, December 1956; and *The Buried Gods; Gog and Magog*.
[2] Joseph Strutt, *The Sports and Pastimes of the People of England*, London, 1833, p. 351.

examination of those relating to the hare might well be worthwhile, if only for the light they might throw on the origin and
structure of those myths that are linked with the other animals
mentioned. But before starting on our inquiry we are putting forward the hypothesis that there is much more involved than this.
The hare is an archetype: that is, as the name implies, it is one of
the original nuclei or formation-patterns of awareness that primitive man used as a tool of communication to come to terms with
his environment and also with the 'internal' environment of his
own instincts and feelings. But in his long evolution since palaeolithic times these early patterns have been long overlaid by his
more recent 'civilized' experiences, just as a man's childhood experiences are buried beneath the happenings of his adult life. And
just as a man's childhood memories have been relegated to his
personal unconscious (though still there and available through
chance association or sudden flashes of insight) so do these deep
racial memories still inhere in the collective unconscious that is
common to man everywhere. We believe that only along the lines
of such a hypothesis as Jung has put forward can the apparently
spontaneous occurrence of similar myths about the hare in the
world's major cultures be readily explained. The fact that the hare
still emerges in its most primitive mythological role in the dreams
of people of the present day adds further weight to this theory.

There is, however, another aspect of myth that concerns us today. In the past, man defined his relation to animals largely
through the kind of myth just mentioned. These myths or stories
were not believed because they were *realistically* true (there is a
strong reason for thinking that the primitive was not as naïve as
this) but because they were a true or poetic definition of man's relation to the animals; of how he stood as opposed to them, obviously
separate from them, independent yet grossly dependent on them
for his own survival. Through the myth, man could both define
his feelings towards certain animals and (before the dawning of
his consciousness of himself as an individual) at the same time
project on to them many of his own barely apprehended feelings
which the animal's behaviour might symbolize or represent.

Today, however, most of the soul and meaning has gone out

of myth. Few people except children get anything out of the old myths: they have outlived their day, lost their pressure, have been de-fused by a scornful reason. At present, for instance, our relations to animals are logical and direct which often means in effect either a cloying sentimentality or an abysmal cruelty. The old role of the animals was to link man, through the collective myth of dream, to a larger 'unseen' environment, to be the mediators between him and his gods. But this mediating role has now been diminished to their sporadic and often unrecognized appearance in individual dreams—unrecognized because man is no longer instinctively equipped to know an archetype when he is confronted with one, or to apprehend the truth that the animals bear a little of man's essence, whether he likes it or not; and that he, with them, is part of the larger 'animal' which includes all living creatures and is life itself. It is likely that man will have consciously to define his relation to the animals as the primitive did, both instinctively and ritually, rather than continue to accept the passive role of a kind of working, neutral proximity. The present world problem of animal conservation could be said to show that such a new definition is needed.

But before we examine the difficult territory of myths about the hare, and before we attempt to understand their origins, we propose to restate as much as we can of the behaviour of the hare in the wild state. By doing this, we hope to decide how far the myths have grown out of man's long familiarity with the hare's natural habits and his apparent strangeness. Can, for instance, the hare's usual behaviour or one of his attributes give a clue to a particular myth? For this reason we have concentrated in the earlier part of the book on the natural history of the hare as far as it is known in Britain.

2

Natural History:
Ancient and Modern

Part of Rachel Levy's thesis in *The Gate of Horn* is that the basic themes of myth originated in the mind of palaeolithic man. There are two main sources of evidence—the mythology of peoples who are still living in a stone age fashion, and the evidence of cave paintings and carvings. In cave art small mammals are rare. In mythology they are plentiful. But man must have known the hare in most parts of the world from his beginning. In Europe hares had existed for about a million years before him, and at least in the legends concerning the moon they appear in the most ancient mythology of all.

Lepus terraerubra and a few other species which have not been named lived near the end of the Villafranchian epoch—which lasted from about three to one million years ago. The two species which now inhabit Europe are first found perhaps in the middle pleistocene, and were certainly plentiful from the beginning of the late pleistocene epoch, about 100,000 years ago. In England, bones almost identical with the modern hare are found in the same strata as animals which have long since died out. Hares flourished during the interglacial climatic phase known as F-Eem, together with hyena, hippopotamus and steppe rhinoceros, and they were numerous during the 4-Wurm at the time of the mammoth and woolly rhinoceros, whose remains are found, for example, in the Tornewton cave in Devonshire beside traces of human occupation.[1]

The order *Lagomorpha* is unusually small. It has only two families, the *Ochotonids* (pikas) and the *Leporids* (rabbits and hares).

[1] Björn Kurten, *Pleistocene Mammals of Europe*, London, 1968.

There are only fourteen species of pikas and fifty-two of rabbits and hares, which shows that since prehistoric times the Lago-morphs have almost stood still in development. The three families of rodents, by contrast, have evolved between them nearly two thousand species. There are 1,183 kinds of rats and mice alone.[1]

In temperate zones, at least, rats are easily distinguished from mice by size. But the hare and the rabbit are mistaken for each other all over the world. The parts they play in fact and fiction are mixed up.

Brer Rabbit was a hare, as Frost's illustrations to Uncle Remus show. The hare in the moon is sometimes called a rabbit by trans-lators from Chinese. And in natural history the same confusion exists, especially in America where the common name for several kinds of hare is rabbit. If you look up Leporidae in Walker's *Mammals of the World*[2] you will find an article headed 'Hares (also erroneously called "Rabbits")' and among the hares described in it are the Snowshoe Rabbit, the White-Tailed Jack Rabbit, the Black-Tailed Jack Rabbit and the Gaillard Jack Rabbit.

The differences between hares and rabbits are greater than out-ward appearances suggest. 'The two basic anatomical features distinguishing hares from rabbits are whether or not certain bones are fused in the base of the skull and whether the posterior naries (opening of nasal passages at the back of the palate) is broad or narrow.'[3] These features are described with illustrations in many modern works.

But apropos popular belief, which is the main concern of this book, two other features both scientifically acknowledged are more interesting. The first is that the hare's heart is very much larger than the rabbit's in proportion to the weight of the body. 'A hare's heart is very large, weighing from 1 to 1·8% of the total body weight of the animal. In rabbits the heart weighs only about 0·3% of the body weight and in squirrels about 0·6% of the body weight. The volume of blood in a hare is also relatively greater than in rabbits or squirrels. The size of the heart and volume of

[1] Desmond Morris, *The Mammals*, London, 1965.
[2] Ernest C. Walker, *Mammals of the World*, Baltimore, 1964, Vol. 2, p. 657.
[3] H. G. Lloyd, personal communication.

blood, together with long hind legs and powerful loins account for the exceptional speed and powers of endurance of the hare.'[1]

The other distinction is very well known but seldom subject to examination. It is the hare's split lip. A rabbit's lip is split up to the nostrils, but there is a membrane near the top which joins the two sides and covers the gums. A hare's lip is almost completely split and is without this membrane. In old age the two sides of the lip become parted and the teeth protrude.

In Great Britain and Ireland there are only three kinds of hare, the brown or common hare, the blue or mountain hare, and the Irish hare, and no confusion of names exists. But in the open at a distance it is possible to mistake any of these three for a rabbit, especially if the one you are watching lies still. It is usual at a distance to judge by the length of the ears. The brown hare, most common in England, has much longer ears than the rabbit but the mountain hare's ears are not much longer and both species vary in colour. The brown is usually a soft fawn, like the rabbit, but individuals vary, as foxes do, from reddish, sandy, greyish to almost black. Piebald brown hares are sometimes seen and even white ones.

Charles Welling, a Norfolk gamekeeper, believes that, apart from such oddities, variations in colour are due to environment. 'It's the district or the place wherein the different places have different coloured coats. Here [in east Norfolk], you'd get a dark sandy colour. Thetford way, that's light, you'd get a light coat, depends on the district and the woods and heather and ling so that they are hard to distinguish at a distance. The only time you'll notice a difference is when the leveret turns into hare. The leveret is smooth—dark—silky. When they get to a hare, they're more coarse, brown, sandy brown, depending on the district where they are.'

His opinion is unusual, but environment certainly governs the changes in the colour of the mountain hare. The mountain hare's colour varies gradually throughout the year. In summer its coat is very like some rabbits'—a light buff with shades of grey. In August it looks bluish grey and in the autumn, as the number of

[1] Ibid.

white hairs increases, it grows as grey as an elderly rabbit until when winter comes it is pure white. The Irish hare is usually light brown, but sometimes sandy coloured. Some Irish hares turn white or partially white in winter.

Hares rely for protection first on camouflage and then on speed and deviation as they take flight. If you approach a rabbit cautiously, he will run towards his burrow immediately he sees or hears you. A hare will wait watching you until you are almost upon her, and then with one bound, long and high, start leaping away, her hind legs reaching out before her forelegs at each leap, her ears erect even in flight—only when pressed at full speed are the ears laid back—her tail horizontal not upturned as a danger signal like the rabbit's, her long thin back now arched, now lengthened, like a snake's. The beauty of the hare is in her speed, her graceful turning this way and that, the subtle wide circles she makes in her flight to elude her pursuer and leave no constant line of scent. When hopping about in a field of sugar-beet or mangel-wurzels she looks as ungainly as a seal on land, because however slowly she wishes to move from plant to plant she does not walk. Rabbits do not walk either but seldom look ungainly. Their eyes do not bulge and stare to make one think of goitre in a human being. Their behaviour is more easily observed and understood; even their underground behaviour has been studied sympathetically, by R. M. Lockley[1] who kept some in an artificial burrow with peep-holes; and as pets they are more easy to make friends with and more easy to look after and hold in one's arms.

Beatrix Potter, during her long life in the country, must have seen as much of hares as of any other animal, but never wrote about them. The English countryside was much wilder in her day. The children, whose imaginations she knew, could wander near home amongst poultry, which were seldom enclosed, or on pastures where at dawn and dusk they could watch dozens of rabbits grazing. They might go further into dark and frightening woods where badgers lived, or across a wide hill to explore a spinney inhabited by a family of foxes, or up a beech tree, near their front door perhaps, where red squirrels climbed above them. They

[1] R. M. Lockley, *The Private Life of the Rabbit*, London, 1964.

divided animals, as she did in her books, into the kind and the cruel, the cuddlesome and those who bit and clawed, those who could draw near and those who kept at a distance. She knew with the instinct of a child the love and fear of mankind for animals. She knew how the shepherd and cowman and gamekeeper of her day identified part of his mind with the mind of the animals about him. And, of course, she unconsciously knew the essence of the truth of mythology and of psychology, that as the limbs, eyes, intestines of man all over the world resemble those of other mammals, then it should cause no one any surprise to find that the feelings of animals are basically the same as the feelings of mankind. But some men are exalted by solitary genius, which usually they hate because it causes loneliness, and can only come near to others on special occasions. And some animals, of which the hare is one, live mostly away from groups. Beatrix Potter wrote of animals which keep a family life such as the child has if lucky, and longs for if not.

The baby hare begins its solitude soon after birth. Its mother gives birth to it, and to two or three brothers and sisters, in an open nest called a form. They are born fully furred and active, with eyes wide open—Eric Parker who has often held babies in his hand says the eyes are blue. Baby rabbits start life pink and naked, blind and deaf and cuddle together with their mother, except when she goes out to feed, in a well hidden cosy place. Baby hares often live alone from a very early age, apart from their mother and brothers or sisters, each in its own separate nest or form. Until they are weaned their mother visits each in turn, and suckles them one by one where they nestle alone. It has been suggested that she gives birth to each separately in a different place, but this seems improbable because new-born litters are very often found in the same nest. The purpose of the separation is clear when one thinks of the dangers of a nursery on the surface of the land; only one can be taken by predators at a time. But how the move is done, if move there is, remains one of the mysteries on which observers contradict each other.

Edward Topsell, writing in the early seventeenth century, says: 'She keepeth not her young ones together in one litter, but layeth them a furlong from one another, that so she may not lose them altogether, if peradventure men or beasts light upon them.'[1]

Arthur Harmer, a Norfolk farmer, was inclined to believe that the doe actually gave birth in two or three forms, and in support of this he added that he had never seen a hare carry its young in its mouth. But Percy Muttit (born 1909) the Blythburgh, Suffolk gamekeeper, while not claiming he had real proof, believed the hare had all its young in one form and afterwards carried the leverets (which were 'all born with their clothes on, with full sight and ready to go') into different parts of the field. He said:

[T][2] 'You'll see the does carry 'em. They'll carry 'em when they're small. They carry 'em about. They'll pick 'em up and carry 'em. When the men are at work in the fields sometimes they'll nearly roll over a little leveret. D'you know, the owd hare will get it and move it: she'll slip in and move it so that—there isn't many people see it but they *do* move 'em. I see a hare only last year come through the hedge when there was a chap a-rolling a piece o' corn; came through the hedge with a little leveret in her mouth on to the field and leave it.—They're born with their fur on, different from a rabbit. They got protection as soon as ever they're born, soon as ever they are dry they'll run about. They are born with their eyes open: nearly every other animal is born blind for a fortnight. I don't suppose they can feed when they're first born but they have to see if danger's coming. They won't move. You can stand right beside them, within an inch of 'em, and if you don't see 'em you wouldn't move. I have just *coached* [stroked] 'em; but then soon as ever you touched them, they're away. They'll allus move 'em then. She wouldn't be long before she moved 'em. If you looked next day they'd be gone.'

Both the Norfolk farmer and the Suffolk gamekeeper are experts, having observed the hare in highly populated hare-country for well over fifty years; and yet they have different opinions about a vital aspect of the hare's behaviour.

Other observers, equally experienced, think it more probable that baby leverets walk to their new forms. Some think that the

[1] Edward Topsell, *The Historie of Four-footed Beastes*, London, 1607.
[2] [T] indicates transcript from a tape recording.

mother will only carry them if she has been frightened. A Yorkshire gamekeeper says: 'The litter is born in one form, but within
a couple or three days is distributed to separate forms. Whether
they walk or are carried I don't know, but I do know they are
quite able to walk.'

Some ancient writers believed not only that the mother gave
birth to the babies one by one, each in a separate place, but that
she had a separate womb for each one. Claudius Aelianus in the
third century wrote that the hare 'carried some of its young half
formed in its womb, some it is in the process of bearing, others it
has already borne'.[1] Aristotle, Hippocrates and Pliny are often
laughed at for making similar statements. They were referring to
the process of superfoetation which has only recently been proved.

'Superfoetation is the fertilization of an already pregnant female
which causes the simultaneous development of eggs of two different ovarian cycles within the genital tract.'[2] Unlike most animals—dogs, foxes, cats—rabbits and hares will accept the male
while pregnant, but only the hare can conceive a second time.

The sex of the hare has always seemed a mystery too:

'A Hare is a four-footed Beast of the Earth, which the Hebrews
call *Arnebet*, in the feminine gender which word gave occasion to
an opinion that all Hares were females, or at the least that the
males bring forth young as well as females. . . . The common sort
of people suppose they are one year male, and another female.
Aelianus also affirmeth so much, and by relations of his friend, he
ventureth the matter and saith, moreover, that a Male hare was
once found almost dead, whose belly being opened, there were
three young ones alive taken out of her belly, and that one of
them looked up alive, after it had lien a while in the Sun, and it put
out the tongue as though it desired meat, whereupon milk was
brought to it, and so it was nourished . . . the Hunters object that
there be some which are only females and no more: but no male
that is not also a female, and so they make him an Hermaphrodite.
Niphus affirmeth so much, for he saw a Hare which had stones

---

[1] *De Natura Animalium*, quoted by Henry Tegner, *Wild Hares*, London, 1969.
[2] Von S. Bloch and others, 'Beobachtungen zur Superfetation beim Feldhasen',
Zeitschrift für Jagdwissenschaft, Hamburg, 1967.

and a yard, and yet was great with young, and also another which wanted stones, and the males genital, and also had young in her belly. Rondelius saith, that they are not stones, but certain little bladders filled with matter, which men find in female hares with young, such as are upon the belly of a Beaver.'[1]

It was said that the female hare escaped from the Ark and was drowned, and when the animals came out there was only one. So God gives him the power to bear children.

Sir Thomas Browne who set out to correct vulgar errors,[2] such as the belief that elephants have no joints in their legs, assured his readers that the hare is of two sexes only, but that the male does occasionally give birth to young; and he lived most of his life in Norfolk where hares abound and, especially in his time, were easily observed. The people of Ancient Greece held the same opinion, and the old laws of Wales, which set out the value of many animals, including the cat, giving different prices for males and females of various ages, put no price on the hare because it was female one month and male the next.

The belief derives from a concept expressed in many religions and myths in which the god or the perfect human being is spiritually and physically hermaphrodite, as Adam was before Eve was taken out of his body and made into a separate person.[3] Shiva and his 'wife' Shakti are often portrayed as one person, the left side being female. The Bodhisattva is both male and female. So was the prophet Tiresias. And so, in some primitive cultures, are the ancestors of the tribe.[4] In this, as in other cases, myth is related to fact. The human embryo is androgynous in its early stages. The girl's clitoris is exterior and identical with the boy's penis. His genital cleft is open like hers, and the seam which closes it at a later stage remains visible throughout his life. At the base of his bladder, embedded in the prostate gland, there also remains a small organ which in a girl has developed into a womb.

[1] Edward Topsell, op. cit.
[2] Sir Thomas Browne, *Pseudodoxia Epidemica*, London, 1646.
[3] Compare Gen. i, 27 with Gen. ii, 18 to 22, which seem to contradict each other unless one bears this concept in mind.
[4] See, among other works, Joseph Campbell, *The Hero with a Thousand Faces*, Princeton, 1968.

In the Old Testament, there is yet another mystery about the hare. In Deuteronomy, the second book of laws, it is named among the animals that chew the cud:

'And every beast that parteth the hoof and cleaveth the cleft into two claws, and cheweth the cud, that ye shall eat. Nevertheless these ye shall not eat of them that chew the cud, or of them that divide the cloven hoof; as the camel, and the hare, and the coney; for they chew the cud but divide not the hoof. . . . And the swine because it divideth the hoof, yet cheweth not the cud. . . .'[1]

Hares do not chew the cud, but in one respect they feed like ruminants. All ruminants need a vast bulk of food to sustain them. They eat it in a hurry and digest it slowly at leisure. Cows lie down with their backs to the wind under the lee of a hedge if there is one, regurgitate all they have eaten and chew it thoroughly before swallowing it again. When they gulp it up into their mouths it has only been partially digested, compressed and slightly softened.

Hares and rabbits eat mostly at night and are often interrupted by enemies and set to flight. There is no time for thorough chewing or digestion, but during the day they lie still for long periods, the rabbit, secure against all except weasels and ferrets, the hare in her sheltered form where though she listens constantly for danger, sniffing every scent in the air and watching without ever closing her eyes, she is physically at rest. At rest, all the partially digested food they have eaten is taken back into the mouth, chewed again and re-digested, but instead of gulping it up as cows and sheep do, they eat it after it has passed through the body. In other words each individual eats its own dung. The dung that lies about on grass where hares or rabbits have been has passed through the digestive system twice and is discarded as useless.

Hares and rabbits do not fraternize. Hares feed on almost every kind of vegetation, even seaweed, mushrooms, puffballs and the leaves of young conifers, but they will not graze on land used by rabbits. It is said that rabbits drive them off pugnaciously, but even when there are no rabbits about they will not feed there be-

---

[1] *Deuteronomy* xiv, 6 and 7.

cause rabbits make the grass seem foul for them, as it is for sheep, and as a pasture is for cattle after geese have been on it.

Charles Welling has seen ghastly evidence of antipathy: 'What used to destroy most hares was rabbits. The buck rabbit used to go and bite the top of their heads when they found them. Of the leveret. Of the young. When you go—you find the form with three or two in it. But going back an hour later—you'd see the heads all smashed and eaten. You'd stand back and say, "Well what's done that?"—and you'd suddenly see a buck rabbit come or a doe rabbit come, jumping out and go round and scratch them out of the nest after they'd killed them. So we'd know that that's what they'd done. But now we've had myxomatosis, the hare population has increased 75%.'

And hares do not fraternize with each other as rabbits do, although they gather together in certain enclosed spaces–aerodromes and parkland—and on some occasions they appear to hold meetings the purpose of which is unknown. Each doe settles down in her own territory and lives there, breeding and rearing her young, changing her form from time to time within its boundaries and venturing further only if food becomes scarce or when she is hard pressed by a fox or by hounds. The hunted hare that runs in circles is usually a doe. If the hounds lose her scent she goes back to the place from which they started her. The hare that runs straight for long distances is usually a buck. He leads a roaming life and makes a new form frequently. Like the doe, he is more often alone than in company. Both are promiscuous. The buck serves as many does as he can find and the doe will accept several bucks one after another. But after mating they do not stay together.

Perhaps it is this lack of family life that makes the hare so much more difficult to domesticate than the rabbit. Of all wild animals, so those with experience of zoo-keeping say, wolves make the most affectionate and gentle pets, if they are first handled when very young. Wolves remain emotionally attached not only to the pack but to their mates. Hares have no pack, a roaming mate and scattered infants. Yet people have kept them as pets since ancient times. If they are caught young they are easily tamed; they can be happy with people they know, but are terrified of strangers and, while a hutch must seem homely to the burrow-loving rabbit the hare does not take readily to a cage of any sort.

Few zoos have been able to keep them. Apart from their dislike of crowds of people, it is said that a fright will make them leap against the wire with such force that they can even kill themselves. Witchingham Wild Life Park, Norfolk, is one of the few places where they breed in captivity and there they are kept in a large enclosure. They are no more timid than rabbits, but they appear to be more emotional, more highly strung.

They have always been thought of as melancholy creatures.

'If they hear the dogs,' says Topsell, 'they raise themselves on their legs and run from them; but if fearful imagination oppress them, as they oftentimes are very sad and melancholy, supposing to hear the noise of dogs where there are none such stirring, then do they run to and fro, fearing and trembling, as if they were fallen mad.'

One unusual feature of the hare's behaviour has caused a great deal of interest in recent years both among naturalists and the general public. This is the hare's frequent choosing of aerodromes on which to congregate and, in fact, to live. Towards the end of 1966 photographs appeared in newspapers showing scores of hares running alongside aircraft as they took off and landed. One of the aerodromes most frequently photographed was at Aldergrove, Northern Ireland; and the following story appeared in a newspaper at the time:[1] 'The hares of Aldergrove Airport, Belfast, are by now well known in many parts of the world. Daily they put on performances for passengers who arrive and fly out in jet airliners. Eyebrows go up and fingers point as aircraft sweep to the tarmac, and green turf rushes past the windows. Up to seventy or eighty hares often course alongside. In miniature, the effect is like the travel films in which herds of zebra and antelope are chased from above. How sensitive is the hearing of hares? Their five-inch long ears at least suggest efficiency. Evidently the Aldergrove hares are more stoical or adjust better to jet-scream than human residents about Britain's airfields.'

These hares are no great hazard to aircraft as are the bigger

[1] *The Times*, 26th November, 1966.

birds like plovers, pigeons or gulls; and they do not appear to set aerodrome authorities a great problem. The watch supervisor in the Aldergrove control tower at this time (1966) drew attention to another peculiarity of the aerodrome hares: when he fired a bird-scaring cartridge over the heads of about seventy hares, not one paid any attention. But when a helicopter appeared over the air-field their reaction was immediate: they scattered at speed and attempted to find cover. This was explained as an instinctive reac-tion to something that looks like a hovering predator, for instance a huge hawk.

Henry Tegner in his book on the hare[1] draws attention to this gregariousness of the hare in Ireland: 'Something has already been said about the mass congregation of the Irish Hare; and it has been stated that this affinity complex in the sub-species, *Lepus timidus hibernicus Bell*, is an innate trait of the animal.' But he acknow-ledges that it is not only Irish hares that have a liking for aero-dromes. Hares, performing the same manoeuvres, are to be seen on many airfields in many different countries: Prague, Frankfurt, Heathrow and so on; and he reports that they also frequent Canadian aerodromes in abundance. This is the kind of behaviour, contradictory and unpredictable as it is, that is nevertheless not too much out of character in the hare. For the common phrase *hare-brained* refers not so much to a lack of intelligence as to a wild impetuosity. Why, for instance, does such a shy and fearful crea-ture choose the noisiest, most dangerous and most frequented spot in the modern urban complex to disport itself in?

There have been many attempts to explain why the hare appears to be so attracted to airfields. Tegner quotes[2] a Natural History Museum expert as saying: 'The hares seem to like the noise and the vibration'; and Tegner comments on this statement, pointing out that hares are themselves noisy creatures on occasion. Percy Muttit, the Suffolk gamekeeper, has also noticed this; and when we talked to him a few months ago (13th February 1970), he said:

[T] 'Now you might see five hares in a field today, playing or fighting, whatever you call it. Next week, as soon as ever the sun

---

[1] *Wild Hares*, London, 1969, pp. 48–9.   [2] Ibid., p. 49.

get out, as it now is, they start to harrow the fields down. They disturb these owd doe hares, and they'll run 'haps across to another field, and disturb another one or two; and then they all get on to one field, 'haps a dozen or fourteen—and they'll fight it out. The does don't fight. They sort of keep crouching about; but the owd jacks they'll fight all day sometimes. In fact, they *do* blind one another: and they sort of get thin for a time. Sometimes I've seen 'em lay dead. You can hear 'em, you know, two hundred yards off when they're striking one another with their front paws, just like two men. They keep *flicking*. You can hear this *flick*. You'll see pieces of down fly off up into the air like as if they were being shot at. That's during the mating season. It's the harrowings. That's when they start to pull these *ploughs* [ploughlands] down. 'Cos they're all a-sitting on the *ploughs* now.'

Frequently, too—so some observers say—hares will play by drumming and thumping with their paws, in the way a buck rabbit will suddenly thump on the ground when he sees danger— a warning to his fellows to take cover. It is related that the poet Cowper's pet hares became excited by the change in atmosphere that precedes a thunderstorm; and, when the thunderstorm broke, apparently enjoyed the noise. A liking for noise may, therefore, be a partial explanation for the airfield's attraction for the hare. But the noise of a modern jet aircraft taking off or landing is of a higher order than even the worst thunderstorm we know in these latitudes (anyone who is prepared to stand near a runway when this is happening can judge for himself); and it is risky to argue that the hare has a natural liking for, or imperviousness to, such a noise as this.

Others have put forward the theory that it is the abundant food they can get on the stretches of well-kept turf between the runways that has drawn hares to aerodromes. Good grazing is undoubtedly a factor in *keeping* them on an airfield; but it is questionable whether it is the main attraction. There is strong evidence that aircraft themselves attract the hares in the first place. For when in recent years an aerodrome frequented by hares was closed for repairs, the hares followed the aeroplanes to the satellite aerodrome which became the temporary landing place. But why should aeroplanes attract hares? We may get some light from what happened in the early days of flying when aircraft engines made less noise than a present-day motor-bike. A former First World War pilot told us his experience:[1]

'It was in January and February 1918. I was at Sedgeford in Norfolk. I was flying Martinsides, B.E.Z.Es, B.E.Z.Ds and D.H.4s; but I had learnt on D.H.6s. My instructor was Captain S. F. Vincent, now Air Vice-Marshal Vincent. About 4 p.m. in the afternoon he used to say to me: "You had better come up in my D.H.6 and let me see how you are getting on." I noticed on the floor of the D.H.6 there was a twelve-bore double barrel shotgun. When we got a bit away from the aerodrome, and he spotted a nice stubble field he would say: "Take over and fly low over that stubble field."

'Invariably two or three hares would get up and race parallel to our line of flight. Partridges did the same thing. When we had a bag of two, three or four hares Captain Vincent used to land; and I got out and collected the game.' On one occasion they took off again just as an angry farmer or gamekeeper came on to the field to see what was happening.

This early report of the hare following aircraft suggests that the hare's reaction is inbuilt, an instinctive impulse to emulate the speed of the aeroplane by running alongside it: it suggests that the hare is purposefully 'taking on' the aircraft, responding to what it interprets as a kind of challenge. This fits in well with what we know of the playfulness of the hare, of its delight in its own swiftness, and its readiness—in spite of its fear—to pit itself on occasion against a fast moving object. The hare's main strength lies in its speed: it does not go to ground and relies on its speed to get itself out of trouble; therefore when it plays, as it appears to be doing when it courses alongside aircraft, it is likely that in showing its speed it is using one of its strongest instincts of self-expression. The same desire may well stimulate birds to fly alongside aircraft; and we can point to a similar kind of behaviour in dolphins. Many of these have been known to swim alongside

[1] James L. Waugh, Hill Crest, Top Lane, Copmanthorpe, York, YO23 UJ, personal communication.

ships for miles, sometimes even 'guiding' them,[1] responding no doubt to the same sort of impulse as the hare when it tries to out-run jet airliners.

Later on in this book we shall examine some aspects of animism, the belief that the phenomena of animal life are governed by an *anima*, or soul, distinct from matter. The old naturalists held on to vestiges of that belief and allowed their feelings to colour what they saw. It was impossible for them, as it is now for anyone who keeps pets or looks after farm animals, not to share emotions with the creatures they observed, not to identify themselves with the animal as children and primitive men still do. Instinctive feeling can be a guide to the deepest source of truth. The purpose of the modern, scientific naturalist is specialized. His pure, factual dis-coveries enlighten us in another way. Even he, with all his equip-ment, has not been able to come close to the living wild hare. The most marvellous knowledge—of the process of moulting or super-foetation—has been gained by dissection of corpses. The life of the wild hare is less familiar to us than the lives of many rare birds which can be watched and filmed from hides.

Familiarity unveils all mystery. Elusiveness and solitude en-hance it. And of all the creatures linked with the mystery of magic, the hare is the most remote. The practice of magic is secret, its conception fearful and imaginative, and to cause fear arouses much the same emotion in a human being as to feel it. You cannot consciously make another person or an animal afraid without fearing something in yourself. The hare fears man as she fears any other beast of prey. Man has for centuries feared the hare because of the supernatural powers with which he has endowed her, in her solitude, her remoteness, her subtle, natural skills.

[1] The famous *Pelorus Jack* is a good example.

3

The Mountain Hare

(*Lepus timidus Scoticus*)

The mountain hare of Scotland is one of sixteen subspecies of the *lepus timidus* which inhabit the northern parts of Europe and Asia and which left behind them in Europe, as they moved north after the last Ice Age, a small colony that still survives in the Alps. They are thought to be the oldest of all the hares in Europe and if we judge by the deposits of the late pleistocene age, it was they and not the common or brown hare of England that flourished in the days of cave art. The few known palaeolithic engravings are almost certainly of the *lepus timidus*.

Some English sportsmen of the nineteenth century, in spite of Queen Victoria's love of Balmoral, despised them in a patriotic way which now seems funny, saying that they cannot run fast and that they look like starved cats, scraggy, ungainly and mean. They are in fact smaller than the Irish or brown hare, and that may make them slightly slower, but their natural terrain gives them a greater advantage over dogs. Any hare will try to run uphill when chased. Long hind legs working with short front ones give far stronger leverage on an upward slope than the legs of a dog which are all the same length. And the mountain hare lives on the hills. Those who hunt them say they 'go to ground' more readily than the brown hare. This is because their ground has safer hiding places, jumbled boulders which hold up pursuers and confuse them, rocks with shallow hollows underneath, small crevices in cliffs. But if one can be stopped from taking shelter and driven to the summit it is easily caught. Dogs and men with guns are sent up the back of the hill to wait while it is being chased up the front and even if it escapes the guns, its downhill gait is so awkward that any dog can snap it up.

C

The idea that this hare is gaunt and scraggy, may be based on observation made during or after hard winters. Visitors to the Cairngorm Mountains, the fashionable sporting ground above Balmoral Castle, could have seen many such. All animals look scraggy when ill fed. But those who have seen the mountain hare on kinder land, the foothills and the undulating moors, describe her as stocky and compact, and no one who has watched her sitting hunched but alert in the snow or leaping and running at a sign of danger can pretend not to love her composure in stillness and her grace in movement. She seems solid and neat when well fed and when she runs she is dainty. 'On the level', says Norman Halkett, 'a hare has a beautiful rocking motion that makes it just about the most elegant runner I know.'

Norman Halkett is one of many accurate and loving observers of nature whose knowledge hardly ever gets into print. He was brought up in a part of Aberdeenshire where brown hares are plentiful but not far from uplands inhabited by the mountain hare. He now lives in Caithness, in the very far north, where mountain hares abound. So he is familiar with both kinds. In Scotland the brown hare is often called a 'baud' and the mountain hare a 'mawkin'.

Both words, like the southern English 'puss', are affectionate pet names shared by hares and cats; 'baud' is short for 'baudrons — kindly designation for a cat' and 'mawkin', 'maldkin' or 'Maudkin', diminutives for Matilda or Maud, are nicknames for cats too; 'grimalkin', probably means grey malkin.

'The mawkin's size and condition', says Halkett, 'obviously depend on nutrition and some of them live at considerable heights where vegetation is scarce indeed. Our Aberdeenshire moors, though extensive and plenty wild, are for the most part not very high and despite the severity of the winters there always seems to be abundant food among the mawkins. I have never found a healthy one thin. Yet it dwells in the heathery places. It will certainly invade a croft or agricultural land adjacent to the moors, but otherwise it is never seen in arable areas. It stays only on the moors.'

In many parts of Scotland the moors and mountains are covered with snow for months every winter and it is difficult to understand how hares reach any food at all. Some say they burrow for it. 'I have no doubt they do burrow, so do rabbits, so do sheep, but I am quite happy that the hare does it as seldom as possible. It can afford to roam the countryside to where the wind has blown most of the snow to the dykesides or the mountain hollows leaving much of the ground only vaguely covered with snow. You will see there hare-scratches a-plenty. [Places where thin snow has been scratched away by hares.] And there are always places that escape the worst of the storm. These animals know where to go. I would almost categorically say that a hare will not burrow where the snow is any depth at all. When I lived in Aberdeenshire, which is, of course, a much snowier country than anything up here in Caithness, I used to be amazed at the condition of hares shot in the midst of the wildest winters. Not a skinny one among them.'

The mountain hare's form, whether made in snow or not, is usually deeper than the brown hare's and some observers say that she digs shallow burrows. Like all hares she lies with her back to the weather, sheltered by the best wall she can find or make, sometimes earth or snow, sometimes heather, grass or bracken; but in soft earth or snow the form may look like the opening of a burrow a rabbit has abandoned after a little work and left as a cul-de-sac.

Norman Halkett thinks: 'Her form in the snow would most likely be heather lined. It is easy enough for her to creep in below a snow-covered heather hummock. Hares do not so much dig a form as shape it and press it into shape with their bodies. An excellent example of this I used to see (with the brown hare) every New Year time down near Turriff where an old uncle of mine had a very fine farm with big fields all of which had been ploughed by New Year time. One would have expected the luscious grassland to be alive with hares. One or two were there right enough but the great majority were lying in forms on the ploughing! They sort of pushed down the front rig so that they could lie with the back rig at their backs, sheltering from the bitter winter winds. In every case, whichever way the wind was coming, the back rig was left untouched and the front one had been levelled. This made room for a sizeable body. Being well fed, there were really muckle hares and I think they must have kept pressing at the earth to shape it to their requirements.' He thinks that the mountain hare shapes her form in the same way. The rig is the ridge of a furrow. The front rig slopes. The back rig is almost perpendicular.

Another informant from the north of Scotland believed in his childhood that all hares were white. He was brought up in Nairn, a small town on the coast of the Moray Firth where the butchers' shops were plentifully hung in winter with mountain hares. He does not remember seeing any in their spring or summer coats, though of course at least in autumn there must have been some bluey-grey ones there. When he came near a hare in summer he either did not notice it or took it for a rabbit.

The mountain hare is not very much bigger than a large rabbit. Its ears if laid forward on the face never reach its nose, whereas the ears of a brown hare extend beyond the nose, and when it runs away its tail shows white, not that it is upturned like a rabbit's but because it is white on top as well as underneath. Its summer coat is an excellent camouflage especially in flowering heather or the mosses and coarse grasses of the moors. On bare stony ground and against the blue shadows of lichened rocks on a sunny day it is perfect. In summer too there are many places where hares can hide in long old heather or grass.

But the winter coat is a terrible danger to the hare unless there is snow. Nairn is only four miles from Cawdor Castle—King Duncan's castle of *Macbeth*—which is in the foothills of the Grampian Mountains, the highest and loneliest range in Great Britain, where rare creatures like the wildcat and the golden eagle live. But its climate and the climate of the lower hills and moors is mild, much milder than the Aberdeenshire moors or any near the east coast of Scotland. When winter comes there without snow, or on Culloden moor not far from Nairn, the white fur of a mountain hare makes it more conspicuous than any other creature.

When he lived in Nairn as a boy, he used to borrow his uncle's field glasses and bicycle out to the moors, usually alone, but sometimes with a friend, and lie down to watch birds and animals. He remembers two with the greatest pleasure: the capercailye, a bird now rare which haunted the woods about Cawdor, and the white hare on the moors above. The capercailye is something like a grouse, but almost as large as a turkey and the sudden flapping of its wings when it took flight among the trees as he crouched watching in the shadows where all had been silent was to him like the Angel of Death. The mystery of the white hare sometimes frightened him too. He says that when it was sitting or lying down it looked as if it had been frozen to death or stuffed in a hunched up position like a cat that is feeling the cold. Its staring eyes were like glass eyes. Then watching through the field glasses he would ask his friend to clap hands or bang two stones together. The hare would crouch even lower in its form. They would approach it cautiously. It would watch them stilly until they were very near. The friend would run on towards it, and he would see through his field glasses how it leapt from the form with a twist of its hind-quarters and land about ten feet away in order to leave no scent from its paws. Then it would bound in an easy regular gait, a series of smooth unhurried jumps that reminded him of a horse gently cantering, to the summit of the nearest ridge usually less than a hundred yards away. It would sit up there with its ears erect and look back to survey the danger. Sometimes when it ran on more level ground it would seem like a puff of smoke rising and falling, blown by the wind. It would often vanish suddenly near a rock or a high clump of heather. When he tried to imagine the Holy Ghost he thought of the white hare. The mysterious sin against the Holy Ghost was to kill a white hare.

He was having private lessons in Latin at that time from a minister of the Episcopal Kirk who thought it his duty to give him religious instruction as well. That may account for the religious images in the boy's mind. But it is significant that of all the birds and animals he saw, only the capercailye and the hare became symbolic.

In those days before the gin-trap was made illegal, he and his friends used often to find dogs, cats, rabbits, and even ptarmigan and grouse caught by the leg. They used to release them all, but kill the rabbits or birds if they were badly injured and wherever they found a trap with its steel jaws open they would spring it to make it harmless. This became a secret mission and a war against adults. There were many dramatic incidents. Releasing a wounded cat was a dangerous business. To protect themselves against its claws and teeth they would cover it with a coat and try to hold it still. And often they were chased by angry trappers. Yet the deepest impression on the boy's mind was made by the sight and sound of a trapped hare—the only hare he can remember finding in a trap. Everyone who has heard a hare screaming agrees that it sounds like a woman or child; it is sometimes indistinguishable from the scream of a baby.

The ptarmigan and the mountain hare both turn white in winter when they live in their natural habitat. The process by which this happens was a mystery for years. Pliny thought the hare went white from eating snow and later naturalists believed that the summer coat became bleached in autumn or that it lost its pigment by the same process that makes human hair turn white. Then it was thought that the summer coat was lost and replaced by white during a single moult in autumn. Then it was discovered that the mountain hare moults three times a year.[1] The brown hare moults only in spring and autumn, but the mountain hare loses its white fur in spring and grows a smoky bluish-brownish coat that lasts only till after midsummer. Between June and August it grows a new coat of almost the same colour but showing some white in places. This coat begins to be shed during the second half of October and by December has been replaced by longer, thicker fur and hair white, or almost white, with variations.

This third moult has been shown by experiments on captive hares to be instigated by a reduction of light received through the eyes. The rapid decrease of daylight in northern latitudes during autumn and early winter suggested it.

'Four hares recently obtained from Nova Scotia were exposed to 12·5 hours of illumination per day in outdoor pens, starting October 5, 1939. The "night lighting" was increased about one hour weekly until, on November 9, they received a total of 18 hours of illumination per day. One of the four animals showed

[1] Raymond Hewson, 'Moults and Winter Whitening in the Mountain Hare', *Proceedings of the Zoological Society of London*, Vol. 131, London, 1958.

white "snow shoes" and the tips of white hair on the lower hips at the start of the experiment, but the other three were still completely brown. On November 15, another animal, which had been so slow in its final normal autumn moult that the growth of white hair had not yet reached the mid-dorsal line, was added to the experimental group.

'In spite of a cold December, all three totally brown animals remained in the brown autumn pelage. One died on December 7, and another on December 27, apparently from effects of the low temperature. The animal which had begun the final moult grew typical winter hair and displaced the autumn hair to the level of the top of the hips, and well up along the sides, but remained brown over the back and on the face, except for the tip of the nose. The animal which was exposed to light later than the others retained a brown streak down the mid-dorsal line, but otherwise developed a modified winter pelage which was slightly flecked with brown hairs over the whole dorsal region.

'Not only did the night lighting completely arrest the moult to the white pelage in three cases, but it also turned all the animals, which were physiologically white at the beginning of the experiment, back to the physiologically brown condition. One totally brown animal was plucked on October 26th and, instead of growing white hair as it did on October 5th, grew typical brown, summer hair. Two other animals tested in the same manner on November 14th also grew brown replacement hair. Five controls, exposed to normal daylight, underwent normal final autumn moults to the white winter pelage.'[1]

Experiments with the temperature of cages show that once moulting has started, its extent is governed by the degree of warmth and this is confirmed by the fact that mountain hares introduced from Norway to the comparatively mild climate of the Faroe islands in the eighteen-twenties turned white at first in winter, but had ceased to turn white by about the eighteen-sixties. The height of the land they live in also seems to have something to do with colour change, for mountain hares introduced into the

---

[1] Charles Peirson Lyman, 'Control of Coat Colour in the Varying Hare', *Bulletin of the Museum of Comparative Zoology*, Vol. XCIII, No. 3, Cambridge, Mass., 1943.

Pennines, at the same altitude as much of their habitat in Scotland, still turn white.

Only the common or brown hare is native to Wales, but colonies of mountain hares have been started there also at various times during the past hundred years. The only survivors, so far as we can ascertain, are in north Wales and these are rare. They still turn white. In the winter of 1969–70, four white ones were seen by observers from the Nature Conservancy. They flourished in parts of south Wales until about 1926, but there, according to the memories of the few people we talked to, they had ceased to turn white in winter by then. In the *Blaenau* or foothills of the Brecknock Beacons both the common and the mountain hare used to be seen. Mansel Davies (born 1879) of Llanfyrnach, Pembrokeshire told us that hares of any kind are now rare:

[T] 'Since then [about forty-five years ago], I've not seen a hare in the district. They tell me there's a hare on the common at Trelech, five or six miles from here; but I've not seen it. It used to be a very good place. You never came home from there without seeing a hare, even if you didn't catch one. I don't know the reason for them going away; perhaps they took up too many in the nets.

'The mountain hare was a bit smaller than the common brown and harder to catch. No, it never did change colour in winter, not to my notice. I used to go out when there was snow on the ground to shoot them. You could track them better then. A farmer near here and I were out together after hares one day and we came to a small field with a lot of tall *trash* in it. And the dog went in before us. How many hares do you think we raised? Twelve. All mountain hares. I think, perhaps, the mountain hares collect together more than the common brown. But I can't be sure as I've only observed them during the [shooting] season.'

4

The Irish Hare

(*Lepus timidus Hibernicus*)

The earliest known description of the Irish hare, distinguishing it from the English, was written by Giraldus Cambrensis
in the twelfth century: 'There are also hares, many but
small; resembling rabbits as much in their habits as in their soft
fur.'[1]

By their habits (*sui modicitati*) he does not mean they burrowed
for he goes on to say that they had, like foxes too, the remarkable
habit of keeping to woods and coverts when hunted, instead of
taking to the open. Ireland was then a thickly wooded country,
which must have made this habit more noticeable, and maybe the
hares were smaller than they are now; for they are now almost as
large as the common or brown hare, except perhaps in the
mountains where country people report small individuals.

By 'their soft fur', Giraldus means to pay no compliment to the
Irish hare. All through the Middle Ages—perhaps even until the
invention of synthetic cloths—felt making from the hair and wool
of various animals was an essential industry. In England, high-
quality felt can be produced from hare-skins and till the nineteenth
century at least they fetched a good price when sold for that
purpose. But the English author of 'An Account of Ireland', who
studied every industry, wrote in 1812 that a hare-skin in England
was more valuable than a rabbit's but in Ireland useless. 'The hair
obtained from it will not felt, a circumstance the more remarkable
as rabbit-hair in this country [Ireland] answers exceedingly well in
the manufacture of hats.'[2]

[1] Giraldus Cambrensis, *Topographia Hibernica*, Chap. xxiv.
[2] Edward Wakefield, *An Account of Ireland*, London, 1812, Vol. 1, p. 356.

People now living can remember hare-skins being put to some uses. Mats:

[T] 'They put some stuff on them to preserve the fur and the skin—turn the skin inside out to preserve it. And when they have that then [when they have cured the skin] they stick it on a stiff piece—a cardboard. And that's your mat. And that's the way they make their mats. I never made them. I could make them if I liked, but I never done it.'[1]

Patrick Johnston who told us that is eighty-eight, William Egan who remembers skins being sold 'in the old times' is only seventy-three:

[T] 'They always sold them—always sold them. Sixpence. Some o'them only threepence. I've always heard it said—the skin of them was used for the binding of the books. They used to send them out to America. Binding the books. Those big books. Like ruled books—it was used for the binding of the back of them.'

Hare-skins were stuffed too and used as scarecrows:

[T] 'What we used to do—a great plan was—skin 'em nice now, head and all. It's hard to skin the head but its not such a job. And you stuff that skin with hair . . . or dry moss. Stuff it in the shape of a hare now. So you have the shape of a hare stood up. Get a needle and thread and stitch it, stitch the belly and round about, and you stuff the legs—you skin the legs and you stuff them down—and you stuff the neck and you fill up the head. And I used to get—I had two small glass marbles and they done for the eyes. And you'd swear they were eyes and they shone so big. I've a piece down there in the field where there'd be corn sown or even cut and the crows would be terrors; they'd rob you. And you put one o' them stuffed hares on the ground and put a bit of a fork of a stick under his neck to hold up his head, so he'd be looking up . . . and no crow would go near your corn. Till dogs and then foxes began to take those—they thought they were natural. They took them and brought them off and torn and bit them away. So I got a high bush, a thorny bush, and I put my man [the stuffed hare] above sitting in it, and I had him always there. . . .

'I don't know whether I thought of it. I think I fired at a rabbit

---

[1] Patrick Johnston, Balinlassie, Athlone, Co. Westmeath.

that was stuffed and I thought that he was live, one morning. I went up, and damn it, he was stuffed! And I lost a cartridge on him. I was sure he was a rabbit, he was alive. His head was up and his eyes was up. And I took aim at him and of course he was turned upside-down as though he was alive. I looked and felt him—"What the hell is it?" So I knew then, and this morning I came home and I told me father. "Oh", he says, "that'll be a great plan. You stuff the hare. Stuff him!" '

It seems surprising that a hare, live or stuffed, should frighten crows, but G. E. H. Barrett-Hamilton,[1] one of the most reliable observers of the hare, also comments on this: 'I have twice in spring seen a hare chasing crows from a field, as if she resented their proximity to her young.'

In most of its ways of behaviour the Irish hare is like its Scottish cousin. It makes deeply sheltered forms like those of the mountain hare and it protects itself in the same way as any hare. Here is one account:

[T] 'The shape [of the form] it's round like a football, first, and it's narrow where he goes in. He doesn't leave a big space for himself. Narrow. You'll be surprised—he'll creep into it. You could see out like that, you know now, and in the form—he lies in it today—well, he could lie in it for a week, then he leaves it goes somewhere else. But the most thing I've often remarked in snow, when I'd be tracing them—I've often traced a hare a half a mile. I followed it up and wouldn't heed any other hares passing; I followed the one. You'll get her somewhere; she has to stop, and she carries on a long way. But when she comes to lie—she'll spot a place there now; there's a lot of bushes up there now or there's rocks; and you'll see her *pups* [footmarks] all right along, and all of a sudden they'll stop. There's no mark of her in the snow. You get the old track in front and you wonder where the hare has gone. She comes back and very same tracks again. But she weakens and she doesn't go more than a perch back, and all of a sudden she gives a spring and goes from here to that window. [About seven feet?]

'Oh more! Clean out of her tracks. She'll go either that side or

[1] G. E. H. Barrett-Hamilton, *A History of British Mammals*, Vol. 2, p. 347.

43

this—wherever she's going to lie, and she'll make no marks. And she'll make her form there then, and she'll lie there. And a man who wouldn't be used to her, he'd be tracking her and tracking her and never be thinking about this spring she'd give.'[1]

And another description of the form:

[T] 'Well it would be wider, like, in one end than the other—seemingly. The head is narrow—the head part of the form is narrow. Well, a hare will make a form in a furrow if it's on dry ground, so long as she has a little cover round. Well, where she comes on old thick tufts of rushes, if it's anyway dry she'll make her form there too. And high old grasses—in old weathered grass —she'll make her form in that too. Well, a hare she never walks into a form. A hare will spring from that table to that one [about eight or ten feet] into her form.

'I've seen them in the form. And I was standing over the hare in the form and I had a stick and I didn't hit her. We gave her the chance for a hunt; and she got away too! And I've seen a hare hunted—do you know what I seen her do? And it happened—and Ned Mannion will tell you this—below in the sallies [willows] just at the back of them houses. Well, she run right into Ned Mannion's house and right into the ash-hole [a hole at the side of the fire-place]. That's the truth! Ned Mannion now, he'll tell you: "That's a wise hare!" And they let her go. Ay, they did! She got into the ash-hole and laid down. They let her alone. Well that happened down there in Ballinahown.

'Now I was telling you about the form. The narrow part was where the head was; the side part was where the hips were and the hind legs. The back part was straight, so she could push with her legs and lep out. The only thing I ever seen happen with a hare [he means the strangest thing]—you know Tom—he was hunting hares below on my pasture, and there was a big rock there below, and there was a big burrow.

'So we always thought the hare wouldn't run into a burrow. Well she run. . . . But she came to where the burrow was in under the rock and ran into it. . . . I never seen a hare going into a hole before. I'd never have believed it. But it does! I seen that happen!

[1] Patrick Johnston.

Just there below. It's very unusual. She was a kind of a young hare . . . she was knocking round there all the time. And seemingly, she used to go in there and lie down under this old rock. It wasn't a right burrow.'[1]

Barrett-Hamilton wrote:

'The Irish Hare if pursued frequently "goes to ground", but it digs no burrow for itself. I have seen one when coursed disappear into a rabbit's burrow and thus save its life, and on several occasions leverets have voluntarily done the same thing, or have concealed themselves in hollow tree-trunks; I also knew two leverets which habitually lived in a rabbit's burrow. My friend, Capt. T. S. Blackwell, once bolted a hare with a ferret in the King's County; and in the summer of 1912 my keeper thus bolted eight leverets, each aged about a month, from two burrows.

'In mountains the habits are thus described: They take to natural fissures in the rocks, or to natural courses, called by the natives water-brakes, formed by the percolation of the water through the peaty formation overlying the rock or other hard sub-soil, often to a depth of several feet. In many localities, as for instance in the Bannermore chain in Donegal where there is little covert, the hares become nearly as subterranean in their habits as rabbits. In these holes or crevices they seek safety from their enemies or shelter from bad weather, coming to the entrance of their "burrows" if such they may be termed, to bask in the sun, their "seats" as they are termed, being clearly marked. It is supposed that hares took to this habit to escape from their chief enemies the eagles, formerly abundant in these mountains. . . .'[2]

It is said that Irish hares are more inclined to congregate in large numbers than either the Scottish or the common hare, and this not only in the spring, but at all times of year, most noticeably in winter. 'An Account of Ireland'[3] says, 'These animals are frequently confined to gentlemen's domains, and in this case they always herd together in flocks.' Seventy years later, a writer living in the north of Ireland 'repeatedly saw from one to three hundred

---

[1] William Egan, born 1898, Clonfanlough, Athlone.
[2] G. E. H. Barrett-Hamilton, op. cit., Vol. 2, p. 344.
[3] Edward Wakefield.

moving together in one drove like deer,[1] and at the beginning of the present century flocks almost as large were seen at all times of the year in the south.

Another quality that seems to be peculiar to the Irish hare is its preference for the bog as habitat even in areas adjoining richer land. The word 'bog' as used in Ireland, does not mean land that is always wet and marshy, but those wide barren-looking stretches, usually flat, where—ten or twenty feet deep—below a shallow top-soil, there is solid black or brown turf. This turf, called peat in Scotland and England, is still the staple fuel of Ireland and the continual cutting of it creates a chopped landscape marked by wide steps, dark precipices and deep rectangular pools of glisten-ing black water. The surface of the bog looks greyish and withered. It is covered with light and rough grasses, many kinds of moss and, in some places, heather. Its verges are cultivated by the people and will grow good crops of potatoes and oats.

Nearly all the Irish people quoted in this book cut their own turf out of these bogs for fuel every year. It is part of their every-day background and in order to understand their frequent refer-ences to it, it is necessary to know what it looks like.

We asked a man from South Roscommon what kind of land the hares in his district preferred:

[T] 'The hare wants the bog if it's dry. If the bog is dry the hare won't come in [to the fields], except in the winter-time if she's short of food. And if she's short of food she'll come into the very yard—and, dear God, I've seen them in the yard eating the cab-bage plants. They want to be in the bog. They won't leave the bog if it's dry and getting enough of food, but if they're running short they'll come into the very yard. I've often seen them passing up the road. Hundreds of times.'[2]

Rumour, which is often discarded without thought, says that large droves of hares are or were to be seen on the bogs of Ireland. We found no evidence of it, but several people had watched small groups:

---

[1] William Thompson, referred to by G. E. H. Barrett-Hamilton, op. cit., Vol. 2, p. 347.
[2] William Egan.

'I've seen them jumping across one another and all like that, and going round in a ring. ... It wouldn't be in the mating season, but maybe when five or six of them would be running round the bog in a ring, when one of them would lay down and another would pop out—like that, that's all. That's the most ever I seen. Except I saw two fighting, all right. I've seen two and they were cuffing one another all right, with the front legs. ... They can give you a bite too. I've seen them clipping one another all right. ... They make the fur fly all right. There's no mistake. Hitting with the nails, you know. He puts out the paw, do you see? And the nails, and the nails will stick and he strikes down. Oh! And he'll— I've seen the fur flying on them all right.

'I often seen [them] going round the bog in a ring, do you know what I mean, go round the bog in a ring, and maybe one will lay down and another pop across him that way. I often saw them, all right. Especially in the mornings. In the mornings.'[1]

Descriptions of hares going round in a ring or sitting in a circle are heard in England and Scotland too. The most characteristic habits are shared by the three types of hare. But the following account of the fearlessness of wild Irish hares towards men has never been paralleled in Great Britain, so far as we know:

'When accustomed to human beings, it becomes anything but timid, and at my own home there are few hours of the day or night when from one up to (occasionally) a dozen may not be seen grazing within a stone's throw of the house. Very often they will not take the trouble to retire on the approach of a human being, and their tracks show that in the night they wander quite close to the house and even ascend the hall-door steps. Even if chased by a small dog they will frequently sit bolt upright to reconnoitre a pursuer. It is a pretty sight when a party of these beautiful animals are feeding at close range in perfect confidence, and in spring their movements are particularly attractive. At that season they are unusually in evidence, and go through many antics—boxing, bucking, dodging, leaping sideways, sniffing at each other nose to nose, or rushing madly round in a circle. Then after a general scurry they settle down to feed, scraping away snow (if present)

---

[1] John Connaughton, born 1899, Lisduff, Belmont, Co. Offaly.

with their paws; or they may roll on their backs or stretch themselves at full length on the ground. In March 1909 two pursued a large domestic cat of colour somewhat resembling themselves; the pursuit was sustained so hotly across the lawn and through a shrubbery that more than one person witnessed it independently; a possible explanation may be that these were two males so blinded with "March madness" as to mistake grimalkin for a member of their own race.

'The eyesight cannot be very good, at least not as compared with that of man, dog or fox. Although a hare, when not lying in her form, will see and move away from a man while still several hundred yards away, she often does not notice a motionless observer, even if he is standing in the open, and will approach him quite closely without suspecting his presence. On such an occasion one has fed a little quite close to me, lingered to clean herself, and passed on without having perceived me. At other times individuals have been so near that their twitching nostrils were plainly visible.'[1]

All hares are good swimmers, yet it is surprising to know that the Irish hare can contend not only with strong tides but with the rough seas of the rocky Atlantic coast:

'This hare swims as well as its allies, and when frightened ventures to face a branch of the tidal estuary of the river Suir at Kilmanock, the width of which may be nearly a hundred yards across near its mouth. The ears are then laid back as when running at high speed, and lie close to the water. In Connemara, Mr. Harding Cox found hares on the islands of Lough Inagh, and they were always ready, if disturbed, to cross the several hundred yards of often rough water intervening between them and the mainland. The above records relate only to frightened animals, but a friend of Thompson's observed one of its own free will enter and swim across a deep pool of a mountain stream, although a short way lower down the crossing was easy. A remarkable instance of swimming was that of a doe which, in order to attend to the wants of three leverets, swam every night to an island on an artificial lake.

[1] G. E. H. Barrett-Hamilton, op. cit., Vol. 2, pp. 338–9.

1. The Irish Hare: summer pelage (*left*) winter (*right*)

2. The Mountain Hare: winter pelage (*left*) summer (*right*)

3. The Common Hare

4. Two hares: a late eighteenth-century design by William Blake. Mrs. Thomas Butts, his friend and patron, worked-over the design in needlework

'Occasionally these hares lie out so close to the sea that it would seem to be not unusual for them to be cut off and have to regain the shore by swimming. Thompson states that he twice in one day came upon hares resting on rocks usually isolated for at least half of every twelve hours.'[1]

The most glorious distinction of the Irish hare, which we have left till last, is the beauty of its coat, especially in summer. It is never the smoky blue of the mountain hare and seldom so dark a brown as the common hare. It has a preponderance of yellowy-orange, a rusty look, rich as a fox, not glossy but reflective of many shades of light. Pale yellow individuals are not uncommon, and dark ones—so dark that two of our informants called them black—are sometimes seen, but rarely. Ears and tail are longer than the mountain hare's but the same shape—the ears somewhat rounded or even squarish at the tips, the tail fluffy and entirely white both in summer and winter. The furry soles of the feet are brownish.

Only a few Irish hares turn completely white in the winter. A great many show no white in their winter coats at all, but the majority have splashes of it especially on the flanks, or spots of white, unevenly shaped, on various parts of their bodies. They have the peculiar charm of incongruity, the magical look of a piebald, which has always stood for good fortune. Those which show no white look darker in winter than in summer.

The common hare has been introduced into Ireland, but like other colonists thrives only in the north. It does not fraternize with the natives, but in contrast to its way of life in Scotland it is often to be seen on the same terrain. This is because the Irish hare does not keep to the highlands like its Scottish relative. In size, and even in their summer colour at a distance, the Irish and the common hare look similar. They can be distinguished close up not only by colour but by the ears. All hares have black tips to the ears, but the common hare's ears are pointed. Irish people have learned to distinguish them at a distance only when they run away. The top of the common hare's tail is dark. From far away it looks as if it has no tail.

[1] Ibid., pp. 345-6.

5

The Common Hare

(*Lepus Europaeus* or *lepus Capensis*)

In Scotland because the *lepus timidus* is common, the common hare of England is called the brown hare. At most times of the year it does look browner than the other two, but there is no word to describe that mixture of grey, fawn, yellow, black and brown which distinguishes it from the even colour of a brown cow or horse. Its winter coat is reddish, though seldom as bright as the foxy russet red of the Irish hare. At a distance, especially on grassland, its summer coat looks darker than a rabbit's, and if you examine it closely which, unless you have a pet one, means examining it dead, you will see that in contrast to the *lepus timidus*, its back is covered with tiny black specks—the black tips of its 'guard hairs' which are longer and coarser than the other hairs. Its chest and abdomen are almost white, also the sides of its face. The inside of its legs and the furry pads of its feet are usually the most beautiful yellowy-gold, often tinged with red. The only part that is pure brown or buff is on the nape of the neck smooth and hidden. Individual colouring varies greatly as we mentioned earlier.

It is very much larger than the mountain hare and slightly larger than the Irish, and is easily distinguished from them by its longer legs and very much longer ears. It is less compact, less rounded. Perhaps it is its slightly flatter, more elongated head that make its eyes appear to be set unnaturally high. Many people think it the most uncanny of the hares. The eyes are distinguished also by a beautiful honey-coloured iris, but like a jewel or the gleaming skin of a frog, they seem cold. Contrast them if you like with the eyes of a golden cocker spaniel.

The adjective *'timidus'* stuck to the mountain and the Irish hares by chance. Neither they nor the common hare are in the least timid. In the mating seasons, they are fiercely pugnacious, and for a creature whose only protection against predators is camouflage and flight they are exceptionally courageous in defending their young. Henry Tegner mentions a female hare that was 'observed to stand up and punch a bullock on the nose, presumably in defence of her leveret', and another which 'was actually seen to ride off a terrier as a polo player will attempt to do with his opponent'.[1]

Charles Welling says:

'The only time I've ever seen them defend their young is from a hawk, a kestrel hawk. They've jumped up and skipped up in the air to try to keep the hawk off. But the hawk always wins. As quick as the hare is, the hawk's always quicker. He swoops in and gets them in his talons and he's gone. Of course they're only small things, about four inches, you know, when they're born—the first week they're born. You see, they can hover just out of the way of the hare—and as soon as ever the hare's jumped at them then he goes in and he's gone. He always watches the hawk—but of course he comes over so quick, he'll perhaps fall over backwards—the hare does, trying to get at it in his anger.'[2]

Percy Muttit said:

[T] 'I've seen a dog pick 'em [the leverets] up and you've heard 'em shriek. Then the old hare will come after him. If that don't see me that will run round him. Yes, oh yes, once the hare *shriek*—we call it *shriek*—once the leverets shriek, the owd hare isn't far off. She'll come then. If she don't see a man, she'll come. If they see a man they won't come. I should say, if a stoat has got a leveret and a owd hare was on its own that would knock it off. I've never seen it happen, but I got some snares along this wood—at the bottom—once; and a leveret got in one of 'em; and as I was stooping down to let the leveret out—it was nearly as big as a rabbit—and when I got hold of it it shruck [shrieked]. And this owd hare come on to the middle of my back. Yes, I was stooped down. I don't suppose she knew what I was. But she hit me in the

---

[1] Henry Tegner, *Wild Hares*, London, 1969, p. 22.
[2] Charles Welling, retired warrener, Norfolk.

middle of the back and I flew round and I thought it was him [his dog]. But he was chasing down the field, and I shouted, "Stop!" He stopped: I thought it was him. It had hit me in the middle of the back and I flew round and there was this owd hare a-scuttling off.

'I've seen a hare travelling—running across the field at tremendous speed to cover in the heathland, and I've gone to see if I could find out what was the matter; and I've seen a leveret drawed into the briars where an owd stoat or something had took it in; and the hare must have heard that shrieking. I couldn't hear it! But I knew she was worried about something the way she was travelling. Then I see the little leveret drawed out on the side like that. So it showed they are a-listening all the time.'

From a lifetime's observation of the common hare in Suffolk, Percy Muttit believes that the fights in the mating season begin when hares invade one another's territory. He was born in 1909 at Blythburgh in the cottage where he now lives and worked in his boyhood as a warrener, catching rabbits on the farms. He started on his own as a gamekeeper in 1925 at the age of sixteen on the same estate, the Westleton estate, a corn-growing land. Here he confirms Norman Halkett's observation from Aberdeenshire:

[T] 'They'll dig a little hole so they can cover, so they're level with the top of the land, so you can just see them as you walk past. A *seat* we call it. They dig it out and they allus sit with their back against—like they scrap it out that was and put the back in there, and they allus set the head on where they've scrapped this little stuff and rest the chin on there. If you shot at a hare sett'n in the furrow like that, you wouldn't kill it. They'd just be under enough so the shot would go right over the top of it. They're just down to the level. When they start to harrow they put 'em all up you see, and they disturb 'em. If they're harrowing on this farm and on another farm they upset the owd hares, and they all get together then. If an owd doe hare run across where there's another one that cause these owd jacks to git upset and they start to fight.'

In captivity, at least, bucks have been known to fight to death. Hares often stand upright on their hind legs to fight. They rely on their hindlegs in most of their actions and their balance is superb as can be seen most clearly in the arctic hare which does not touch the ground at all with its front paws at high speed. But it seems that they do not use their hind feet as weapons. Norman Halkett has watched them boxing with their forelegs:

'The hind legs do not so much kick as thump the ground much in the same way as we would stamp our feet rather than give an outright kick. I have heard the thumps quite distinctly; the object seems to be to make a noise and therefore attract attention—possibly some kind of display before the female. Both fore and hindlegs are armed with strong claws, sharp and long enough to inflict wounds.' Halkett never saw much damage done.

'I have heard them make funny noises with their feet, sort of thumping on the ground, and occasionally one punches another like kangaroo boxing, or again you couldn't quite say it's punching; it's more like poking at the other fellow. But again one has to be so far away—I never was lucky enough to have a pair of field glasses or anything with me when I saw this, so that I couldn't get near enough to make out exactly what they were doing.'

But he is one of the few people to have seen the mysterious circular assembly of hares, at which some say fights take place.

'No one has ever been able to explain to me fully just why hares do on occasion sit in a wide circle with one or two or even more of their number having gambols or frolics inside the circle. I have heard that it is supposed to have something to do with mating, but no one has ever been explicit on the subject. I have seen it at least three times in my life, from as small a circle as say ten or twelve, to as many as thirty or forty hares, all performing at once. Some standing up on their, bolt upright on their hind-legs, others sitting on their hunkers, as we say, and some actually lying down as though they weren't paying much attention. But it does happen and I would honestly like to know what it really means.'[1]

Walter Flesher, the Yorkshire gamekeeper and naturalist, has seen the circle too and believes it has to do with breeding:

'I have seen this gathering of hares in a circle, sometimes five or six, and on one occasion eleven, but they are usually running

[1] Norman Halkett in *The Hare*, BBC 3rd Programme, December, 1966.

round and round and striking or kicking out at one another, and I have never seen them sit for very long. It must be something to do with the breeding or mating season, for it is always in March or April when I see it. I am pretty certain that it's only the Jack hares that indulge in this performance, because when I have seen it taking place I have usually seen three or four does feeding not far away, and when the circle breaks up the Jacks start chasing the does around—sometimes three or four after the same doe. Then there is more boxing and kicking until one Jack goes off with the doe. I have never seen hares drumming or thumping with their hind legs. I don't say they don't do it, but I have never seen it and I've a notion that only rabbits do it, as a sort of alarm signal.'[1]

And Percy Muttit has seen a peaceful gathering. He thinks that certain bucks can agree with each other on one piece of land:

[T] 'Yes, they do get together; four or five jacks and a doe got together on a field; and if they don't get disturbed they'll keep hopping around there all day; and they'll keep—well, just a-playing about or sitt'n or cleaning themselves. But if anyone goes on and disturbs them and they go on to the next field where there's some more; that's when the fight starts.

'We don't see many hares after we've done partridge driving. We don't go across these *ploughs* [ploughlands]—they set on there. And if you get a heavy rain or a cold, wet owd night and then the sun come out, you can see them then; they'll have got up in the seat, you know. They'll all come out and put their head out, and set so you can see 'em. They'll just get their legs and head up out of their little seat, to let the sun get on them. You'll count 'em then. You'll see eight or more on some fields. They'll set there just half out of the seat getting the sun. But if anybody else walk there I don't suppose they'd see 'em because as soon as ever they see a man they'll go down again into the seat. But if you go quietly and stand and look on a ploughed field after you'd had a heavy rain when the sun come out, they draw out of the seat half-way and sun themselves. But they don't come out of the seats till evening unless they're disturbed.'

It is natural to be surprised at the powers of survival of the

[1] Walter Flesher, unpublished notes, 1970.

mountain hare on snowy hills and frost-bound plateaux, but Muttit after nearly sixty years of watching wild creatures still wonders how the common hare can survive even in the low-lying countryside of East Anglia where snow is infrequent.

[T] 'They are a most peculiar animal. How they live we don't never know, and yet they *do* survive in hundreds. They are born in the open and there they take all weathers until the corn is green enough to hide them up a bit. I've seen heavy thunderstorms, and afterwards some come out of their forms; they are dried out again.

'Well, I go about: I've done nothing else all my life only wandered about here, and I fell in with these little leverets; and I've seen 'em as I've looked for plovers' eggs. I've seen two little leverets on an owd stubble, on an owd corn-stubble. They make little seats just like their mothers do, just backed in, you know. Before I left that field there was a tremendous storm; and I was back on to this field after this heavy storm because I thought they must be dead; and there they set—just the same; and everywhere all over was all water. I saw these little owd chaps there and I said to myself: "Well, they can't survive." (But we used to look at the field every four days, so we used to look at 'em twice at that time o' day, look at 'em twice to pick these owd plovers' eggs up, years ago.) They'd moved about two hundred yards away, and they'd grown. They were four or five days old, nice little chaps; they were alive and well. Well, anything else—that would have been killed! They have to be out in the open till the corn get up and they can get in out of sight.

'They are born next month, March I mean, when there's no green stuff; they just had 'em on this owd heather or on the walks on the bracken land. And then they go up on to the land when the corn begin to get a bit green. Then you'll see the leverets a-feeding and playing about then. They used to reckon years ago if you could see a hare hopping about on a piece of wheat in March it wouldn't be no good. Well, nowadays it would never cover a skylark. Do it? Things have altered.

'Yes, poor owd things; they got a job to live today [in February, at time of interview]. When they get the corn up, then they're away with it. You don't see much of them then unless they get heavy rain; then they'll come out [of the seats] and get dry. Otherwise they'll keep out of sight.'[1]

For the common hare, the best place to keep out of sight is a wood and in spite of the vigilance of warreners such as Charles Welling, large numbers frequent the Forestry Commission plantations at certain times of the year. Welling says they don't live in the woods:

[T] 'No, no, they don't live in the woods at all. Only when they're frightened or to get away from the personnel on the land. Their habitat is on the land in clover fields and stubbles at this time of the year [August]—sugar beet when it's very hot. They'll get in that to keep cool. They go in there [to the woods] to shorten their teeth. It keeps the teeth down. Something hard they must gnaw. The bark, or the top of a young Scotch pine they'll nibble out—cut out the top, because they have a reach of somewhere between three feet and—or—to stand on their hind legs and reach up into the top of a Scotch pine—four foot high. And I've stood and watched them and they've even used the front, as they've stood on the hind legs, bouncing the tree to pull the top down.

'And then he's paid the penalty and I've shot him. Yes, because one hare in a Forest Commission wood can cut sixty to a hundred and sixty trees up in one night. Hop from one to another and of course they're spoilt. And of course you know a Scotch pine or a Corsican pine grows a foot to fifteen inches every year. So you know that once they're cut down they're useless—the top has gone out. A hard winter will put them into the woods and a dry time like we're having now—they'll go in. They must have moisture.'

Wire-netting fences which keep out rabbits are no protection:

'Oh, they can leap over the top of that. That's no hindrance to them whatever. When they come out they'll go to a post what's half-way along the wire and they'll go up the post and sit on top and look at you. Make a laugh of you.

'They used to be a nuisance in the apple orchard too. I used to

[1] Percy Muttit.

go round every year and stop all the women and men—about forty or twenty in the apple orchard—[picking apples] and drove them [the hares] up into one corner and shoot them. I've shot as many as a dozen. Because at this time of year they'll stand on their hind legs and they'll go up the apple trees. And they not only eat in one place, they nibble all round and kill it. Take the bark off all the way round. What they call ring barking.

'They don't breed in the wood. They breed out on the edge of the wood or on fallow fields where there's a tuft of grass, or in a thorn bush, they'll tuck into a thorn bush. Always to the sun.'[1]

The 'madness' of the March hare cannot be attributed solely to the courting instinct, because courting and breeding goes on for nine or ten months of the year. The mad March hare most often described is the common hare which has the longest breeding season of all. Its gestation period appears to be shorter too—42 to 44 days, compared with the mountain hare's 50 days.[2]

The comparative lengths of the breeding seasons were calculated by the post-mortem examination of some of the hundreds of hares that are shot every year by gamekeepers and farmers to control the numbers and by Forestry Commission workers to protect young trees. Samples of common hare does in north-east Scotland in 1960 and 1961 showed the earliest date of conception to be about 10th January. Samples from the Cambridgeshire–Suffolk borders in 1965 showed that a large proportion of does became pregnant between 15th and 28th January.[3] Mountain hares examined in Moray and Aberdeenshire, also in 1960 and 1961, showed the earliest dates of conception as about the 22nd and the 4th of February respectively. The last pregnant common hares were found during the last four days of September and the last pregnant mountain hares on the 19th of August 1960 and the 11th of August 1961.[4] All of which shows that the common hare's

[1] Charles Welling.
[2] Raymond Hewson, 'Reproduction in the Brown Hare and the Mountain Hare in N.E. Scotland', *The Scottish Naturalist*, 1964, Vol. 71, pp. 81–9.
[3] H. G. Lloyd, 'Observations on Breeding in the Brown Hare (*Lepus Europaeus*) during the first pregnancy of the season', *Journal of the Zoological Society of London*, 1968, Vol. 156, p. 524.
[4] Raymond Hewson, op. cit.

breeding season is probably more than two months longer than the mountain hare's. The number of babies in each litter is larger too.

6

Hunting the Hare

As man down the ages has gained most of his knowledge of the hare through hunting, we are including here some of the methods he used in taking the animal. The hunting and killing of the hare also lays bare our attitude towards it; and man must early have come up against the paradox of having to kill a creature he admired.

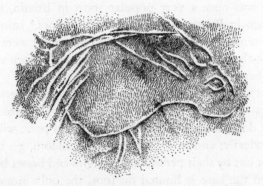

Fig. 1.   Wall engraving of a hare at Le Gabillou

Men have hunted the hare from at least the earliest period about which we have any record. The hare was represented on both Egyptian and Assyrian monuments; and there is evidence[1] that the Egyptians kept hares in special preserves, as we do pheasants, presumably for the purpose of sport. But the remains of the arctic hare have been found among the debris in some of the cave dwellings of palaeolithic man,[2] and the engraved hare on the wall of the

[1] G. E. H. Barrett-Hamilton, op. cit., Vol. 2, p. 243.
[2] Ucko and Rosenfeld, *Palaeolithic Cave Art*, London, 1967, pp. 16, 126, 190.

Le Gabillou cave in the Dordogne area of France, suggests that the hare was hunted during this early period. The question whether the engraving was made simply as a direct, magical aid in the hunt or as a representation of a totem animal, which would give it a wider though essentially similar significance, does not concern us here; for either interpretation would presume paleolithic man's concern with the pursuit and taking of the hare.

Xenophon, writing in the fourth century B.C. described[1] the pursuit of the hare by dogs. Hounds, fast enough to outpace the hare, were unknown at that time; and the dogs which Xenophon described were scenting hounds similar, at least in method of pursuit, to the modern beagles, basset hounds or harriers. The Greeks, too, were interested in the taking of the hare by large birds of prey, even if they did not themselves practise hawking; and there are a number of descriptions in Greek literature.[2] Hawking was once a very popular sport in Britain, but half a century ago in Britain it was practically extinct,[3] being revived only in recent years. Both the hare and the rabbit were favourite quarries for hawks; and there is a description of a hawk attempting to take a hare in a later chapter (p. 209).

But the pursuit by dogs—either fast dogs like greyhounds or scent dogs—has been the usual way of killing the hare for sport. The scent dogs, though comparatively slow of pace, will follow a hare relentlessly; and as it will never, or seldom, go to ground they tire it out by their persistence. Beagles and basset hounds are used when the hare is hunted on foot, the only proper way to hunt the hare in the opinion of many. When the hunters are on horseback they use harriers; and this sport has been aptly called foxhunting in miniature.[4] But the hunting of the hare with dogs is very much older than foxhunting, and undoubtedly began long before the Greeks took up the sport. It is certain that hare hunting was once preferred in Britain and had much more acclaim. The fifteenth-century Edward Duke of York in his treatise on hunting,

---

[1] In his *Cyneticus*.
[2] *The Iliad*, Bk. xxii, 1, 390; *The Agamemnon* of Aeschylus, and in Aristotle.
[3] Barrett-Hamilton, op. cit., Vol. 2, p. 248.
[4] Brian Vesey-Fitzgerald, *It's My Delight*, London, 1947, p. 40.

The Master of Game,[1] gave the hare precedence even over the deer:
'It is to be known that the hare is the king of all venery; for blowing and the fair terms of hunting cometh of the seeking and finding
of the hare. For certain it is the most marvellous beast that is.'
And according to *The Master of Game*: 'It is a fair thing to slay her
with strength of hounds, for she runneth strong and cunningly.
A hare shall last well four miles more or less if she be an old male
hare.'[2] The writer of *The Boke of St. Alban's* (1486) was even
higher in his praise: 'The hare beest Kyng shall be calde of
venery. . . . He is the marvellest beest that is in any londe.'

But many people today raise the question: should we hunt the
hare at all for sport—with greyhounds, scent-dogs, or by any
other means? And many appear to take up the absolute position
that no hares should be destroyed in any way. Alongside this
viewpoint we can place the opinion of a countryman:[3] 'For my
part, as I have written before now, I wish that hares were rarer
animals. No more graceful creature moves in the English fields;
but hares unhappily do not suit with harvests. And to see them as
they flock over the Oxfordshire downs, or as you may watch the
whole plain in Wiltshire moving with them, is to realize that in
these places the only useful hare is a dead hare. Who would shoot
a hare unless he must? But unfortunately, must is often the only
word.' This attitude is undoubtedly the only one for farmers in a
region like East Anglia where hares are traditionally plentiful and
generally heavier than those in other parts of Britain. Here, a fully
grown hare often weighs up to eleven pounds, whereas elsewhere
in Britain its weight ranges between seven and eight pounds.[4]
Many East Anglian farmers have strong views about keeping
down the hare population. They used to say that ten hares will eat
as much as a sheep; therefore the damage they can do to a field of
young corn is considerable. A Norfolk farmer of the old school
estimated that in the farming year one hare would cost him two

[1] Written between 1406 and 1413. It is largely a transcript of Count Gaston de
Foix's *La Chasse*, known as *Gaston Phoebus*. Ref. *The Master of Game*, London, 1909,
pp. 136–46.
[2] Ibid., p. 137.
[3] Eric Parker, *Game Birds, Beasts and Fishes*, London, 1935, p. 139.
[4] Ibid., p. 138.

sacks of corn. Consequently, if there were forty hares on the farm his yield would suffer by eighty combs—a loss that no farmer could afford to stand. He said that hares work during the day; and they eat the 'knots' out of the wheat-stems thus preventing the plants coming to maturity. Moreover, they work out in the middle of the field, unlike the rabbits which keep to the edge where damage is immediately visible. But as the hare likes to live in the open where it can use its speed to best advantage, the farmer will suddenly come across huge, ruined patches in the centre of his corn, perhaps the first indication he has that hares have been at work. A good keeper, he said, was a great boon to him: he would know where the hares had their forms; and even if he could not see them he could find out by using his device of *calling* the hares and bring them towards him.

In recent years, too, hares in East Anglia have done extensive damage to sugar-beet crops. This happened particularly in the 1954 season when hares were unusually plentiful. At that time West Suffolk farmers estimated that in some areas hares had reduced the crop of sugar-beet by as much as two tons an acre.[1] Here, however, is the experience of another farmer of the old school. We recorded it after he had retired from a lifetime of farming in Norfolk where hares have always been abundant, and where he was continually forced to keep them down. His account has been transcribed in full, with his references to other creatures besides hares, because it shows the attitude of the old countryman who respects and is fond of animals but whose situation has compelled him to sterilize this attitude of any trace of sentiment. He is Arthur Edward Harmer of Upgate Farm, Shottisham, Norwich:

[T] 'I was born in 1893 on a 250 acre farm at Arminghall, Norfolk. Then we farmed at Potash Farm, Hethel. There used to be a lot of hares there. I remember going out one morning and getting into a ditch to shoot at two; and when I got there, there was a bunch; and I shot three at one shot. Then I shot two more of the remaining ones. I went home with five, and I hadn't been gone out but half an hour. There was a lot of hares about there, full grown; and there was one run away into the wood to tell the tale. This was

[1] *Evening Standard*, 13th July 1954.

fifty-five years ago. There was a lot of hares about that part then. And we lived tucked into a wood nearby, you see, so they were out; early in the morning it was when I got there. They were just a little way in the wood; and they come out at dusky time.

'They used to go out into the fields to feed. In the day time a good many of 'em would sit out on the ploughed land in a cover in a little place set in a hole in the land. They never used to have a hole like a rabbit. They just had a seat; and they'd *scrap* [scrape] this seat and sit with their hind-part into the seat and lay their head out so they could see anyone coming. And by scrapping this little hole, when they sat in it, it used to bring them on a level with the land. You couldn't see the hare, not if she squatted herself down then. But they were all ready for a bolt. They used to set with their front feet like that [stretched out before them] and the head out of the hole, and the rump used to be down in the hole. When they sprang out they were ready for going. But when you went across the field—if you could see the hare before you went on the field, you couldn't see it when you come near it because they squat down so close. They go down into this hole. That was the seat, or *form* we used to call it. That was their idea of setting without being seen; and you could walk within a yard or two of them and still you couldn't see them—till they sprung out. They were quick on the run and could see to get away. But they got no hole to run to. They never run home to a hole anywhere.

'And the young hares, when they were quite the size of a rabbit, we would chase them on a field and they wouldn't leave that field. They keep going round and round; if they got in a ditch you could catch them. But they had nowhere to hide up; and they never hardly leave the field (unless they were frightened badly) until they were getting a big size. But the old hare have the little ones in bunches of grass out on the field: we used to find an extra dark bunch of grass, a high bunch, and that's where they had them, in there. There'd be two in one field and two in another field perhaps, when they had four. These little hares could see quite plain when they were first born, not like rabbits. They were born so they could see and jump about. They were funny little things, pretty little things. We used to like to see them. We could always catch them till they were a good size in the field because they would never run out of the field: they didn't know where to go. The mother used to come, too, of a night. She'd sit on a field nearby; she could come and settle 'em, look after 'em. They'd never protect them like cats, and that kind; they'd never protect the young ones. The mother would keep nearby. Mostly in the ploughed land they used to get. You couldn't see them in the ploughed land; they scrap this little hole and set in there. Well, when I used to go after them to kill them I used to walk up the furrow, then they'd jump out and I'd shoot them on the ploughed land, in the winter time.

'But of course they had a season. They were not allowed to be shot in the summer time. But if the farmers shot them they couldn't sell them. They can shoot them all the year round but they aren't allowed to sell them. They aren't allowed to sell them from late February to the cutting of the corn. That is the breeding season. When they were cutting the corn; that's when they used to shoot 'em again. But in the summer months—well they used to shoot 'em, farmers used to keep 'em down; but not to sell 'em. They mustn't sell 'em in the summer months.

'There used to be another thing with farm-laws. If I was a farmer I could go and shoot a hare coming out of the corn on my own land without a game licence. But if I went on to my neighbour's and shot one coming out of his corn I got to have a game licence. Time I was on my own farm I could shoot it without a licence; but to go on to another neighbour's and shoot one I'd got to have a game licence. That was done so that people working for them [the farmers] you see, could shoot rabbits coming out of the corn but they weren't allowed to shoot the hares; they were game, ground-game, while rabbits were not. They put them down as vermin. A man didn't allow the men that worked for him to shoot hares on anyone's land. They could shoot rabbits but not hares. Hares were game.

'I've never seen much difference in the buck and the doe. In the spring time we used to see three or four chasing one another about in the field—about March time. They used to be about the time of the year when the wheat was beginning to grow. They used to say

6. Hare hunt, Ancient Greece. From a phial, showing four hounds chasing a hare which flees towards a net and a crouching hunter (*British Museum*)

7. Hare and Hound. The handle of a Roman knife

5. Return from the hunt (detail), Egypt. New Kingdom. About 1500 B.C. (*British Museum*)

The Frightened
Hare

The Mother Hare
and the Tailor

Hares Investing
a Castle

The Hare as
a Soldier

8. From the Metz Pontifical

then if the wheat didn't cover a March hare it wasn't a good piece of wheat. That's what they used to say. It had to be high enough to cover a March hare; when the hare was setting on the ground on these little forms the wheat had to be high enough to cover it.

'Often when we used to be on the stacks sometimes, or if we got upstairs [in the farmhouse] and looked around with a glass you could see a hare or two a-sitting out in the fields. But you go into the field and look for it you couldn't see it; it was squatted down close then, you see. Well, then we used to walk out to where we knew it was, and it would jump up and run off, or we'd shoot it. But when they were down you couldn't see 'em, just like a pheasant: you'd see a pheasant do the same thing. They squat down so you can't see them.

'Yes, I think the hare is an intelligent animal, and they are a very shy animal. A clever animal, too, but easier caught than rabbits because they can't go to ground. That's why these greyhounds can soon catch hares. I myself... now they say about the coursing-hounds. I don't see coursing-hounds so cruel as the hunting hounds. Because a coursing-hound only runs a hare about two minutes at the most, and it's killed. They catch it nearly in the same field. Well, a hare-hunt, that will last twenty minutes or half an hour; until that hare is racing about so it can't run any more. That's a terrible run!

'I once shot one running from the hounds. And I got it away before the hounds got it. I shot it and covered it up so the hounds didn't find it. Well, when I opened that hare I was never so much surprised. There wasn't a mite of blood in it! That blood was all gone to pink bubbles. She'd been chased then for over a quarter of an hour and her blood was all gone to pink bubbles. There wasn't a mite of blood in her. I couldn't . . . I never. When I opened that hare I never used it because I couldn't fancy it. I never see such a thing in my life. It had run the life out of herself. It had run until the blood had gone all bubbles. That was the state that hare was in when it was killed. I shot it. But if them hounds had got it they would eat it up you know, pull it to pieces. But that was the only one I ever see; I shot it in front of the hounds. They'd been hunting that thing for nearly half an hour. But if it had got away from the hounds it would never have lived because the blood had gone to froth. It would have died; it would never have gone back to blood again. But that was the state; that will tell you how these stags and hares must be that have been hunted all that time.

'I've seen stags hunted with their tongues hanging out and nearly done, after they've been hunted for nearly an hour. They don't get a dog that can catch 'em. They want a dog that will chase 'em a long while; and they'll even . . . when . . . we've known one get into a cowhouse to hide up, they want you to turn it out again so it can run a bit further. Well, that isn't . . . I can't see that's right! Well, when they put these coursing-hounds on a hare —I don't say it's not cruel—but the hare is killed in a minute and a half or two minutes at the most. They never hardly run more than two fields. The hounds are quick and they catch it. But these other hunting [scent] hounds they can't catch a hare. They got to run it and tire it out can catch it so. They aren't quick enough. But you get a lurcher, they'll catch a hare in five minutes, less than that, you see. They'll soon catch them. They [the hunters with their hounds] want to have her to hunt. That's put in the paper that they had a rare good hunt! Well, that's the thing. That's sport! But it's jolly cruel for the hare.

'I think the same about foxes. They don't try to catch these foxes, although they hunt 'em. If one of them get to ground, they don't dig it out and kill it. They let it be there for another day. Well, they were hunting here over one season, and they never killed only one fox. I've shot eight foxes since October. It's not cruel to kill a fox like this. I've shot one myself. I don't think it even knew I shot it. I see it come down the wood: it gave about two jumps and I shot it. I never see it move no more. But to go and hunt a thing for half an hour or an hour—well, what would they feel if they got something chasing them all that while and they hear them a-coming? They [the animals] run till they can't run. And, as I say, I see that one hare and I never want to see a thing like it again. I shot thousands of rabbits but I don't shoot to let them keep living. There's hundreds of 'em never feel a thing when you shoot 'em. But that hare was being chased by about twenty-two hounds and twenty horses; and it had been running up to half an hour—round miles and miles. But they hadn't caught that one. I shot it when it was a good field in front of these hounds; got it away from them; they didn't know where it went!

'I remember once hearing my grandmother say when she had a farm at Horstead, Norfolk; and the river run through her meadows; and she saw the hounds catch a deer on the other side of the river and the horses and the men couldn't get to it. The hounds pulled that deer to pieces, joint from joint. And when that was killed it was like a copper of boiling water, my grandmother said; and there were two little ones inside the animal while it was being hunted. And two young ladies that used to hunt from Colonel Herring's—his daughters they were—never went hunting again after they saw that. They sold their horses. And my grandmother told us the tale; and it was in her meadows at Horstead near Narborough. When they had the farm there: Mrs. Ireland my grandmother used to be, Mrs. Emily Ireland, and that was Horstead. I didn't see this but my grandmother told us this story, and that was Colonel Herring's daughters at Narborough Hall witnessed it. That must be eighty years ago—more than that. My father used to be the steward for Colonel Herring.

'Yes, my family has been against blood sports for a long time. That's one of the reasons why we shoot the foxes. Yes, we do. We take against it. We know foxes cause damage and things on everybody's poultry. But I don't believe in chasing them to kill them off. I believe in shooting them; killing them properly. They've done a lot of damage round our way. They've got Mr. Cawston's four stock turkeys last year, hen turkeys when they were worth about £4 each. I'm afraid they're a-going to do it again, now because we've heard 'em round after the wild ducks. There was a dog fox and a vixen out here the other night. My son went outside and he could hear them. The dog fox will bark and vixen makes a high squeaking kind of noise. They were right close; and we were down there and saw the footmarks all round the moat, that same day. So we know they're still there.

'I used to go out a-shooting of hares in the morning. I used to go out before breakfast. I used to get a lot like that. We used to sell them about two shillings to half a crown each. We used to cook 'em too, the nice young ones. They used to make a lovely dish, too. But we used to kill ours and bleed them. We never used to keep them like the gentry used to keep them; hang them up for a fortnight or three weeks. When we killed one we opened it and bled it. It was more like a rabbit then. But when the gentry used to get them they'd hang them up for a fortnight with their insides in. After bleeding my mother used to put them in salt and water and draw all the blood that was left out of them. And then we used to cook them: they were lovely. We used to think so. But I've known a gentleman bring my father a hare after it was shot on our farm a fortnight before.

"Take that away again," he said, "I don't want it. I like mine fresh killed."

'We do with everything. We don't believe in hanging things up till they get high. We like to have one what's fresh. They [the gentry] used to dress it with all sorts of wine—port wine and herbs and so on—to disguise it when it was high. And I've known lots of cooks when they're dressing it wanting to throw it away rather then cook it up. I remember two girls going from Norfolk, going up to London. And one of 'em had to go and pluck the pheasant. She said that when she started plucking it she saw some maggots falling out of it; so she went and threw it all in the dustbin. She hadn't been long before the cook wanted to know if she'd done the pheasant, and the girl said:

"No, I couldn't pluck that because of the smell of it, so I threw it over into the dustbin."

"Well," said the cook, "I tell you, you'll have to go and get that out of there again. It will have to be done!"

'That girl didn't want no pheasant all the while she was up in London.'

Another Norfolk farmer, Albert Hupton (born at Mettingham, Suffolk, in 1889) spent a lifetime observing and catching hares; and he told us some of his experiences:

[T] 'When the hare first comes off the form, for about a hundred yards it's not so fast as a rabbit. But the further the hare goo after a hundred yards, the faster it get. That's the reason it takes two

greyhounds to catch it. But I did have one dog that would catch a
hare—when I was thirteen year old. That could really run and
catch a hare. His mother was a spaniel and his father a cup-winner
greyhound. I used to go into a field of beet [cattle-beet] every
Saturday morning, a ten acre field of beet, and come out with three
or four hares. I used two dogs; but that dog used to catch 'em; the
other one used to turn 'em in between the rows. That dog was
very fast; one of the fastest dogs there was about here, I should
say. There was two: a gamekeeper brought them up in a big wood
because the mother was a spaniel; and he asked me whether I'd
like to buy one; and I had the first pick of the two. That could run
and catch a rabbit when it was four months old. I gave three
shillings for this dog. I was thirteen.

'One night, evening time—closing-in time, there was about
two or three inches of snow on the ground; and I went and stood
up the corner of a meadow where there was a field of mangels
next to it; and there was a road in between the wood and the
hedge. And I had about fifteen snares in that hedge to catch these
rabbits going down. And all at once I heard a patter-patter (it was
a little bit frosty) and out come an owd hare across the road; went
to the first *smile*[1] where I got a snare; and it went—just put its
nose up and down three times, and it hopped away from that and
went to the next smile and put its nose up and down the bank like
that; and it went to the next one: it went to all those smiles what
I'd got snares in for rabbits, and that didn't go through one. It
kept a-cocking up its nose to these smiles; and when it came to
the gateway it went through and down the field.

'Well, this time—during the First World War; and this was in
Brooke—I was coming home on leave one morning, and I met a
coalman, right the other side of the *King's Head*; and he stopped
(he was in his coal-cart and he could see over the hedge on to that
little meadow against the *King's Head*). So he said to me:

"Goo you and see Colman (that's the one who had the *King's
Head* those days) and ask him for a gun. Tell him that the owd
hare is on that meadow."

[1] *Mewse* or *meuse*, the opening in a fence, hedge or gate through which a hare
habitually passes.

'There was nearly a foot of snow on the ground. So I went to the door and I said:

"Hullo, Mr. Colman. Have you got a gun?"

"Why?"

"Well," I said, "Potter now tell me the owd hare sit on thet meadow agen."

"Weh!" he say, "you'll never git thet!"

'So I said: "Have you got a gun?"

"No, not a twelve-bore," he said. "But I got a four-ten."

"Well that'll be better than nawthen."

'So I said to him:

"Which way do thet owd hare get up when anybody goo through that gateway?"

"She goo straight to thet corner."

"Now," I said, "will you do what I ask you to do?"

"Certainly," he said, "I will."

'So I said:

"Go you through there to that hedge; go up with the hedge and get into that corner where she allus goo through when you go on to the meadow," I said: "When you get to that corner I'll go alongside the road-hedge, and I'll meet you; and you come and meet me."

'So that's what he done. Away I goo. When I went up opposite where this hare sat on her seat amongst the snow, I could just see the top of her brown back; and I was getting close to shoot her setting—with this four-ten, really. But the owd hare got up and away she goo. I up with the four-ten and knocked the owd hare over. Well, she kicked about; turned and come back again and dodged between my legs. And I picked the owd hare up and waited for Mr. Colman what kept the *King's Head*. "Well," he said, "thet's a rum 'un. You'd better come in and have a drink."

'So I went in and he gave me a drink and a shilling. He was so pleased to think he'd got that owd hare that a lot of people had been trying to get. Of course, I'd never have got it but for him up in thet corner! She could see him, and she could see me; and she didn't know which way to goo.

'Another time: it was a Saturday—dinner-time really. I'd been snaring rabbits alongside this thick owd wood; and instead of getting twenty or thirty rabbits I was getting down to two. So I said: "I've had enough of this!" So I put some snares across a meadow. There was a large run near, like a sheep's walk, right across this meadow; and I thought I'd plant a couple of snares down there—it looks like a likely spot—fifteen yards apart. And when I went on a Sunday morning to look at these snares—I didn't take a game-bag; of course, I didn't think I'd get anything —there was an owd hare in one alive, and one got the snare round the neck and round a hind leg and it lay there dead. I thought to myself: What am I going to do now? Of course, you shouldn't be in possession of hares on a Sunday morning, owing to the game-laws. So I thought to myself—I had a scarf on: it was a wind-frosty morning; I had a scarf on; I undone my jacket and put the two owd hares on the top here and tied another bit of string around the top of them to keep 'em in position. And I got hoom all right with them and walked into the dairy as Mother was doing the milk churns and pans.

"Mind the way, Mother," I said, "I'm going to have twins this morning!"

'And I undone the top buttons of my breeches and let the two owd hares out! Mother laughed! Of course, I was quite young then: full of devilry—about seventeen to eighteen.'

Arthur Harmer's, the Norfolk farmer, attitude towards hunting, and towards hunting the hare in particular, appears to be the norm for those who work on the land and come into daily contact with animals and wild creatures. A few years ago a twenty-three-year-old Hertfordshire farm-worker took similar action in the face of a hare-hunt. He shot a hare that was being closely pursued by beagles; and he was later fined—for not possessing a game licence. His defence was: 'I don't like the idea of a hare being hunted by hounds. I think it is cruel.' His fine was paid by The League Against Cruel Sports.[1]

William Cobbett, in his writings about his early days,[2] related how he once foiled a hunt of hare-hounds. But on this occasion,

---

[1] *Daily Telegraph*, 30th April 1957; *The Guardian*, 2nd May 1957.
[2] *The Autobiography of William Cobbett*, London, 1969 (Faber Paperback), pp. 13–15.

at least, Cobbett was not animated by a humaniatrian concern but was paying off an old score:

'A huntsman, named George Bradley, who was huntsman to Mr. Smither, of Hale, very wantonly gave me a cut with his whip, because I jumped in amongst the dogs, pulled a hare from them, and got her scut, upon a little common, called Seal Common, near Waverley Abbey. I was only about eight years old; but my mind was so strongly imbued with the principles of natural justice, that I did not rest satisfied with the mere calling of names, of which, however, I gave Mr. George Bradley a-plenty. I sought to inflict a just punishment upon him.

'Hounds (hare-hounds, at least) will follow the trail of a red herring as eagerly as that of a hare, and rather more so, the scent being stronger and more unbroken. I waited till Bradley and his pack were trailing for a hare in the neighbourhood of that same Seal Common. They were sure to find in the space of half an hour, and the hare was pretty sure to go up the Common and over the hill to the south. I placed myself ready with a red herring at the end of a string, in a dry field, and near a hard path along which, or near to which, I was pretty sure the hare would go. I waited a long while; the sun was getting high; the scent bad; but by and by I heard the view-halloo and full cry. I squatted down in the fern, and my heart bounded with the prospect of inflicting justice, when I saw my lady come skipping by, going off towards Pepper Harrow; that is to say, towards the south. In a moment, I clapped down my herring, went off at a right angle towards the west, climbed up a steep bank very soon, where the horsemen, such as they were, could not follow; then on I went over the roughest part of the common that I could find, till I got to the Pales of Moor Park, over which I went, there being holes at the bottom for the letting-in of hares. That part of the park was covered with short heath; and I gave some twirls about to amuse Mr. Bradley for half an hour. Then off I went, and down a hanger at last, to the bottom of which no horseman could get without riding round a quarter of a mile. At the bottom of the hanger was an aldermoor, in a swamp. There my herring ceased to perform its service. The river was pretty rapid: I tossed it in, that it might go back to the

sea and relate to its brethren the exploits of the land. I washed my
hands in the water of the moor; and took a turn, and stood at the
top of the hanger to witness the winding-up of the day's sport,
which terminated a little before dusk in one of the dark days of
November. After over-running the scent a hundred times; after
an hour's puzzling in the dry field after all the doubles and turns
that the sea-born hare had given them, down came the whole
posse to the swamp; the huntsman went round a millhead, not far
off, and tried the other side of the river: "No! damn her, where
can she be?" And thus, amidst conjectures, disputations, mutual
blamings, and swearings a-plenty they concluded, some of them
half-leg deep in dirt, and going soaking home.'

Two records from nineteenth-century East Anglia relate to the
problem of hares in this highly cultivated corn area and to the
methods of keeping them down. The first comes from a book by
Herman Biddell, the writer on Suffolk farming;[1] the date was
about 1850: 'Five and twenty years ago when Mr. Crisp lived at
Chillesford Lodge all the farms in that quarter were game farms—
"game farms" as the word is used to express a state of things
scarcely to be credited. This was in the time of the late Marquis of
Hertford. Stover stacks close by the premises were undermined by
the hares till they had to be hurdled round to save the remnant
from burying up the swarms that would come for a meal on a
frosty night. Not a turnip could be left unclamped after October,
and boys had to keep the pheasants off the pea-stacks. There were
hares there at that time grey with age, with teeth turned up outside the jaw like the tusk of a wild boar. In 1849 three thousand
were killed on the estate between Monday morning and Saturday
night, and on one occasion two hundred and forty were killed in
three hours, and then forty more alive and hungry were counted
on a field close by where the slaughter had just taken place. They
were coursed with greyhounds till at last the dogs would wag
their tails, turn their heads, and refuse to run another hare.'

The other estate, also highly preserved for game, was in West
Suffolk. Stowlangtoft Hall was owned by the Maitland Wilson
family who let the Hall and the estate to the Jamesons, the Irish

[1] *The Suffolk Stud Book*, edited by Herman Biddell, Diss (Norfolk), 1880, p. 643.

whiskey distillers, from 1889 to 1910. The Stowlangtoft estate game-book has been preserved, and it shows that over the period 1853 to 1911 (59 shooting seasons) 41,593 hares were killed on the estate; and it is probable that quite a few more were poached. On 2nd October 1896, a distinguished party shot at the hares. They were: 'Mr. Jameson, H.R.H. The Prince of Wales [afterwards King Edward VII], Lord Enniskillen, Lord Chesham, Lord Londonderry, Capt. Fortescue, Capt. Haig [afterwards Earl Haig, British commander in the 1914–18 war], Col. Oliphant.' They shot over Pakenham Fields and although they got only six hares, they were more successful with the birds, shooting 697 partridges and 59 pheasants. They also got two rabbits. H.R.H. was back again the following season, shooting on 1st October over the same fields. In his party were Capt. Haig, Lord Londonderry, Sir H. Bunbury, Mr. la Touche, Lord H. Vane Tempest, Lord Kenyon, and Capt. Holford. They got one more hare this time but no rabbits; and they do not appear to have been outstandingly successful shoots as far as hares were concerned, and added few to the overall total. Some years before (19th November 1873) a shooting party at Stowlangtoft killed 236 hares in one day at Hunslow Woods. But it is probable that the number of hares shot had little relation to the skill of the shooting party. East Anglian farmers and gamekeepers have remarked on the fluctuation[1] in the

---

[1] The Game Book shows that there was a considerable fluctuation in the number of hares killed:

1865–66	943
1866–67	1,170
1867–68	1,281
1868–69	1,653
1869–70	1,367
1870–71	950
1871–72	1,050
1872–73	833

A 'thin' period occurred about ten years previous to this:

1855–56	790
1856–57	722
1857–58	635
1858–59	780

A note for the season 1856–57 reads: 'Great rabbit year (1473 killed), murrain amongst the hares, supposed to be caused by artificial manure: not grand for birds or pheasants.' But in 1871–2, which had a 'cold and wet June—a rascally bad year for Partridges', 1,050 hares were killed.

hare population in this region over the years; and no one as yet seems to have given an adequate explanation of it.

It will be noted that the Master of Game in his reference to the hare already quoted was in some doubt about its sex, referring to it in the same sentence as a *he* and a *she*. Cobbett in his account, called the hare 'my lady'; and we can assume that this was the conventional phrase at that time. For even today in East Anglia the survivors of the old rural community still refer to a hare, irrespective of its sex, as *Owd Sally* or *Owd Sarah*.

An unusual method of catching hares should be noted here. It appears to have been extensively used by poachers in addition to the more common devices of snaring or netting at the *smiles* or *meuses*, the places where the hare runs through gates or hedges. Though, however, this is one of a poacher's tricks, we first heard of it in connection with a gamekeeper. Stanley Threadkell of Ipswich told us:

[T] 'It was during a holiday I was spending with my aunt on the Yorkshire Moors. It must have been well over sixty years ago. My uncle was head coachman; and one day he introduced me to the gamekeeper and sent me out with him. The gamekeeper said to me:

"Can you do what you're told, boy?"

"I'll try," I said.

"Well," he said, "do you see that hare over there, sitting on its form? I'm going to walk out in a half circle ahead of it. You go behind the hare; and when I start throwing my cap up, walk up to the hare; and when you come to it fall on it."

'The keeper started throwing his cap up. I walked quietly along behind the hare till I got close enough to fall on it; and I grabbed it in my arms. And the keeper came across and took it out of my arms. He was very pleased, and so was I.—Throwing the cap up attracted the hare: naturally the hare was watching the keeper ahead of it; and I was behind it and it could not see me coming up.'

Harold Jenner, another naturalist, learned a similar method in the St. Olaves district of Suffolk:

[T] 'I'd heard about this picking up of good, live hares; and this I was taught by an old boy from this part of the world. He made his living by poaching. He told me this was possible—which I doubted. He took me out; told me what he intended to do, and we went out and did it. This is a question of two of you finding a hare. It has to be at the right time of the year, in March when they are a little peculiar—the mad March hare—and finding a hare which is sitting out in the open. There needs to be a cross wind. One person comes up towards the hare and walks up towards it, as close as he can get without upsetting it. This is a question of doing it very carefully: as soon as the hare begins to show signs of agitation and going off, of standing still and waiting for it to settle down again; and of coming up and dropping a handkerchief—in this case, Owd Billy's was a red-spotted handkerchief which he dropped over the top of a piece of ragwort. Then he walked backwards—walked away completely. Then I came up from the other side, having been told what to do. And the hare was sitting watching this red-and-white handkerchief waving in the breeze; and I simply walked up behind the hare and picked it up. I've done this quite a few times since: I've even done it on my own. Yes, if the hare happens to be in the right place so that I can approach it from one side, and put an ordinary handkerchief down and then go backwards and come round behind it; come up behind it fairly quickly. I've done this several times. I've picked up at least a score at that time of year. It doesn't make much sense: I don't really know why it works; but it does. The hare seems to be fascinated by whatever it is—something that has been brought up and wavers in the breeze. It won't work except in the mating season when they're punching and fighting and acting, fooling generally. I've never been able to do it at any other time of the year other than March or very early April. But I've picked up a score this way over a matter of thirty-five years. But the conditions have to be right: if they aren't it just isn't possible. I've had a great many failures. It doesn't always work by any means. You got have a cross wind.'

The sport of hunting the hare in Wales is of a different character from that, say, in East Anglia. There are two chief reasons for this: the terrain is different, and also the weather. Frequently, the presence of deep snow on the hills during the hunting season calls for an entirely different technique as the following accounts show. Our Welsh informants also had experience of hunting the mountain hare which was present in south Wales nearly fifty years ago. Mansel Davies of Pembrokeshire recalled:

[T] 'I remember I went out with my brother-in-law who had a farm near here to look for hares; and there was a tremendous thickness of snow on the ground. But he had a sheep-dog; and his sheep-dog was making points at a part where the hedge was—though there was nothing of the hedge to be seen. Snow right up to the top, you see. He told me there must be a hare in there else the dog wouldn't do like that. So he went there and knelt down and picked up some of the snow with his hands. And three hares jumped out! But the dog wasn't fast enough to catch one of them; and the three got away.

'I'll tell you a little yarn about this bloke who had this whippet; Ben Richards was his name. He was a deuce of a poacher—the one I was telling you about. And one of the mansions there, they had a shooting party every year, do you see. Invited their friends from very far to shoot pheasants. There were hundreds of pheasants there. They were breeding them up themselves. And, anyhow, the crowd now had come on this particular day from far away. And there were very few pheasants to be had, anyhow! A lady was the owner of the mansion, and of the pheasants of course; and she was "down at the bottom", you see, when all these people had come there and the shoot was so bad. Now when they were having food after they came back one of them said:

"What has happened, do you think?"

"Oh, the poachers must be there."

"Well, who is the biggest poacher? Do you know the name of the biggest poacher in the district?"

"Yes, Ben Richards. That's the biggest poacher in this district."

"Well, now take a tip off me," this man said. "You hire this poacher, Ben Richards, as your gamekeeper; and give him double the money any other keeper is getting."

'And by Jove, it paid! He put down wires and so on where they were trapping the hares and rabbits and so on. Putting wires down to stop them. And, anyhow, the next shooting party came. Damn! there were hundreds of pheasants and hares and so on. That was the poacher who had that fast little whippet. Ben Richards was his name; but he's dead now, years and years ago.'

We also talked to two countrymen, Evan William Davies and Howell Jeffreys from Coelbren and Dyffryn Cellwen on the borders of Glamorgan and Breconshire. The common brown hare is abundant around Coelbren, and the mountain hare—the blue-back, as they call it here—used to be found a few miles farther north in the Sennybridge district. Howell Jeffreys told us:

[T] 'They make tunnels in the snow, have a lot of sport in the snow. I think they're sort of intoxicated with snow sometimes when they are feeling healthy. They sleep very soundly in the snow because you can get very close to them; and even pass them; and they won't notice. When you are tracking them in snow it's no use you starting from their feeding ground. You got to guess where the form is or else they'll keep you walking all day. You can easily say where a hare goes to its form (*gwâl* in Welsh) on the snow, see, and where it got out. Because it comes out of its form straight. When it goes into its form it's doubling back this way and that, making tracks difficult for you to find. But when you've seen a hare doubling back, her form is not far away in the snow. I don't say that they stop in their forms in the same place all the time; but it's in a matter of an acre or two [where they make them]. They have a glorious time in the deep snow because they make tunnels and they trample it down. I think they are sort of intoxicated when they get snow.'

Evan Davies also said:

[T] 'I've seen hares now in the snow up country there (in Breconshire). Walking on, on; follow the tracks; lost it; can't see it at all. But there was a little breathing hole with her. When once we got on a few yards that hare would work herself out and go. I was telling my *butty* [mate]; "Look at her going now!" And I've seen hares after that hard weather frozen on the seat. Dead! Yes, on many occasions I've seen that.'

Evan Davies has also done a great deal of coursing:

[T] 'We used to go out to Forest Lodge coursing hares with

greyhounds. Slip two dogs and away they go. If you slipped two dogs out of your turn, you'd be sent off the ground.'

He gave a good picture of the advantage a hare has—either mountain or common hare—while it is running up hill:

[T] 'I know when we went to Forest Lodge we rose eighty-five hares, and never caught one, near Sennybridge, Breconshire, where the blue-back was. This was in 1926. Mr. Rhys Rees, Pantscallog, was running it then. He used to have it there. Those hares just came down from the hills to the corn or to the clover; and then they lay in the marshes before going up to the Forest. And he started two hares with a beater or a spaniel which works close; and once the hare was up, slipped two greyhounds. Once she was up that mountain, putting her ears back and changing gear and everything. Well! The hare can run faster up hill than down it. You'll never catch her!'

7

Ancient Ways of Taking the Hare

We referred in the previous chapter to the method of *calling* hares used, by poachers and gamekeepers alike, to bring hares in sight of where they are standing. Two Suffolk gamekeepers, Archibald Tebble of Helmingham and Percy Muttit of Blythburgh, had both used the device at various times when following their occupation. Percy Muttit called hares some years ago by making the appropriate sound through his teeth. Archibald Tebble demonstrated how he made the calling sound by placing the back of his hand to his mouth and *squeaking* or *sucking*. He was out one morning with his grandson:

[T] 'This hare came out of the sugar-beet and was quite unaware of our presence, and we watched it quite a while. It was having a peck at this plant and that plant and various other things.

"We'll make a note of that!"

'And I squeaked on my hand—like that; and of course it sat up. But eventually the wind was in the hare's favour. It winded us and went on rather fast.'

Gamekeepers enticed the buck hares by imitating the cry of the doe. The scream of a leveret in difficulties invariably brings the doe; and a successful imitation of this by the caller would bring her within sight in a few seconds. But the caller has to have a good ear, and skill in interpreting and reproducing the hare's cries. In addition to the above two methods, calling was also effected by placing a blade of grass to the mouth and blowing against it, a device that is known to most schoolboys when they want to produce a high-pitched squeak. Hare-calling does not appear to be much practised now, though it was possible—not many years ago —to buy an instrument for making hare-calls from a gun-maker's shop. Hare-calling appears to be the same as hare-piping, but there has been some controversy about hare-piping and hare-pipes. Brian Vesey-Fitzgerald has briefly summarized[1] the different viewpoints which largely centre in the interpretation of a law passed during the reign of Richard II 'prohibiting the use of un-authorized persons of dogs for hunting, ferrets, nets, hare-pipes or other engines to take or destroy hares'. Similar laws with similar intent were passed in later reigns and 'the word hare-pipe does not disappear from the statute-book until 1831 when the Game Act came into force'.

From the above context people have argued that the hare-pipe was some sort of trap or snare. But Brian Vesey-Fitzgerald points out that no one in the countryside of Britain knows of a trap or snare that is called a pipe; but many of the men who call hares refer to it as *piping*. He rightly argues that country words last much longer than the distance in time from the reign of Queen Anne when a law mentioning hare-pipes was last passed; and he has a strong case when he identifies hare-piping with hare-calling and interprets hare-pipes as some sort of device or instrument for calling. He himself has seen hare-pipes made of plaited grass. Additional evidence also seems to be on his side when we record that, 'In March 1910 two men were convicted in the north of England for killing six bucks by use of such a call'.[2]

But it seems that we can be absolutely certain of nothing whenever a hare is concerned. Just as we were about to enlist ourselves on Brian Vesey-Fitzgerald's side along comes a fifteenth-century poem[3] which apostrophizes the hare in this manner:

> *Go forth, Wat! with Christ's curse!*
> *And if I live thou shalt be take.*
> *I have a hare-pipe in my purse;*
> *It shall be set all for thy sake.*

[1] *It's My Delight*, London, 1947, pp. 75–6.
[2] G. E. H. Barrett-Hamilton, op. cit., Vol. 2, p. 282.
[3] The complete poem is in Appendix Two. It is from the *Dunbar Anthology* (1401–1508), ed. Prof. E. Arber, 1901. It is also printed in *Early English Miscellanies* (Warton Club), 1855.

We have to leave the reader to decide whether an engine or device lethal to a hare will go into a man's or a woman's purse, or whether a hare-pipe was simply a small instrument, something like a whistle or tin *noise-maker* that boys used to delight in, or like the device which we know was sold by the gun-makers for this very purpose of calling. Yet—do we *set* a whistle or for that matter a musical pipe? Unless the word has radically changed, we would be more likely to set a snare than anything else; and a snare perhaps that could easily be concealed in a purse.

We have mentioned the use of greyhounds in coursing and how difficult it is for even two fast dogs to catch a hare which has started moving and is properly in its stride. This is chiefly due to the hare's ability to sight the following dog even when it is moving forward, and to turn abruptly away from it at the very moment the dog is about to strain his jaws to take it. This action has been vividly described in a sixteenth-century book[1]: 'It is gallant sport to see how the Hare will turn and winde to save hyr selfe out of the dogge's mouth. So that sometimes even when you thinke that your Greyhounde doth (as it were) gape to take hyr, she will turn and cast them a good way behind hyr; and so saveth hir self by turning, wrenching and winding, until she reach some covert and so save hyr life.'

Two Irish countrymen have described how skilfully the hare uses its ability to turn sharply and alter its course. First, John Kenny:[2]

[T] 'The hare often tricks the dogs that are after him. Well, that's no lie. The dog is tight on the hare, and she comes to a wall —and she takes the wall. And when she hits the ground she lies flat and the dog goes over; and she comes back, and by the time he gets up she's two hundred yards gone. I once saw them going to a gate and getting over the gate, the hare turning to the left: the dog would go on straight. And when he'd come back over the gate he'd go down straight; and she'd be gone away out in the next field. Fooled!'

[1] *The Noble Art of Venerie or Hunting*, attributed to George Turberville, 1575; reprinted, Oxford, 1908.
[2] Newtown, Kiltoom, Athlone.

The hare also has this tremendous ability to leap, not only over obstacles but across the ground, as for instance many of our informants have told us, when she leaps over a considerable distance into her form, and thus eludes a pursuer of her tracks in the snow. This leaping power of the hare has been confirmed by an English observer who once saw a hare clear a wall seven feet six inches in height.

The other example of the hare's skill in the quick turn comes from the same district of Ireland, the midlands near Athlone. William Egan:

[T] 'I seen a hare hunt once, and they were coming from the place where we call *The Hill*. Well, we were watching this hunt coming in the bog. We had a right view and we were right up. So they came in the bog, two hounds after the hare. She turned straight to the bog-hole where we cut the turf out of. You know, that would be the height of that ceiling, into the water where the turf was cut away. She came; and she came to the edge of that. She wheeled short; went out of the bog; in went the hounds and in to the bog-hole. Couldn't stop themselves! They throwed water up to the clouds out of the bog-hole. She was gone out of the bog; and there was neither tell nor count of the dogs. What was the use of following her then? She was beyond the other side of the Shannon before they knew where they were!'

Another old countryman, Patrick Johnston, described vividly how a greyhound broke his neck in chasing a hare. He went after the hare at speed, and in attempting to snap at it as she came alongside, it turned suddenly and eluded him, leaving him gaping the air.[1] As he said:

[T] 'When she turns she mesmerizes the greyhound. He doesn't know where she's gone. Well, now she's gone. She has the good odds of them then.'

He also described how some greyhounds had been trained not to attempt to get up alongside a hare to try to take her from the side:

[T] 'There's more greyhounds then, can follow the hare straight behind her; and they speed up, and when they come up they'll throw their nose right in between her hind legs. The little

---

[1] Cf. Ovid: *Vacuos exercet aëra morsus.*

tip of the greyhound's nose pegs [throws or pitches] her up in the air. It's a great thing. It's lovely to see 'em. There's no worry on them then. They'll get her coming down.'

This method of catching hares was also practised in south Wales on the Glamorgan–Breconshire border at Cefn Coed y Cymer, near Merthyr Tudful. *Cwrso pryfed*, coursing hares, on the moorland above the valleys was a common sport among coalminers at one period; and it appears to have been carried on into the Thirties. Seven years ago Lynn Davies, now of the Welsh Folk Museum, St. Fagans,[1] recorded two ex-coalminers, Ned Powell and Noah Evans from Cefn Coed. They were both born *c.* 1895 and the period they refer to is roughly 1910–20, when they were young men. The sport was also followed by Monmouthshire miners during the same period. The Merthyr men coursed the hare with specially trained whippets. It was a sport that was very popular; and the taking of the hare for the pot seems to have been a secondary motive: the excitement was mainly in the whippet's ability to turn the hare over a number of times before it was actually caught—'turn it over so you could see the hare's white belly uppermost'. If the dog happened to catch the hare immediately, within a short distance—thirty yards, as Ned Powell remembers on one occasion—there was a certain disappointment: such an encounter was not considered a good, sporting one. One man's dog was often pitted against the other; and there was betting on the result.

As we see from Noah Evans's testimony, the above method of catching the hare appears to be identical with the Irish:

'My uncle, Twm Noah, had a very fine bitch. Ship, he used to call her. That was one of the best dogs I've ever seen for hunting. She could always be relied on to raise a hare on Cilsannws over there. Always! He'd trained this old whippet so she'd be following the old hare with her nose right under it! The result, of course, she could tumble the hare right over, completely. That's the way she used to catch 'em; turn the hare right over; and then at last grab it in her jaws!'

[1] Tapes nos. 30 and 36 in the *Merthyr Tudful and District Dialect Collection* in the archives of the *Welsh Linguistic Research Unit*, University College, Cardiff.

Ned Powell, the other informant, also emphasized that he trained his whippet, Silver, to swing with the hare and to catch it after it turned. It is probable that the smaller whippet was able to follow the turn of the hare much more effectively than the larger greyhound.

Patrick Johnston described another unusual way of taking a hare by a snare. He had often found that when he had fixed his snare in the traditional way, the hare was strong enough to break the wooden peg that held it to the ground, or to tear it up and make off with both snare and peg. When he was a young lad, an old poacher told him a way of avoiding this: instead of fixing the snare to a peg driven in the ground, tying it to a branch of a hawthorn bush, cut off for the purpose:

[T] 'I never set one snare after that but I caught a hare. I never missed a hare. In her path as she goes along she makes *pups*— what we call *pups*. It's a hole, a mark on the ground, a little round spot [where the pads go]. When you get that you put this snare right on that hole over that pup. Set it to the height I showed you now—me thumb. Put down your snare; and you have a small bit of a stick now, about as thick as my little finger— about eight inches long. And you split that at the top—a middling split—and you leave the snare down in this, in that bit of a stick; and put that stick in the ground by the side of the pup. Right! Well, that holds the snare the height you want it. And it's no obstruction to him when he gets it: it's gone and out of this split bit. It's a grand turn!'

The bush is then tied to the snare:

[T] 'When the hare gets into the snare he'll stir the bush; and he hears this noise and he'll make a drive round; and when he hears, of course, the snare is on him and tightens on him. Well, the little bush will come out; and he'll make a drive far off. And the moment he does, the bush will come and hit him in the front: it will go before him and he'll lep [leap] back. He chucks it off the ground; and, of course, when he does it hits him behind. He makes another lep on and the bush will hit him on the head again —and so on until in a few minutes the hare chokes himself.'

The following methods of catching hares in Ireland and Wales are given in some detail because they are undoubtedly some of the most ancient, especially those which forgo the use of dogs. Catching a hare with a hunting- or throwing-stick probably goes back to the Stone Age. The Australian aborigines still use a stick that is described as being very much like the Irish one; and they can kill a running animal with it just as some of the Irish countrymen we talked to can 'turn over' or kill a hare running at a distance of twenty or thirty yards from the thrower. The Irish throwing-stick is about thirty inches in length and is a little heavier than an ordinary walking-stick. Blackthorn, hazel, or sally (sallow) or willow were commonly used to make a stick; but one of our informants made a stick from an old broken fork-handle. Patrick Johnston preferred a hazel stick, and one that had a slight bend about a third of the way down the stick.

[T] 'And what you would want now to be accurate—get a bend in this stick so it would come out crooked that way, with a hump in it. And whatever it does in there, it makes the stick carry accurate. I know that! I tested that. I tested it with a straight stick first, you know. And when it was *pegged* it always took this side of the object. You see, I always peg a little out when I use the stick. But you should always, when a hare is passing you: peg a full yard in front because he'll be there agen the stick is there. How I used to do: I'd put my cap in the field, practising to peg. And the straight stick would always bring it this side of the cap. And the other was accurate; used to cut the cap out of it. I never hunted hares without—I always carried two: two sticks with a different kind of bend in them, because if I did chance to miss with one. I hadn't to be looking for it. I had another chance in hand. Experience it is! You'll see your fault after a couple of turns; and if you're anyway smart, you'll pick up something; then you'll try some other game.'

John Connaughton told us that you could knock out a hare with a throwing-stick:

[T] 'Anywhere up to twenty yards—maybe more. Mightn't kill him. You'd knock him out, anyhow. You'd leave him where you'd get him, anyhow. Curl him upside down. A hare is different to a rabbit. You can knock a rabbit out quicker than a hare. You could hit a hare, and you could curl her upside down, and she could get up and go.

'Oh, practice! They would practise. That was every Sunday when they came home from Mass. Put up anything for a target, anything at all; maybe a lump of stick, a kettle, a teapot, an old tin can, maybe a bottle sometimes. Well, when it was after a certain time, the rabbits get fit to hunt (they'd got to be about three-quarter size). Up to then they'd be at the fishing every Sunday when they came home from Mass. From that time till the spring-time, they'd be off hunting somewhere or another.'

The use of the throwing-stick was not solely confined to hares and rabbits:

[T] 'Four guns were out after woodcock; and the dogs raised one. They fired and missed her. A man with a throwing-stick saw this woodcock coming; let fly and cut the wing of her—clean off.' This is exactly how the Australian aborigines used the stick as the following quotation shows:[1]

'The woomera, which white men sometimes call the throwing-stick, is a hooked stick that hurls the spear. There is another throwing-stick, one that is itself thrown; it is made of heavy hard-wood, and can be thrown with destructive force a considerable distance to break the legs of game, or hurled with a whizzing, circular motion up into a flock of wild duck or pigeon or other flock birds to bring down half a dozen crippled birds at the throw. In the hands of the Kimberly natives these sticks are thoroughly nasty weapons, really clubs, called the dowak and the quondi.'

Here are two stories told by John Connaughton about the 'old times' (the end of last century and the beginning of this) when the throwing-stick was still in common use:

'Devery was out hunting with the landlord, General l'Estrange, together with greyhounds. They were after hares. Now Devery was an expert with the throwing-stick. He was watching a hound chasing a hare that made for a gap. The hare was getting away from the hound; and Devery, who was standing near the gap, up and let fly with his throwing-stick and killed the hare.

[1] Ion L. Idriess, *Our Living Stone Age*, London, 1964, p. 24.

"Why did you do that?" the landlord said angrily as he came up.

"Your old dog is no good!" said Devery; "I had to kill her. I wanted soup!"

John Page was born about 1840 in the midlands near Athlone; and he was well known for killing hares with a throwing-stick:

'This was in the landlord's time—Lord Mount Sandford. Now Sandford heard about Page's skill with the stick and asked him whether this was true. He denied it for fear of the landlord's power. But he coaxed Page to come shooting with him into the bog. Sandford had a gun and dogs to raise the hare. After a while the landlord made a bargain with Page "to take every second chance"—that is, the landlord to shoot with the gun and then Page to try at a hare with his stick. So the landlord fired three volleys at a hare and missed. Page let fly with his stick and tumbled the hare at the first throw. Sandford said:

"Now I can see that you can do it. It's true what I heard about you!"

'And he made John Page his gamekeeper: he gave him land and a cottage and made him keeper over a big tract of his estate.'

But it is very likely that the throwing- or hunting-stick was in common use in the rest of Britain a few centuries ago. There is a reference to it in the thirteenth-century poem (p. 202) from Shropshire; and we know from the Dorsetshire mummers' play, an excerpt from which is included later (pp. 100–2) that the belligerent Father Christmas carried a hunting-stick when he went after the jack hare he had brought home with him.

Allied to the use of the throwing-stick is the method of getting a hare with a pebble or stone:

[T] 'Michael Mc Cormick, an old postman, lived in Sally Grove, Roscommon. There was a tradition there of killing a hare with a stone. Michael Mc Cormick used to have one. It was a round pebble from the seashore—about the size of a good hen-egg—smooth and made so it would fit nicely into the hollow of the hand. He always had this stone with him in his pocket as he was going round with the letters. He killed a hare in a ditch one morning as he was travelling on his rounds.'

Another ancient way of catching a hare was practised in Ireland until recent times: the digging of a pit-trap. This was called a hare-hole, and was usually dug in a bog. The hole was about a yard square—sometimes less—and was dug down to about the depth of a spade, two and a half to three feet. The sides, however, were not dug down straight: they sloped outwards from the centre of the hole. Patrick Johnston made his trap like this:

[T] 'You'd scoop it out like a pot inside. Scooping in, not straight. If you did she would be up out of it. But you have to cover the hole. You get strands of heath [heather], and you lay them across on that square hole. If it's heath she's travelling on there, then get the short heath and shake it over, and you could stick an ordinary strand down now as if it was growing. (I was accurate.) Or if it was mould she was travelling on, shake the mould on the whole along. Get a bit of the heath, and it would hold up the mould for you. And put the mould along; peg it along, and she'll come on. She'll land on that and that snaps.

'I cotched what they called hedgehogs—*gráinneog*. I caught them buggers in it. He'd be below; and I'd think now it's fine as I see it snapped overhead: I am all right! And I'll go and look at my buck below, and I'd seek round. And I'd be mad when I saw this *gráinneog*!'

The hare-hole usually started to fill with water as it was being dug; and overnight it would often collect water to a depth of two feet or so. Another Irish countryman, William Egan, told us his experience:

[T] 'I catched them [hares] in traps myself; and I made hare-holes in the bog. Have you ever heard a hare dying in a hare-hole? You'd never suffer one again while you're living! The mournful cry of them is frightening. She cries like a child. You'd never set a hare-hole again!'

Patrick Johnston also caught hares in a bag after making a kind of bridge-contraption up to an old tow-path or high-bank. He laid poles from the bank down to ground level so that there would be a space of four or five feet underneath. And after fixing lathes across the poles he nailed a bag, with its mouth open, to this structure. Then he covered the surface of the contraption and the mouth of the bag with vegetation in a way similar to the covering of the hare-hole. When the hare crossed the trap she fell into the bag:

[T] 'The bag slackens, drops with her, and she has no power; and its swings this way and that way. But I now have her in the bag. That's what they call the Hare in the Bag.'[1]

As a coda to these accounts of hare-hunting in Ireland we include these two pictures of a fox going after a hare—both gathered in the same district. First John Kenny:

[T] 'Well, she [the hare] is on her form, and the fox wants to get her. And he creeps along on his belly, and he keeps dragging himself along (I was watching them). And when he gets within five yards of her he makes the charge and gets her. I was watching them. I thought he was going to take the young lambs—I had sheep at the time and I thought he was watching the ewes he was. And he was watching the hare he was. And he got her! He had her killed when I landed there. And he left her there and skedaddled: he wasn't able to bring her; she was big; she was heavy. And she died there, the poor thing; and I left her there. But when I returned again she was gone. That's the fox had her.'

And John Connaughton:

[T] 'I know. It is true as to tell you a fox will know the way a hare is lying: whether she is facing him or not; and he'll always go for the hare from the front. And the reason for that is he'll steer his course as carefully as he can before he. . . . The hare has a turn, one side or the other; and it's on the turn the fox will take him. If we were to take him coming from behind, he [the hare] would have gone out straight from him. I've often heard it said by an old man over here now—Pat Callan—if you're facing a hare you'll take him, if a fellow is looking at her. She'll see more behind her than straight in front—always!'

[1] A phrase that seems to echo the *Badger in the Bag* of the *Mabinogi*.

8

The Hare as Food

The same ambiguity, and the same differing view-points as we meet when discussing the hare's behaviour, are still present when we consider the hare as food. Even in the catch-phrase which comes so easily to mind when we think of the hare in this connection, *First Catch Your Hare*, Mrs. Beeton's 'classic mot of culinary philosophy'—as a cookery book expert once called it—is not what it seems. But we might have expected this. Mrs. Beeton, presumably a practical woman, would not have been likely to amuse herself by trying to elevate the obvious into a principle. Like many of the beliefs about the hare, the saying has been grossly changed from its original form. It started out in life in a much more sober dress:[1] *Take your hare when it is cased*, and it was not written by Mrs. Beeton.

It can be assumed that hares were hunted for food from early times. A fully grown hare has a lot of meat on it; and would have been worth the chase even though it probably would have been a hard one. But how extensively it was hunted is not known; for there appear to have been two long-standing reservations about the hare as food, one of them very ancient. First, hare's meat is dark and rather 'strong' and unsavoury unless it is skilfully prepared and cooked. The Master of Game advised that after a day's hunting of the hare the animal's flesh should not be given to the dogs because it is indigestible. They should have only the tongue and the kidneys and some of the blood soaked in bread.

Robert Burton in his *The Anatomy of Melancholy*, also warned

[1] *The Oxford Dictionary of Quotations*, London, 1943, p. 571.

against hare meat: 'Hare is a black meat, melancholy and hard of digestion; it breeds *incubus*[1] often eaten, and causeth fearful dreams, so doth all venison, and is condemned by all physicians. Myaldus and others say that hare is a merry meat, and that it will make fair as Martial's epigram[2] testifies to Gellia; but this is *per accidens* because of the good sport it makes, merry company and good discourse that is commonly at the eating of it, and not otherwise to be understood.'

If we can judge from East Anglia, ordinary country people agree with these writers. We have asked a number whether they like hare meat; and most have never tasted it. Whenever they poached a hare, unless circumstances were exceptional, they sold it; and as the hare usually fetched a good price this was the more worthwhile course for them. Country people much preferred a rabbit to a hare; and the reasons they gave for not liking hare's meat can be summarized by the experience of a sixty-nine-year-old countryman[3] who poached hares but had never tasted the meat:

[T] 'I remember poaching hares in the early Twenties, and the price that time would be about 7s. 6d. for a hare—much more than you got for a day's work; because I remember thrashing corn then for 5s. 0d. a day. No, I don't like eating hare. In fact, I've never tried it. Well, I think it's because of the meat; it's very dark, and they are so bleedy. There's a lot of blood: people don't like the blood; and they also—there's a smell that a lot of people don't like. The meat is very strong.'

A farmer's wife[4] occasionally cooked a hare:

[T] 'The blood! Murder! Oh, yes, in this district joints of hare were steeped in a pail of milk to draw out the blood before they

---

[1] (*a*) A lascivious spirit appearing only by night, credited with the power of producing supernatural births by actual intercourse with women,

(*b*) (pathological) A sensation of an oppressive weight at the epigastrium during sleep, and of an incapability of moving or speaking; a nightmare.

[2] *Epigrams:* 'Whenever you send me a hare, Gellia, you say to me: "You will be beautiful for seven days." If you are not making fun of me, my love; if you actually mean what you say, then you Gellia—poor girl—have never tasted the tiniest bit of hare in your life!'

[3] Joe Thompson, Helmingham, Suffolk.

[4] Mrs. Phoebe Lockwood, Thorndon, Suffolk.

started the cooking. I'm talking about years ago when a pail of milk, you know, didn't cost so much. But the hare was costly to prepare. Well, I had to doctor it up. Just look at one of the old recipes. In 1910 it cost about 6s. 6d. to jug or roast a hare. A woman needed the animal plus one and half pints of good stock, a glass of port or of claret, a tablespoonful of lemon juice, three ounces of butter, an ounce of flour, an onion, four cloves, twelve peppercorns, parsley, thyme, a bay-leaf, seasoning, veal, forcemeat and redcurrant jelly.'

To prepare a hare in this way so that it would be palatable, was beyond the means of the ordinary countryman who in this area was earning between nine and twelve shillings a week at that period. 'That's why the women preferred a bunny because by adding pork they could make a jolly good pie for next to nothing.'

A Suffolk gamekeeper[1] thought that country people do not like the hare's meat because they have not tasted a hare done in the proper way. It seems clear that the hare was gourmet's meat, eaten chiefly if not exclusively by the 'gentry'; and the cynical would say that they were unaffected by the blood and the smell because they were removed from it. But they were very careful to select the hares that went into the kitchen. The Stowlangtoft Game Book shows that only young hares went to the table:

'1863, 22 Jan.   6 killed coursing
                    23 leverets killed for house
      26 Feb.   30 leverets killed for house'

Mrs. Beeton, too, recommended that you should choose a young hare for the kitchen. It may be known by its mouth and sharp claws and the narrow cleft in the lip. An early nineteenth-century book[2] written by *A Lady* had, as its object, cookery for rich and poor; but even if the cost of preparing the hare was not prohibitive the manner of preparing it (especially old hares) would suggest that those who prepared it would not be inclined to eat it. Here are three of the recipes:

[1] Archibald Tebble, Helmingham.
[2] *Domestic Economy and Cookery: For Rich and Poor*, London, 1827.

The Hare as Food

'To Roast an Old Hare

'An old hare is very easily known, from its weight and skin. If the ears tear easily, it is supposed still fit for roasting; if new killed, it will be stiff; but if long kept, it will be limber, and of a mawkish smell. The condition it is in ought to fix the time and the mode of dressing.

'If an old hare is to be roasted, prepare it in the following manner: Prick the neck, and squeeze out the blood with the hands, till it is quite clear. Lay it on a cloth, and wipe it well and stuff it with a high-seasoned bread stuffing; sew it up, and skewer it in a sitting posture. Have ready a strong garlic, allspice, vinegar, and sweet herbs braise; lay in the hare; let it come gently to a simmer: if it never boils at all so much the better. Leave it two hours, take it up, and, if to be larded, let it cool on a cloth; if not, it may be spitted and barbed immediately, and basted continually for ten minutes with the braise, and afterwards with cream and butter. Serve the gravy from the dripping-pan, with red-currant jelly sauce, or cold jelly in a crystal dish.'

'To Roast a Hare

'Skin and prepare it, wipe it well without washing, slit it a little under the jaws to let out the blood, and stuff it with a savory or sweet stuffing, or with a gratin; sew it up, and lard or barb and paper it. Put it into the dripping-pan half a pint of ale, a gill of vinegar, a clove of garlic, pepper and salt; baste it continually without stopping, till it is all dried up. If a pint of good cream or a quart of fresh milk can be spared, baste it with it till ready and finish frothing it with butter and flour. Serve as above.'

'To Roast a Leveret

'Leverets are roasted in the same way, either barbed or larded. They may be stuffed with a sweet pudding, and basted with butter or clarified dripping and the liver mixed in the sauce from the dripping-pan.'

A Lady advises leverets in March and hares in September; and this further nicety may well confirm the suggestion that in East Anglia, at least, there was a definite division in regard to the hare as food, and that this division followed a more or less horizontal class line: those who were well off could afford to prepare the hare in the accepted way in order to make its meat pleasantly edible; those who could not afford to preferred to do without it.

But here are two very early recipes for *cyue*[1] (onion broth: mixed meat stewed with onions), a manner of cooking the hare which has lasted in Wales and Ireland to the present day:

> '*Harus in cyue*
>
> '*Perboyle þe hare and larde hit wele,*
> *Sethyn loke þou rost hir everydele;*
> *Take onyons and loke þou hew hom smalle,*
> *Frye hom in grece, take peper and ale,*
> *And grynde togeder þo onyons also;*
> *Coloure hit with safrone and welle hit þo;*
> *Lay þe hare in charioure, as I þe kenne;*
> *Powre on þe sewe and serve hit þenne.*'
>
> *Harus in cyueye*

'Take Harys, & Fle hem, & make hem clene, an hacke hem in gobbetys, & sethe hem in Watere & Salt a lytylle; þan take Pepyr, and Safroun, an Brede, y-grounde y-fere, & temper it wyth Ale. þan take Oynonys & Percely y-mynced smal togederys, & sethe hem be hem self, & afterward take & do þer-to a porcyon of vynegre, & dresse in.'

There must be more in the reluctance of country people to eating the hare than just a natural distaste for the flesh of the

---

[1] *Liber Cure Cocorum* and *Early English Meals and Manners*, quoted in 'Names of a Hare', A. S. C. Ross, *Journal of Leeds Philosophical Society; Literary and Historical*, Section III, 1935, pp. 369–70.

animal—its dark colour and its 'mawkish' smell and to the amount of blood it has in its body. There is another reason (this is the second of the reservations we mentioned earlier): country people are those who have kept the old traditions in their pristine form, and a certain attitude to the hare is one of them. Up to recent years in Britain they still followed beliefs and customs whose origins are to be sought in the remote past before recorded history; and over the centuries—although these beliefs have lost their original purpose—they still persisted like a hard shell after the kernel it once held had long since withered away. If, however, in its newer setting a belief, or custom, now appeared irrational, they did not find it difficult to bring forward a reason for still carrying it out; and, what is more, vaguely believing in it. For traditional belief is not perpetuated by reason alone but by the vague awe that was once the most vital part of its make-up; and a deficiency of reason is no barrier to its continuing. Moreover, this awe, which is maintained by the knowledge that this has always been so and that their ancestors had always responded in a similar way, would ensure that they could always put forward a negative reason, saying it is *safer* and *luckier* to follow the custom or to retain the belief rather than to risk the penalties of ignoring it. The repugnance in Britain to eating horse-flesh can be quoted as an example. Most people would regard it as a 'natural' reaction, and they would take the stand: 'Why! You just don't eat horse. I wouldn't like the idea of sitting down to a plate of horse-flesh!' Yet they would laugh, or perhaps be a little indignant if it were suggested that their distaste for regarding the horse as food has been brought about by the religious beliefs of their very remote ancestors. But there is a strong reason for maintaining that this is so:[1] the horse was once a sacred animal in Britain and his flesh was never eaten except on rare, ritual occasions when the taboo was broken. There can be no doubt at all that the animal was so regarded here; and our foremost authority[2] on the history of the horse has recently stated his opinion that it was possibly for reli-

[1] George Ewart Evans, *The Pattern Under the Plough*, London, 1966, Chapters 18–24.
[2] Anthony A. Dent, in *The Pure Bred Exmoor Pony*, Dulverton, Somerset, 1970, p. 19.

gious and not utilitarian reasons that the horse was first introduced into Britain.

The hare, too, was sacred here as it was in other parts of the
world. It was taboo because—like the horse and the pig—the hare
was sacred to the White Goddess, the Earth Mother, who was
worshipped in varying forms and under varying names all over
the world. Robert Graves[1] reminds us that the hare was a royal
animal; and it was taken into battle by Queen Boadicea; and undoubtedly the religious taboo was reinforced by sympathetic
magic in the mind of the primitive: 'If I eat hare-flesh it is likely
that I myself shall become as timid as the creature.' Sir James
Frazer gives an instance of this kind of thinking:[2] 'The Namaquas
abstain from eating the flesh of hare because they think it would
make them as faint-hearted as the hare.'

There is also a vestige of the former religious significance
of the hare in the belief about it still held in Ireland.[3] An old
countryman, John Gately (born *c.* 1870), of Curraghboy, Co.
Roscommon told how a man went to shoot at a hare, and the
hare spoke and said:

'You wouldn't shoot your old grandfather, would you?'
We can assume that here the belief did not emerge from Pythagoras's
doctrine of the transmigration of souls, but from the conviction—
which we will discuss later—of the hare's close connection with
witches, those relics of the pre-Christian religion. Therefore in
abstaining from its flesh people would be spared the possible em-
barrassment of eating one of their own family. It is hard, at first
glance, to see how a statement of this sort could be taken seriously;
but if a person did believe it, this would be enough to make him
abstain; just as the long-standing, almost unconscious, taboo is
enough to keep him from fancying horse-flesh. Moreover, an
experience we had in the early Fifties in the Suffolk village of Little
Glemham convinced us how ancient—and therefore how irrational and 'unmodern'—are many of the beliefs held by the survivors of the old rural community in Britain. This particular

---

[1] *The White Goddess*, London, 1961, pp. 293 and 404.
[2] *The Golden Bough* (abridged ed.), London, 1947, p. 495.
[3] Op. cit., p. 657.

incident may also throw a possible light on the strong reaction of country people to the amount of blood there is in a hare.

We met an old man who lived alone; and we talked to him about the old way of life before the First World War. The talk was mainly about the farming methods and the crafts and home life of the village. In the course of it he digressed to tell us of a strange thing that had once happened to him. One day a sparrow flew up against the window of his living-room as though it wanted to come in. He took little notice of it at first; but the bird returned to the window again and again; and this persisted over a few days. Then he began to wonder about it, and became obsessed by the sparrow's effort to get inside the house. This is no ordinary bird, he told himself:

'I made up my mind not to let it in,' he said. 'I dussn't let it in!'

And at last he took a shot-gun and went outside into his garden; lay in wait until the sparrow returned to the window and then killed it. He then told us, as though in full justification of what he had done:

'The blood that came from that sparrow! No bird could have had all that blood in it!'

An example of the taboo on hare-flesh comes from Ireland:[1]

'In Co. Leitrim people wouldn't eat a hare. They say they are bewitched or that there is something uncanny about them. *They are not right.*

'Mrs. May Morris, of Carrigamguirke, Granard, Co. Longford, told me that a woman from Leitrim was visiting her not long ago. In general conversation, the subject of hares came up, and Mrs. Morris remarked:

"I haven't eaten a hare for ages. I wouldn't mind having one now."

'The Leitrim woman was shocked at the idea of anyone eating a hare:

"Surely to God, you're joking!" she says to Mrs. Morris. "You surely wouldn't eat a hare, would you?"

"I would indeed," said Mrs. Morris, "and I often did."

"Well," said her visitor, "I wouldn't eat a hare if I was never to

[1] Collected by James Delaney.

eat anything. There was an ould woman died up near us long ago. Just after her dying, didn't the *street*[1] fill up with hares! There were about forty hares. The old woman must have been a witch or something." '

Two Irish countrymen already mentioned had a definite attitude towards killing hares. First, John Kenny:

[T] 'Nobody liked to kill them. And above all things, nobody wanted to shoot them. And they were tee-totally against people coming to shoot them. I remember when I was a little fella— about twelve year old; and I saw two men having an awful fight over a hare. One fellow fired at her, and she passed him, and the other fellow took the gun off him and threw it down on the ground; and they fought it out. The fellow that took the gun was the best man, and he put the other fella down. And I ran away crying. I was afraid.

'The people got that into their head that it wasn't right to kill them, right to shoot them in any case. The old people didn't want them shot; and they didn't want them hunted with a pair of dogs. They objected tee-totally to a man letting out the second dog after them. There was a many a big row over it.

'Many people didn't like the flesh either. They didn't like them [hares]; they were black. Something like a water-hen; she's quite dark, too. And a lot of people used to bind them first, and then bake them; and that would put a bit of a change on them—but at the same time they weren't as nice as the rabbit. He was tender, and more of a chicken—more like a chicken.'

John Connaughton said:

[T] 'They say it's unlucky to make a practice of killing hares. Something always turns up. Something happens. They say about poachers—that if something happened to one, they'd say: "He can't have better luck! He's always going about killing and catching hares." '

But John Connaughton himself used to catch hares; and when he took it home he had it made into broth:

[T] 'The broth of the hare: that's the best. *The broth of the hare and the meat of the rabbit.* The meat of the hare is darker in colour;

---

[1] *Street* in Cos. Longford and Leitrim means the yard or bawn in front of the house.

but the broth is the best. Oh, the soup! That's the best of it. I flayed the hare, and the blood was still in her. It's best not to bleed them at all. Let the blood in them. The soup and the broth is the best!'

This is the *cyue* referred to above, and also mentioned later by the Welsh countryman (p. 210). This broth, *ius nigrum*, is essentially the black broth of the Spartans and was celebrated in antiquity: it was made from the blood and bowels of the hare.

But here, as always with the hare, there is contradictory evidence: some liked its flesh: most did not. Cato the Censor frequently ate hare-flesh with cabbage; and, as Sir Thomas Browne wrote,[1] the ancients were fond of the hare's flesh and believed that it would make anyone who ate it handsome. There are also two instances from Dorset[2] of a belief in the efficacy of hare's brains as a method of soothing fractious infants or of 'satisfying their *longings* when the special thing for which they crave cannot be guessed'.

From the same source,[3] too, comes a version of the mummers' Christmas play in which a hare is a central figure in one of the scenes. There seems to have been no argument between Old Father Christmas and his wife Bet whether it was good to eat hare-flesh or not: the dispute was about the right way to cook it:

Enter Old Bet

Here comes I, Dame Dorothy,
A handsome young woman, good morning to ye.
I am rather fat, but not very tall,
I'll do my best endeavours to please you all.
My husband he is to work, and soon he will return
And something for our supper bring,
And perhaps some wood to burn.
Oh! here he comes!

---

[1] *Pseudodoxia Epidemica: Enquiries into Vulgar and Common Errors*, Vol. 2, London, 1927, p. 247.
[2] J. S. Udal, *Dorsetshire Folklore* (reprint), Guernsey, 1970, p. 234.
[3] Pp. 93–5.

The Hare as Food

(Enter Jan *or* Old Father Christmas)

Well, Jan!

Old Father Christmas

Oh, Dorothy!

Old Bet

What have you been doing all this long day, Jan?

Old Father Christmas

I've been a-hunting, Bet.

Old Bet

The devil a-hunting is it! Is that the way to support a wife? Well, what have you catched today, Jan?

Old Father Christmas

A fine Jack hare, and I intend to have him a-fried for supper; and here's some wood to dress him.

Old Bet

Fried! No, Jan, I'll roast it nice.

Old Father Christmas

I say I'll have it fried!

Old Bet

Was there ever such a foolish dish!

Old Father Christmas

No matter for that, I'll have it done; and if you don't do as I do bid I'll hit you in the head.

Old Bet

You may do as you like for all I do care,
I'll never fry a dry Jack hare.

Old Father Christmas

Oh! you won't wooll'ee?

(He strikes her and she falls.)

Oh! what have I done! I have murdered my wife!
The joy of my heart and the pride of my life!
And out to the gaol I shall quickly be sent,
In a passion I did it, and no malice meant.

But the outcome was not as tragic as it appeared: there was magic as well as a hare about; and the Doctor soon put Bet on to her feet again. For this was simply a rehearsal of the old symbolic ritual, celebrating the eternal cycle of life when the death of winter is followed by the rebirth of spring. And in this kind of context it is not surprising to find the hare.

9

The Hare in Mythology

It was suggested earlier that the hare's place in mythology might be explained—partially at least—by taking into account early man's observation of its strange and contradictory behaviour in the wild state. In the next two chapters an attempt is made to show how the hare became associated with the moon, and also with sacrifice by fire.

Yet even if we are able to point to a strong link between the hare's behaviour and a particular myth in which it figures, we should still have only a small clue to the meaning of the myth itself. For the connection would be little more than a glimpse of the myth's probable origin: it would throw a little light on the reason for a particular animal being both the protagonist of the myth and its carrier down the ages, but it could enlighten us hardly at all about the myth's essential meaning. To fathom the meaning of any particular myth we have first to understand the structure of myths in general; for the myths that men have constructed are essentially about themselves and their relation to the world they lived in. They were early man's science and his history, and the animals that carried the myth were simply the mediators and the symbols of its deeper meaning. Myths, in other words, are historical statements if we look at them from the right angle; that is, if we regard a myth not as a logical statement in the ordinary sense but as a logical statement in 'illogical' form, not verbalized directly but presented in images or symbols which were originally used with the same force and the same intensity to communicate an intuition of an almost incommunicable knowledge as the poet uses to transmit an experience or an awareness that cannot be told by any other means. It will therefore help us, we believe, considerably in our understanding of myth if we go back to a very early period in man's evolution.

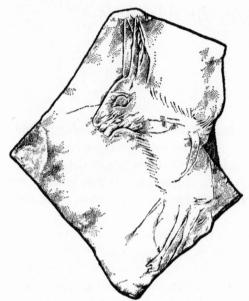

Fig. 2. Magdalanian mobile engraving on stone from Isturitz

Rachel Levy has shown in her inquiry[1] into the roots of myth and religion that it was in the cave that palaeolithic man began his long quest to discover his own identity, his relation to his fellows, to the animals and to the unseen powers he felt to be in control, powers he believed to be so much greater than himself. Again, as we already suggested (p. 18) the hare developed to its present form before palaeolithic times and has not evolved in any appreciable way since: this would seem an additional reason for going back to the dawn period in an attempt to uncover the genesis and meaning of those myths particularly linked with the hare.

Early man made his home in caves as the only available places of shelter. In recent years, archaeologists—Rachel Levy among them—have been able to reconstruct how he lived and to gather what were his main preoccupations. They have done this through excavations at the cave mouth, and also through exploration of

[1] *The Gate of Horn*, passim.

the cave's inner galleries and then through the subsequent discovery and interpretation of the paintings and signs that Stone Age hunters made on the cave walls. These paintings confirm that early man in many parts of the world was at first almost entirely dependent upon animals: he lived upon them, hunting and killing them for his food and covering. But the purpose of the paintings was not simply representation or description. They had both a magic and religious purpose; and by comparing the paintings of palaeolithic man with similar paintings and beliefs of primitive peoples studied by anthropologists, mainly within the last hundred and fifty years, Rachel Levy has been able in her book to put forward a theory which helps to define in detail the magical purpose of the paintings (mainly to help the hunters to success in their hunt) and, at a more general level, to show that the ceremonies performed in the cave were in fact those of an embryonic religion, helping man to sustain the precarious position he occupied at the crux point of an external environment that was actively hostile to him, and an internal environment (his thoughts, his fears, his yearnings) of which he was barely aware.

The choice of the cave as a place for man and animals to seek refuge from an aggressive climate can easily be understood; and it can be surmised that he came into close contact with certain animals like the cave bears because he was forced to share many of the caves with them. But what has the cave to do with the development of religion and myth? For primitive man the earth was the provider of all things: the earth was the Mother, the fount of all life for man, animals, birds and plants. The Earth Mother was the Supreme Being, and the cave where both man and animal sheltered was not only their place of refuge, it was their place of origin. The cave was the womb of Mother Earth, the place of mystery and the place of increase. It was in the darkness of the cave that man made his first attempts to placate and influence the powers upon which his life depended. At that remote period animals formed the major part of his life: they were at once the object of his quest and the focus of his admiration and awe. For he recognized the animals as beings like himself, but they were able to manage much better than he could. They were better able to survive, being much more smoothly adapted to the environment in which they lived together. Early man admired their splendour and celebrated it in the images he drew of them upon the cave's wall; and he attained an art in the drawing of animals that has never since been surpassed.

Yet there was still another aspect of the paintings. The tribe's or group's life was bound up with the beasts', but only by killing them were they able to survive. Therefore their feelings for the animals went beyond admiration: they worshipped them as beings who had preserved their ancestors, who were also saviours of themselves and potential saviours of their descendants. In the animals inhered the Supreme Being, the Earth Mother, the force that kept life going. Through the animals—and, as time developed, through a particular animal—the clan or group was assured of survival, of continuity. The group's relation with the animal it had identified itself with was immensely subtle and was compounded of a divinity, the Earth Mother (or one of her avatars), the group's ancestors whose embodiment the animal was thought to be, and the enduring fertility both of the group itself and of the group animal or totem. The group animal, as it was supposed to enshrine the spirit of the ancestors, would voluntarily submit itself to be killed in a sacrifice to ensure the group's survival; but it would do this only as long as the proper ritual seeking forgiveness for their action was addressed to the animal and to the spirit of the ancestors. And in the later form of totemism that lasted up to modern times among primitive tribes, the group refrained from killing its totem animal, preserving it for the use of cognate groups and only partaking of its flesh on certain solemn, ritual occasions.

The wall paintings and the symbols which accompanied, and were a necessary part of these rituals, were for palaeolithic man and for his counterpart, primitive man who has survived in decreasing numbers to the present, bathed in a sacred light. They were religious in the sense that they were an affirmation of the group's identity with Mother Earth in whose cave or womb they celebrated and ensured the renewal of life—a renewal which depended ultimately on her alone. The paintings were also magical in the sense that many were drawn to ensure that their hunting of the animal would be much more effective if a powerful and permanent 'rehearsal' of the hunt was painted or engraved on the wall. Moreover, the painting of the animal images on the walls of the cave and the deposit of clay figurines of the animal in the cave itself were an earnest that the animal would multiply and make quite certain the group's survival and a continuance of the line of their ancestors. For where was there a more potent place to celebrate the perfect image of the animal and to invoke magic so that like images of the animal should be created outside the cave, in mountain, plain and forest, than in the very womb of the Earth Mother herself, in the secret creator and the secret place of all increase, of man, beast, flower and plant?

Palaeolithic man living in an aggressive environment, just as the Australian aborigine living in hostile bush or desert, was bound up in a circle of necessity with the animal; and this was the basic economic reason for the animal's veneration and his consecrating in a rudimentary religious system. And there can be no doubt that, as Rachel Levy claims, the roots of all religions are to be sought in the prehistoric caves; and it is by starting from this source that we must endeavour to explain the symbolism of animals in modern religions: the Lion of Judah, the Christian Lamb of God, the Cat of the Egyptians, the Sacred Cow of the Hindu, and so on; and it is from this level that we should hope to extract the meanings of those myths which have various animals as their centre figures. To the Mother Goddess, under whatever name she took—Ga Mater, the Great Mother, Diana, Hecuba, the White Goddess, and so on—certain animals were sacred because they had been identified with her and with man in the chain of necessity that was imposed by the unrelenting conditions that hedged in primitive man's life and challenged his survival. This was one of the most powerful and vital complexes in man's evolution, and we cannot be surprised that vestiges of it have survived to the present day in, for instance, the shell that remains of the horse cult in Britain, the cult of the bull in southern France and Spain, in the myths about the hare, the seal and the wren; and also in the numerous superstitions about animals. We see a glimpse of it in the theme developed by the Irish poet, W. R. Rodgers, who suggested[1] that near his home in Northern Ireland, the dogs and the hare, both pursuers and pursued, were part of the same total situation and that each was necessary to the other.

Someone might well object at this stage that a great deal of what has been written in the present chapter is irrelevant for the simple reason that in the various cave paintings that have so far been discovered the hare is represented rarely. But few small animals appear, presumably because they were not hunted to the same extent. The bigger animals were an easier and more rewarding quarry; for a determined group, even though badly equipped with weapons, the labour of digging out a pit to trap a bear or even a mammoth would be well rewarded by the amount of meat the captive beast afforded. It is likely too that the hunting of the smaller animals had to wait until the domestication of the dog as an aid in the pursuit; and we can infer that the hare, along with other animals like the cat was made sacred much later, drawn into the pattern of veneration and worship whose origins Rachel Levy has so convincingly described.

It has been suggested that many if not all the animal myths stem from this early palaeolithic period, directly or indirectly, for the reason that early man linked the beast with a higher form of existence. And when one of the group's number had attained, as shaman or medicine-man, the higher state they all aspired to, he himself had full rapport with nature and all creatures; and like Daniel could lie down with lions and like St. Francis enter into the winged world of the birds. This was the period that some Australian natives call the *Alcheringa*, the dream time (a similar time and state of being to the primordial Garden of Eden) before each individual had become aware of himself as a person with a separate identity; when he was integrated fully into the group and little of his spiritual or physical life was lived apart from it. At this time the myths were constructions by which the group acted out their relationship to the world they knew and experienced and to its unseen Creator. These myths were symbolic representations, collective dreams of the reality that primordial man experienced; and

[1] *Essex Roundabout*, Benham (Publishers), Colchester, 1962.

since his life was so much involved with the animals, the animals figure largely within them. It should not, therefore, surprise us that mankind's terrible initiation during the period of the cave should have stamped itself upon him indelibly, and that the myths, those expressions of the collective experiences of this time, should remain deep within the racial memory.

They also remain in the unconscious mind of the individual as the depth psychologists, notably Freud and Jung, have discovered, and they are revealed in his dreams. As we have already stated Jung has put forward the hypothesis of the existence of certain dominant patterns or nuclei in man's unconscious: around these nuclei his early experiences were constellated. These were *archetypes*, symbolic images or foci in the unconscious of each individual; and though the individual is unaware of them, much of his conscious experience is drawn towards them because of their potency. They become fully activated when modern man becomes involved in those fundamental questions which myth and the ritual clearly tell us were vitally present to man in the cave: How do we stand in relation to all that is around us? What keeps things going? and what is the purpose of living? Creatures figure as archetypes because of their close link with the beginnings of the race: as we have seen, they were invoked as symbols of man's own feelings; they were admired. He was drawn to the high soaring of the eagle, to the relentless pursuit of its prey and its swift plummet to the kill: he marvelled at the anger and courage of the lion, the energy and speed of the horse. Knowing little of himself as an individual and little of the working of his own mind, he projected all his own qualities on to the animals and the objects outside him. And this tendency long outlived man's infancy in the cave and—well into historical times—caused him, for example, to project his own qualities on to the gods, and even on to the stars so that the Signs of the Zodiac (many of them animals) remain even to this day as symbols for the whole gamut of the human temperaments by which, it is claimed, we can calculate and know their many permutations.

These early structurings also come alive at a more superficial level and insinuate themselves into our waking lives as superstitions—discredited beliefs that stand over from an earlier period in our history. But, most interesting of all, we sometimes encounter them in our dreams following the activation of that deep area of our psyche that knows nothing of reason but has a logic of its own, the old symbols and images that our remote ancestors used for most of their thinking.

10

The Hare and the Moon

If the theory put forward in the previous chapter is accepted it will be clear why animals have become the mediators of the sacred and why they figure so largely in those myths which, in a sense, are the dogma of very ancient religions. But even if we accept this explanation it still remains to trace the steps by which a certain animal symbolized a specific aspect of the sacred—how the animal became an image that would contribute to an understanding of, for instance, the cycle of being as imagined by early man: birth, growth, reproduction, death and rebirth. The hare was undoubtedly one of these animals by its association with the moon. For the moon is perhaps the most manifest symbol of this universal becoming. At one part of its cycle the Moon disappears—dies—and is born again three nights later; and it is not only an emblem of the natural process of birth, growth, decay and regeneration but of the mystical idea that underlies most primitive initiation rites:[1] that a being must first *die* before he can be born again on to a higher spiritual level; and this symbolic death is the central meaning in initiation to manhood or entry into a secret society or brotherhood. The moon, that is, is remade every month, and is a homologue of the process that is fundamental to life.

Now the moon and the hare occur together in myth and folklore—in India, China, Africa, Mexico, North America and Europe; and the immediate question we have to answer is: why is it the hare rather than any other creature that is so identified? Here we can return to our former suggestion that we try to discover if there are any aspects of the hare's behaviour in its natural

[1] *Mircea Eliade*, London, 1968, p. 187.

environment that can help us to understand its link with the moon. First, the hare is nocturnal and spends most of its day in a shallow *form* on the ground; and unless someone approaches very closely it will not move away from its resting place. Apart from certain times of the year, in the spring mating season or during the corn-harvest when the hares are disturbed, there are few to be seen about the countryside. But you will frequently see them out at dusk or in the light of the moon, moving about and feeding in the fields. If they have lain in the open or in the woods or reeds of a marsh for the best part of the day, they will come out into the open at night to feed and disport themselves. A Suffolk naturalist[1] has observed them closely over a fairly long period. When he was a young man he went out regularly at night—poaching; and he saw that on moonlight nights there were many hares out in the open field where hardly any other creature was to be seen. He did not, of course, infer that hares came out into the open only on moonlit nights but at this time they were more clearly observed than on others. But rabbits and smaller vermin feed at night: how were they not to be seen also? These, he said, kept to the hedge-rows near their burrows, or cover and they could go to earth quickly as soon as danger threatened. The hare, however, pre-ferred to be in the open where there was plenty of room to manoeuvre; and if an enemy threatened him he could use his tremendous speed to get himself out of difficulty.

The hare, through its gestation period, is also traditionally linked with the moon. More than one East Anglian countryman has reminded us of the old saying: *A hare and a mare goo a year*. That is, a mare carries her foal for eleven months from the date of conception, and the hare's period is a month. It has been estab-lished in recent years,[2] however, that the hare's 'time' is longer than this—over forty days—yet this does not invalidate our using this saying as evidence for the hare's link with the moon. For it is on traditional observations, however inaccurate, that myths are founded and not on modern scientific findings.

Another instance of the hare's identification with the moon

[1] Harold Jenner of Lowestoft.
[2] See p. 57.

9. Japanese myth of the giant boy dancing with his companions: the
hare, the monkey, and the bear. Woodcut by K. Hokusai (1760–1849)

10. The Moon Palace showing the Hare of the Moon with three
children. Detail from a Japanese woodcut by Totoya Hokkei
(1780–1850)

came out of a conversation we had with a Suffolk farmer[1] who recalled a saying that used to be repeated at the end of the month:

Let the owd hare set.

This, on the surface at least, is cryptic; but the saying is understandable against the belief, widely held among farmers and countrymen, that the moon and the weather are closely tied. Thus you will often hear in East Anglia during a spell of bad weather: 'We'll just have to wait: it won't break, you ma' depend, until we see the new moon.' In other words: '*Let the owd hare set*: when we've finished with the old moon, let's see what the new one will bring.'

Primitive man, who was the father of myth, tended with his keenness of observation of natural phenomena to link together things which appeared to him to have like attributes. The hare-moon parallel would not have escaped him. The moon is the emblem of inconstancy: it is always changing its place in the sky, and even over two consecutive nights its shape, point and time of appearance in the sky are different. The hare has a similar attribute. It will appear suddenly in an unexpected place; stand up or leap precipitately out of its form or cover in the undergrowth. It will pause a moment, dart off at speed, only to reappear a few moments later running in an entirely different direction. In the popular imagination, too, the moon (*luna*) is equated with lunacy; and there is a traditional belief that if you sleep out in the moonlight you are inviting madness, which is presumably the danger which the Psalmist gave assurance against: 'The sun shall not strike thee by day nor the moon by night.' The hare's apparent madness at the chief mating season is also well known. It throws all its natural caution to the winds and becomes the opposite of the timid creature that will leap precipitately and hurl itself away from danger. The irrational behaviour of the March hare is therefore another reason for labelling the hare as mad or *moon-struck*.

Undoubtedly, too, early man with his faculty for projecting all his thoughts on to beings and objects outside himself, identified

[1] George Garrard, born 1891.

the moon with his intuition, that quality that gives unexpected light in darkness. The hare, also, with its quick darting and leaping is like the sudden thought that comes, bearing conviction but no hint of where it comes from, or any warning of its coming. There are, in fact, many folk tales illustrating how the hare's quick wit and intuition is able to overcome a much stronger adversary. One of these is an Indian tale where the moon and the hare figure together:[1]

'There is a great lake abounding in water, called Chandrasaras [Moon Lake], and on its bank there lived a king of the hares, named Silimukha. Now, once on a time, a leader of a herd of elephants, named Chaturdanta, came there to drink water, because all the other reservoirs of waters were dried up in the drought that prevailed. Then many of the hares, who were subjects of that king, were trampled to death by Chaturdanta's herd, while entering the lake. When the monarch of the herd had departed, the hare-king Silimukha, being grieved said to a hare named Vijaya in the presence of others:

"Now that the lord of elephants has tasted the water of this lake, he will come here again and again, and utterly destroy us all, so think of some expedient in this case. Go to him, and see if you have any artifice which will suit the purpose or not. For you know business and expedients, and are an ingenious orator. And in all cases in which you have been engaged the result has been fortunate."

'When dispatched with these words, the hare was pleased and went slowly on his way. And following up the track of the herd he overtook that elephant-king and saw him, and being determined somehow or other to have an interview with the mighty beast, the wise hare climbed up to the top of a rock, and said to the elephant:

"I am the ambassador of the moon, and this is what the god says to you by my mouth: 'I dwell in a cool lake named Chandrasaras; there dwell hares whose king I am, and I love them well, and thence I am known to men as the cool-rayed and the hare-marked;

[1] G. H. Tawney (translator), 'The Elephants and the Hares', from *The Ocean of Story*, London, 1924, Vol. 1, 121 BB.

now thou hast defiled that lake and slain those hares of mine. If
thou doest that again, thou shalt receive thy due recompense from
me."

'When the king of the elephants heard this speech of the crafty
hare he said in his terror:

"I will never do so again: I must show respect to the awful
moon-god." The hare said:

"So come, my friend, I pray, and we will show him to you."
After saying this, the hare led the king of elephants to the lake and
showed him the reflection of the moon in the water. When the
lord of the herd saw that, he bowed before it timidly at a distance,
oppressed with awe, and never came there again. And Silimukha,
the king of the hares was present, and witnessed the whole trans-
action; and after honouring that hare, who went as ambassador,
he lived there in security.'

It was in India, also, that there originated the most widely
known story connecting the hare with the moon;[1] and it is likely
that the rich, moon-hare myths were diffused by the spread of
Buddhism from India to much of Asia, particularly China. Here is
a Chinese version of the story[2] of how there came to be a hare on
the moon:

'Once upon a time there was a forest glade where holy men
came to meditate, a beautiful, natural garden filled with fruits and
flowers, carpeted with tender grass and refreshed by the waters of
a sparkling stream, blue as lapis-lazuli. Now in this little paradise
there lived a hare, a creature whose many virtues gave him
ascendancy over all the other animals. By precept and example he
taught his companions to perform their religious duties in a
manner approved by the pious, until "their renown reached even
the world of the Devas".

'One evening the Buddha came to his garden. Certain of his
disciples accompanied the Holy one, sitting reverently at his feet
and listening while he preached the Law. All night long he dis-
coursed and until the next day at high noon, when the sun darts

[1] Ibid., Vol. V, 84D.
[2] Juliet Bredon and Igor Mitrophanov, *The Moon Year: A Record of Chinese Customs and Festivals*, Shanghai, 1927.

115

his sharpest beam; when the horizon, enclosed in a net of trembling rays of light and veiled with radiant heat, does not suffer itself to be looked upon, when the cicadae shriek their loudest; when no living creature leaves the shelter of the shade, and the vigour of travellers is exhausted by heat and fatigue.

'In that time of the day, the Buddha chose to assume the figure of a Brahman, crying out like one who has lost his road and is consumed with weariness and sorrow:

"Alone and astray, having lost my companions, I am a-hunger and a-thirst! Help me, ye pious!"

'All the little forest-dwellers heard the cry of distress, and one by one they hastened to the Holy Man, begging him wander no further but remain with them and accept their hospitality. And each, according to his means, brought food for him. The otter brought seven fishes, saying: "Accept these, and remain with us." The jackal brought his kill, saying: "Honour us with they presence and grant us Thy instruction." When it came to the turn of the hare, he approached empty-handed and said humbly:

"Master, I who have grown up in the forest, nourished by the grass and herbs, have nothing to offer thee but my own body. Grant us the boon of resting Thy Holiness in this place, and vouchsafe to me the favour of feeding thee with my own flesh, since I have nothing else to give thee."

'Even as he spoke, the hare perceived a heap of magic charcoal burning without smoke nearby. He was about to leap into the flames when he paused and began gently picking out the little creatures lodging in his fur. "My body I may sacrifice to the Holy One," he murmured, "but your lives I have no right to take." He placed the tiny insects safely on the ground, and then with the utmost gladness, like one desirous of wealth on beholding a treasure, threw himself into that blazing fire.

'Resuming his own form, the Buddha praised the loftiness of the sacrifice:

"He who forgets self, be he the humblest of earthly creatures, will reach the Ocean of Eternal Peace. Let all men learn from this example and be persuaded to deeds of compassion and mercy."

'Moreover to reward the hare Buddha commanded that his image should adorn the disc of the moon, a shining example for all time. As for the other animals of the forest, they were translated to the world of the Devas, thanks to their holy friend. Ever since these happenings in the forest, the moon has been known to the Buddhist world as the "Hare-marked".'

The moon-hare soon established himself as an image on Buddhist family-altars all over China. This was a challenge to the Taoists. Not hoping to displace him they adopted him and renamed him *The Jade Rabbit*, more properly *The Jade Hare* as the true rabbit is said not to have existed in China. According to Taoist legend, the Jade Hare pounds, with mortar and pestle, the *Jade Elixir* in the moon. This, like the mythical *Elixir Vitae* of the West was thought to bestow immortality on anyone who drank it.

The hare (*lepus Sinensis*) is common in the Yangtze basin and the northern regions.[1] 'It is an emblem of longevity, often depicted on porcelain, and it represents the fourth of the Twelve Terrestial Branches. This animal is reputed as deriving its origin from the vital essence of the Moon to the influence of which luminary it is consequently subject.' The Twelve Terrestial Branches are the twelve signs of the Chinese solar zodiac which contains six wild and six domestic animals. The hare is the sign for the East which coincides with the *Second Moon*; and it also gives its name to *The Year of the Hare*.

The connection of the hare with the moon and immortality comes out in a well-known Hottentot tale:[2]

'The Moon dies and rises to life again. The Moon said to the Hare,

"Go thou to Men and tell them, 'Like as I die and rise to life again, so you also shall die and rise to life again.' "

'The Hare went to the Men, and said,

"Like as I die and do not rise to life again, so you shall also die, and not rise to life again."

---

[1] C. A. S. Williams, *The Encyclopaedia of Chinese Symbolism and Art Motives*, New York, 1960.

[2] W. H. I. Bleek, *Reynard the Fox in South Africa*, London, 1864, p. 71.

'When he returned, the Moon asked him,
"What hast thou said?"
"I have told them, 'Like as I die and do not rise to life again,
so you shall also die and not rise to life again."
"What," said the Moon, "thou hast said that?"
'And she took a stick and beat the Hare on his mouth, which
was slit by the blow. The Hare fled, and is still fleeing.'

The old man who told his tale added: 'We are angry now with
the Hare because he brought such a bad message, and therefore
we dislike to eat his flesh.'

The hare was also associated with the moon in Ancient Egypt
particularly with a moon-god, *Un-nefer*, to be mentioned later in
the book.[1] It appears, too, in a similar mythical setting among
the Indians of North America. An Indian tribe, the Déné Hare-
skins, worship a moon-god and have the following tradition:

One of their number was unlucky enough to be enticed down
into the underworld where all the ways and paths were like a
maze. His task of finding his way out was made much more difficult by the thick darkness that enveloped everything. He saved
himself, however, by throwing the head of a white hare into a
fire. For after he had done this, dawn appeared and he had light
enough to make his escape.

Coming nearer home we find that in the European myths the
hare was also associated with the moon.[2] A Saxon goddess whose
name-day was Monday (Moon-day) was represented in a short
coat like a man's and wearing a kind of hood with two long ears
(see illustration on p. 119). It is not known whether this is an
avatar of Nerthus, the earth or fertility goddess mentioned by
Tacitus (*Germania*, chapter XL), but Nerthus was probably a
form of the Mother Goddess, and linking her with the hare
would not therefore be unjustified. As we can see from the illustration, the figure is holding a moon-disc containing a human profile
before her as though to clinch her identity; and the fact that there
was a hare-headed goddess in Ancient Egypt proves that the
'Saxon Idol of the Moon' is not a kind of mythic *hapax legomenon*

[1] See p. 197
[2] Andrew Lang, *Myth, Ritual and Religion*, London, 1887, Vol. I, p. 184.

but simply another link in a chain of belief that once encircled the world.[1] The significance of the Saxon hare-headed goddess and her relation to the witch-cult that hares are so strongly identified with need little emphasis. It is enough to say here that it can help us to a fuller understanding of the numerous witch beliefs that

Fig. 3. The Saxon Idol of the Moon in the form of a goddess wearing a chaperon representing the head and shoulders of a hare and holding a moon-disk containing a human face. (from R. Verstigan, *A Restitution of Decayed Intelligence*, Antwerp, 1605, ch. 3)

have lasted up to the present day in Britain, especially if we remember the hare's universal identification with the Mother Goddess and the moon which is one of her symbols. For instance, one of the Mother Goddess's names, Diana, will help to set up the essential background to an understanding of the ancient belief that a hare crossing the path of a pregnant woman is a bad omen. Interpreted in the light of the moon-hare complex of myths it means that Diana—goddess of childbirth as well as of the moon—

[1] See also Layard, op. cit., p. 126.

has sent the hare, her familiar, as a warning or negative indication of the outcome of the woman's pregnancy. Similarly, in deference to the Mother Goddess, who in her capacity of moon-goddess also controlled the tides, fishermen must never mention the name of the hare while at sea or take a hare aboard their vessel.

11

The Hare and Fire

In discussing the hare's connection with the moon we came across two instances of his involvement with fire: the hare voluntarily sacrificing himself in the Buddha tale, and the Déné Hareskin who got himself out of a difficult place by throwing the head of a white hare into a fire. This again is not a chance association, and tradition in many parts of the world carries this same linking of the hare with fire and burning. The sacrificial element is present in most of these universal traditions as it is in both instances quoted above. The hare, in other words, is like the phoenix a symbol of regeneration or rejuvenation, as John Layard points out.[1] The Buddha myth implies that it was not an ordinary fire that the hare prepared to throw himself into (although he himself did not know this) but the divine fire that burns away all dross and impurity and makes a being anew. This is the rationale of all sacrifice by burning. It is a symbol of the cleansing by the heavenly fire and the resulting 'birth' of a new man, following exactly the same pattern as the symbolic death mentioned above as an essential to the beginning of a new life. And in actual sacrifice by burning this is considered to extend to the participants in the ceremony, the group or the community that celebrates it, as well as to the victim. This ancient belief was undoubtedly behind —if not consciously so—the ritual burning of witches. Their persecutors could have justified the burning, as some of them did, by declaring they were saving the witch's soul, purifying it, searing it of all its devilish contamination. At the same time they and the community were taking part vicariously in

---

[1] *The Lady of the Hare*, p. 105.

the cleansing and renewing process symbolized by the actual flames.

Primitive man poured himself into objects and living creatures, peopling them with part of himself through the mechanism of projection. He thought through objects and persons and used them as images or symbols for his own mental life of which he was largely unaware. Modern man, on the contrary, has allowed the object to invade and take possession of his consciousness. We have become so materially minded, through abstracting the objects into our own psyche, and so literal that we insist on taking obvious symbolism at its face, and not its implied or concealed, value; and, having once taken it in this way, dismissing it as trivial. This is probably the reason why many people today consider orthodox religion irrelevant. The religious symbols have lost their numinous quality, their *mana*; and we ourselves regarding them simply as objects—which of course they are once they have been depotentized—decide understandably that they are hardly worth our attention. Today the conventional religious symbols move the majority of people as little as would a hare that had strayed into a main street, though not so long ago even this would have caused a decided reaction in many people's breasts. Symbols are displaced; there is a relentless evolution and it is difficult to know what we can do about it. For symbols cannot be invented: they grow from the largely unconscious, but purposeful, imaginings of men throughout the centuries and throughout the world.[1] And if we need a demonstration of this, albeit a negative one, we have only to look at the attempts of those writers, poets and others, who in desperation at the ineffectiveness of the old traditional symbols have been rash enough to invent some of their own.

Therefore to our ancestors there was nothing contrived or artificial in taking a creature—the dove, the lamb, the eagle, the lion or the hare—as an image of part of their own experience. These archetypal images evolved as part of themselves, and although it may seem to some of us, out of our enlightenment, a fruitless exercise to pursue this old way of thinking, and to quote

[1] Ibid., passim.

the myths and stories that have been woven to typify and embellish it, we do at least get an insight into the consciousness and thoughts of people who have gone before us—incidentally a very necessary piece of equipment for the historian—and, what is of more immediately practical value, we may possibly become aware of the limitations of our own sterilized and dehydrated way of thinking, realizing at the same time its provisional nature in phylogenetic terms. This may even induce a new insight which will prompt us to ask ourselves: if we believe thinking has progressed from the primitives, should we not ask ourselves which way it is going to progress from us?

It would be possible to give other instances of its connection with fire, but all merely emphasize the role already discussed: the hare was an archetype and symbol of the sacred. Instead we can point to the remnant of this former sacredness of the hare in a widespread country superstition in Britain:[1] if a hare runs through a village street a fire will break out in one of the houses very shortly afterwards. This is only a faint echo of the deep-toned myth linking the hare with sacrifice. But this is the usual fate of even the central myths and beliefs of former religions: they are demoted to the rural underground or linger on in thin disguise in the harmless games of children. But why, again, should the hare and not some other animal have been chosen for this particular role? Following a note in John Layard's book,[2] and in pursuit of our conviction that a great deal of myth concerning animals is based on some basic natural attribute that fits the animal to carry the myth which has become identified with it, we tried to find whether the hare is in any way linked with fire in its natural state. This is what we found.

A Suffolk gamekeeper[3] told us about the feeding habits of hares (this was in February 1970):

[T] 'I don't know . . . some of these hares today, now all the stubbles are ploughed up, they have to go two or three miles to

---

[1] W. B. Gerish (1915), *Hertfordshire Folk Lore*, S. R. Publishers, 1970; 1911 List of Material, p. 5. Also G. L. Gomme, 'Totemism in Britain', *Archaeological Review*, Vol. 3, 1889, p. 454.

[2] Ibid., note on p. 106.

[3] Percy Muttit, Blythburgh.

feed. They all go where there's a piece of green—rye or an old clover stubble or a maiden layer. They'll go miles to feed. They know all over [the district]. They goo miles at night. If you see their footmarks in the snow or anything—they'll goo miles. They're like the old fox. When they get disturbed in the fields here they go right across from Blythburgh Lodge. If you was to see some particular hare—well, there was some about here two or three years ago as though they'd been scorched on the back. Their fur was of a different colour. We've seen 'em perhaps fighting one day, and then you'd see them back here the next day. These hares had been burnt when they burnt some reeds down here [in the marshes]. They'd got scorched and then that fur was a different colour in the middle of the back.'

The hare will stay in a heath-fire till the last:

'Well, you see, what they do is this: they don't go out to run with the smoke. They turn round and try to get through the fire that way. They don't like the smoke coming behind them. They seem as though . . . well, they go by scent, you see; and they seem to think that if they get back clear on to the fire, in a way, they'll get out of the scent of it. They jump into the fire. I allus see them come through the fire, come right out of it; and they'll nearly all do that, get through the fire to get back. When all the heath get on fire, March time (of course, if they get fire in the summer-time the hares are not there; they're in the corn) when there's no cover on the land, they go right through a fire. In a fire an owd hare will jump right over the top of a fire. He'll come through it: they wouldn't go the way the smoke is going. He'll come through it. I've seen them while they've been a-burning the stubble. The stubble will be burning across the field, and you'll see the owd hares get up on to the stubble and go towards the fire and keep smelling, and go in between the rows; go right through it, and come out to the clear behind. And then they're away with it. They don't seem to like the way the smoke is going: whichever way the smoke is going they seem to think the fire is going that way, and they'll try to get back behind it. They go by the scent; that's a lot of it. I mean, if you stood five or six guns up by the hedge, and the wind was a-blowing from them on to the field, and someone went round to try and drive them they [the hares] wouldn't go where the guns were. They'd come past us what were driving them. They won't go near anyone standing: they'll go back. It's no good a-trying to drive them into the wind. Always drive them with the wind, so your guns will stand so the wind is blowing the other way. Do [if you don't do this], you'd never get one unless the people who were driving them shot them as they goo back. They'll go past them. But anyone standing in a hedge they'll smell 'em. If you watch them at night, when you stand to see if they'll come to you, they'll smell you. They'll know you're there. They'll come about fifty or sixty yards of you and then turn off.'

The gamekeeper believed that the hare's behaviour in a fire, as in the field, was conditioned by his sense of smell. Earlier we had talked with an East Anglian chief fire-officer[1] who had long experience of bracken- and heath-fires both in Wales and in East Anglia:

[T] 'They [the hares] don't retire immediately from the smoke and flames. They seem to hang on to the last minute and then make a dash for it. Yes, normally they hang on longer than rabbits and the other vermin. From my experience I have noticed that, and that's why they get scorched up, you know, and then they're away.' We asked him what was the reason for this reaction of a hare in a fire. He answered: 'Well, it could be fright, of course. You know, sort of frightened to come out. Especially during the hours of daylight and . . . then it leaves it until the last minute and it's away!'

An East Anglian naturalist[2] also took the view that the hare's distinctive behaviour in a heath-fire may be due to simple fright:

[T] 'I have seen this happen. We had a fire several years ago, quite a bad heath-fire, and rabbits and partridges, wood-pigeons and hares were coming out from the advancing fire. The hares— I put it down simply to the fact that they are more nervous than the rabbit—but some of them certainly will turn and run back into the fire and get burned in consequence of this. I've seen rabbits do it, not necessarily directly into the fire but into the area that is burning, and which will be burned. But I don't think this

---

[1] R. H. Bishop of Lowestoft.　　　[2] Harold Jenner.

is peculiar to the hare. I've certainly seen this with rabbits, but the hare does it too.

'You don't get many chances to observe the behaviour of hares in this kind of situation. Fortunately, we don't get too many heath-fires. I have seen hares run back into the fire when there've been people out fighting a heath-fire. They've seen the people and have gone back. I've seen them come out very badly singed. In fact, one that came out and we caught was very seriously burned before it ever came out. I think it's the lesser of two evils. And if they've got to come through the trouble such as humans (they are the hare's main enemies I suppose: humans, dogs and foxes in this part of the world) they tend to go back from whence they came, rather then face the line of people either watching a fire or trying to put it out.

'I've heard about the hare running and a fire coming afterwards. In fact, an old character out this way used to reckon that they were bad luck to have run through your garden because you'd probably have your house on fire before the end of the year. I've had them run through my garden since 1946 and so far I'm all right! But I'm not superstitious.'

12
The Hare: A Symbol of Increase

SPRING

There is visible evidence for one of the instincts we have inherited from the early cave dweller—his need to express himself in the arts of painting and sculpture. Others are hidden not only in our dreams, but in our ecstasies and fears and can be recalled in certain moods or by remembrances of childhood. Fear of the dark is instinctive, not caused by physical danger. It is just as strong in a safe, familiar bedroom as anywhere else. Imaginative fear of the elemental powers of destruction, flood and fire, exists where neither has been known for generations. But darkness is driven out by daylight and the destruction of life is succeeded by new growth. Fear is succeeded by the joy of re-creation, which in a minor way can be experienced every morning. But while the darkness or the flood is going on there seems to the frightened person no certainty that it will ever end. The same is true of a depressive state of mind. Spiritual enlightenment or mere happiness strike the depressive man from time to time like the sun through a window from which a black blind has suddenly been torn. The hare is a symbol of enlightenment, not only of the spirit but of the dawn, the dawn of the day and the dawn of the year which we call spring.

 Fig. 4. The hieroglyph depicting a hare with a ripple of water below means 'to exist'

The ancient Egyptian hieroglyph—a picture of a hare—stood for the auxiliary verb 'to be', but auxiliary verbs come late in the development of language and all are derived from words of independent sense. The Egyptian 'to be' was associated with creation and had the senses of being, existing and persisting,[1] which are in mythology often represented by the hare. Myths and picture-writing often use the same symbols.

A symbol is a sign or object that stands not exactly, but by association or resemblance, for something else. In primitive writing a picture stands for the object named, but as the art of writing develops the same picture is adapted and used for abstract ideas. This process can be traced in language too: 'haring away' for running off in action or thought, 'hare-brained' for foolish or a mind that takes unpredictable leaps. The hare is, literally in several languages, the leaper, the one who springs or starts up, and so becomes linked with creation, the springing up of life, and with the quick mind. We often speak of an intelligent mind as one which leaps to a truth where others plod their way by stages; the fool and the genius share essential qualities. (See Chapter 14, pp. 181-2.)

If we cannot understand a phenomenon our instinct makes us name it, or embody it in a form we do understand. In mines, though everybody knows the scientific reason for disaster, a cat can still be blamed.[2] R.A.F. crews in the Second World War spoke of gremlins not entirely as a joke. There seemed to be an unpredictable force stronger than mechanical faults, enemy planes or storm. To call it fate was not enough. They gave it a human shape, grotesque and miniature, and they named it.

It is necessary to name the phenomenon. It is impossible to think about it clearly until it has a name and a form; once it has those one can at least confront it and at best control it. Everybody learns this in the early stages of illness or unaccountable pain. As soon as a doctor gives it a name some of the loneliness of suffering is taken away. Usually the name gives hope of cure and even if not the patient knows what he must face. The same was true of all the hidden natural powers that govern fertility.

'In the beginning God created the heaven and the Earth. And

[1] John Layard, op. cit., pp. 151-2.
[2] E. & M. A. Radford, *Encyclopaedia of Superstitions*, revised and edited by Christina Hole, London, 1961, p. 87.

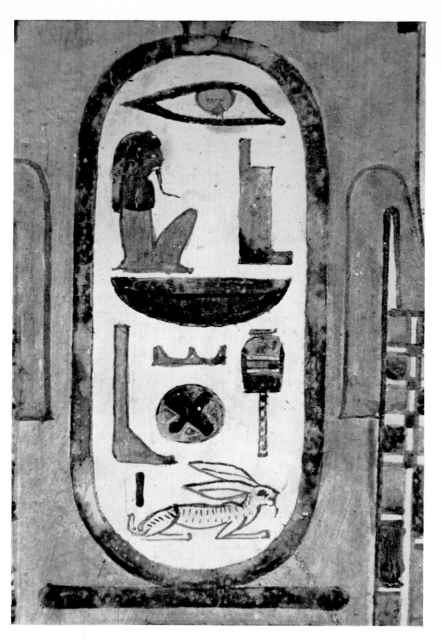

11. Hieroglyphs from the coffin of Djedhoriufankh, Thebes, twenty-first dynasty *(British Museum)*

12. *Below left:* Hare leaping towards elderly satyr's feet as he looks at young satyr. Maenads; *top centre:* Dionysos and Ariadne, with maenads and satyrs. From a bell crater, Ancient Greece (*British Museum*)

the Earth was without form, and void, and darkness was upon the face of the deep. And the Spirit of God moved upon the face of the waters. And God said, "Let there be light" and there was light. And God saw the light that it was good; and God divided the light from the darkness."[1]

The original creation is repeated every morning and every spring but there is always the fear that the little death of sleep and the longer one of winter will one day last for ever. What could look more barren than a dried-up seed in winter, its husk as hard as the frozen earth? This fear is expressed in the story of the Flood. The conception of flood as the end of life on Earth is universal. Stories almost identical with the Old Testament one occur all over the world. But as those who know them are alive to tell the tale, and have animals and plants about them, it is clear that the seeds of life were saved. The Flood is the story of death and resurrection, winter and spring, the darkness of the soul and its creative light. The survivors mark time, so to speak, in some kind of boat, a coconut-shell or an eggshell.

Noah's Ark itself is symbolic of the egg or the husk of a seed, and there are stories of how it sprang a leak and the last hope of new life on Earth seemed about to be lost. It is usually a hare, hedgehog or snake that saves it:

'All through the days of the Flood, the Devil tried to sink the Ark by making holes in it. Noah put in a plug every time. But at last he had no plugs left. He cut off the hare's tail and stopped the last hole with that. When the Devil saw this he fled. But since then hares have no tail. [*sic*]'[2] In another version Noah cuts off the foot of the female hare for a plug. She dies, and that would have been the end of all hares. But when the animals leave the Ark God allows the male hare to give birth to one child, a female. And so the race goes on. This female can be recognized by the white star on its head.[3]

When the flood begins to subside, a bird is released to discover land, but in an American Indian legend a hare is sent out. In that

[1] Genesis i, 1–4.
[2] Oskar Dähnhardt, *Natursagen*, Leipzig and Berlin, 1907–12, Vol. 1, p. 277.
[3] Ibid., p. 278.

story the survivors did not have to use a boat. They took refuge on top of a mountain from which presumably they could not see the extent of the waters. They brought a hare with them and knew that the flood had subsided when one day, after its release, it did not return.[1]

In the mythology of Easter, the hare lays eggs like the bird, and stands for re-creation. In the myth of the Algonquin Indians it is the first creator, the maker of the sun, moon and Earth. It is called Michabo, the Great Hare, and is the ruler of the winds, the guardian of the people, the inventor of picture writing and many other arts.

In 1610, an official of the colony of Virginia questioned several 'Indians' about their religion:

'I will conclude these points with opinion of the Indians of *Patawomeck*-river the last yeare 1610. about Christmas when Capt Argole was there trading with Iopassus the great kings brother, after many daies of acquaintaunce with him as the Pynnace road before the Towne *Mattchipongo*, Iopassus comming abourd and sitting (the weather being very Cold) by the fire upon a harth in the Hold with the Captayne, one of our men was reading of a Bible, to which the Indian gaue a very attent eare and looked with a very wish't eye vpon him as if he desired to vnderstand what he read, wherevpon the Captayne tooke the booke, and turned to the Picture of the Creation of the world, in the beginning of the book, and caused a Boy one Spilman, who had lived a whole yeare with this Indian-King and spake his language, to shew yt vnto him, and to enterprett yt in his language, which the boy did, and which the king seemed to like well of: howbeit he bade the boy tell the Capt, yf he would heare, he would tell him the manner of their begynning, which was a pretty fabulous tale indeed: "We haue (said he) 5. godes in all our chief god appeares often vnto vs in the likewise of a mightie great Hare, the other 4. haue no visible shape, but are (indeed) the 4. wyndes, which keepe the 4. Corners of the earth (and then with his hand he seemed to quarter out the scytuation of the world) our god who takes vpon

---

[1] James Hastings, *An Encyclopaedia of Religion and Ethics*, Edinburgh, 1908–26, Vol. 1, p. 518.

this shape of a Hare conceaved with himself how to people this
great world, and with what kynd of Creatures, and yt is true (said
he) that at length he divised and made divers men and women and
made provision for them to be kept vp yet for a while in a great
bag, now there were certayne spirritts, which he described to be
like great Giants, which came to the Hares dwelling place (being
towards the rising of the Sun) and hadd perseveraunce of the men
and women, which he had put into that great bag, and they would
haue had them to eate, but the godlike Hare reproved those Cani-
ball Spirritts and droue them awaie. Nowe yf the boy had asked
him of what he made those men and women and what those
spirritts more particularly had bene and so had proceeded in
some order, they should haue made yt hang togither the better,
but the boy was vnwilling to question him so many things lest he
should offend him, only the old man went on, and said, how that
godlike hare made the water and the fish therein and the land and
a great deare, which should feed vpon the land, at which as-
sembled the other 4. gods envious hereat, from the east the west
from the north and sowth and with hunting poles kild this deare
drest him, and after they had feasted with him departed againe
east west north and south, at which the other god in despight of
this their mallice to him, tooke all the haires of the slayne deare
and spredd them vpon the earth with many powerfull wordes and
charmes whereby every haire became a deare and then he opened
the great bag, wherein the men and the women were, and placed
them vpon the earth, a man and a woman in one Country and a
man and a woman in another country, and so the world tooke his
first begynning of mankynd, the Captayne bade the boy aske him,
what he thought became of them after their death, to which he
answered somewhat like as is expressed before of the Inhabitants
about vs, howe that after they are dead here, they goe vp to the
toppe of a highe tree, and there they espie a faire plaine broad
pathe waye, on both sydes whereof doth grow all manner of
pleasant fruicts, as Mulberryes, Strawberryes, Plombes etc. In this
pleasant path they run toward the rysing of the sun, where the
godlike hares howse is, and in the midd waie they come to a
howse, where a woman goddesse doth dwell, who hath alwaies

her doores open for hospitality and hath at all tymes ready drest greene *Vskatahomen* and *Pokahichary* (which is greene Corne bruysed and boyld, and walnutts beatten smale, then washed from the Shells, with a quantety of water, which makes a kynd of Milke and which they esteeme an extraordinary dainty dish) togither with all manner of pleasant fruicts in a readines to entertayne all such as do travell to the great hares howse, and when they are well refreshed, they run in this pleasant path to the rysing of the Sun, where they fynd their forefathers living in great pleasure in a goodly feild, where they doe nothing but daunce and sing, and feed on delicious fruicts with that great Hare, who is their great god, and when they haue lived there, vntill they be starke old men, they saie they dye there likewise by turnes and come into the world againe." [1]

The mystical concepts in that account belong to all mankind. There is no death without resurrection and the house of the creator, the bringer of light and life, is in the East.

According to Bede the name of the Christian festival of Easter was adopted from an Anglo-Saxon goddess called Eostre, spelt by other writers Eastre, Ostara, or Eastur. The name is cognate with Aurora, Eos and with Ushas, the Sanskrit for dawn. [2] The month of April was called Eostur-monath, the Dawn month, and the pre-Christian festival of Easter included rites symbolic of death and resurrection. Few details are known, but there is no reason to think that it differed basically from other spring festivals such as that of Adonis. 'At the festivals of Adonis, which were held in Western Asia and in Greek lands, the death of the god was annually mourned, with a bitter wailing, chiefly by women; images of him, dressed to resemble corpses, were carried out as to burial and then thrown into the sea or into springs; and in some places his revival was celebrated on the following day. . . . In the great Phoenician sanctuary of Astarte at Byblus the death of Adonis was annually mourned to the shrill wailing notes of flutes, with weeping, lamentation and the beating of the breast; but the ·

[1] William Strachey, *Historie of Travell into Virginia Britania*, London, 1953, pp. 101-3.

[2] E. Cobham Brewer, *A Dictionary of Phrase and Fable*, London, 'New Edition', p. 381.

next day he was believed to come to life again and ascend up to heaven in the presence of his worshippers.'[1]

The natural sequence of winter and summer, darkness and light was compressed in most spring festivals into a few hours or days. In the north where Eastre was worshipped the sequence is more impressive than anywhere else. Winter daylight only lasts for a few hours. The further north you go, the longer the nights become until, within the Arctic circle, there is complete darkness for months. In spring the process starts to be reversed. So great was the fear of early man that the dearth brought by cold and darkness might never end, that he had to bring back light and life by magic rites. And of course in years of famine, it does not end. Drought, flood, disease stop growth. People who depend only on hunting are also starved. The animals die or move away.

Eastre's mother was Jörd, the Earth; Persephone's was Demeter, the Earth Mother. 'In various parts of Germany stone altars can still be seen, which are known as Easter-stones, because they were dedicated to the fair goddess Ostara. They were crowned with flowers by the young people, who danced gaily around them by the light of great bonfires,—a species of popular games practised until the middle of the present [19th] century, in spite of the priests' denunciations and of the repeatedly published edicts against them.'[2]

Eastre's favourite animal and attendant spirit was the hare. Little else is known about her, but it has been suggested that her lights, as goddess of the dawn, were carried by hares. And she certainly represented spring fecundity, and love and carnal pleasure that leads to fecundity.

The hare was a companion of Aphrodite too, and of satyrs and cupids. Wedding rings in Ancient Greece bore its image and in the Middle Ages it appears beside the figure of Luxuria (Plate 15.) Everywhere it represented love, fertility and growth. It is associated with the moon, dawn and Easter not only in this respect—as a symbol of physical growth—but in their deeper, spiritual, meanings: the enlightenment of the soul through death,

---

[1] Sir James Frazer, op. cit., p. 335.
[2] H. A. Guerber, *Myths of the Norsemen*, London, 1908, p. 56.

redemption and resurrection. Like the Easter egg itself the hare is an emblem of body and soul.

One of the Easter games that died out in England and is to some extent revived is the search for eggs laid by the Easter Hare. That a hare should lay eggs seems at first a ludicrous idea. So does the tale that storks bring babies, and the tale that used to be told to children in Swabia that they had been found by their parents in a hare's nest.[1] But as soon as one thinks of the need for symbolism, even in present-day life, such images become poetic; they are a transference of the miracle of creation into a tangible form. The egg is the epitome of this wonder. To feel its hard shell, to break a fresh one and see nothing but liquid, gives no idea at all that it contains a little creature.

Some images have their origin in the observation of nature, and that may be true of the Easter Hare. Birds, like the plover, that make nests on the ground lay their eggs near the hares' forms. They may even choose a deserted form and convert it. Their eggs and baby leverets are frequently found on the same terrain in spring (see p. 55).

The celebration of birth was preceded by the sacrifice of the symbolic creature and concluded by the joyful eating of its flesh. Vestiges of both these rites survived in England at least until the eighteenth century—the sacrifice in the custom called 'Hunting the Easter Hare' and the feast in a rough game called 'The Hare-Pie Scramble'. The Town Records of Leicester for 1668 refer to the hare hunt as an ancient custom, and in the chamberlain's accounts for 1574 there is an item of 12d 'given to the hare-finders'. But the only description we know of was written after it had become a drag-hunt. A dead cat was substituted for the hare, probably because it is easier to drag without disintegrating, but it may be that the choice of a cat had some symbolic meaning too. The cat and the hare were both corn spirits.

'*Hunting the Hare at Leicester:*—It had long been customary on Easter Monday for the mayor and his brethren, in their scarlet gowns, attended by their proper officers, in form, to go to a certain close, called Black-Annis'-Bower Close, parcel of, or border-

[1] James Hastings, op. cit., Vol. I, p. 518.

ing upon, Leicester Forest, to see the diversion of hunting, or rather the trailing of a cat before a pack of hounds: a custom, perhaps originating out of a claim to the royalty of the forest. Hither, on a fair day, resorted the young and old, and those of all denominations. In the greatest harmony the Spring was welcomed. The morning was spent in various amusements and athletic exercises, till a dead cat, about noon, was prepared by aniseed water, for commencing the mock-hunting of the hare. In about half an hour, after the cat had been trailed at the tail of a horse over the grounds in zig-zag directions, the hounds were directed to the spot where the cat had been trailed from. Here the hounds gave tongue in glorious concert. The people from the various eminences, who had placed themselves to behold the sight, with shouts of rapture gave applause; the horsemen, dashing after the hounds through foul passages and over fences, were emulous for taking the lead of their fellows. . . . As the cat had been trailed to the mayor's door, through some of the principal streets, consequently the dogs and horsemen followed. After the hunt was over, the mayor gave a handsome treat to his friends; in this manner the day ended.

'(This description is by an eye-witness of this old municiple custom, which began to fall into disuse about the year 1767. . . .)'[1]

The Hare-Pie Scramble took place at Hallaton (Hallowed or Holy Town) which is also in Leicestershire.

'A piece of land was bequeathed to the rector conditionally that he and his successors provided annually, "Two hare pies, a quantity of ale, and two dozen penny loaves, to be scrambled for on each succeeding Easter Monday at the rising ground, called Hare Pie Bank," about a quarter of a mile south of the village. This land, before the enclosure, was called "Hare-cropleys". . . . A benevolent rector of the last century made an effort to have the funds applied to a better use, but the village wags were equal to the occasion, and raised the cry and chalked on his walls and doors, as well as on the church, "No pie, no parson, and a job for the glazier"; and again, in 1878, when the railway was in course of

[1] C. J. Billson, 'Folklore of Leicestershire and Rutland', *County Folklore Extracts*, No. 3, London, 1895, pp. 76–7 quoting John Throsby, *History of Leicester*, 1791.

construction, parish meetings were held to consider the desira-
bility of taking the money and appropriating it to sports of other
kinds, and more in character with the tastes of the age; many of the
inhabitants, however, wishing to retain the old custom, the pro-
posal fell through. This year the two benefit societies, as usual,
held their anniversary. . . . About three p.m. a selected deputation
called at the rectory for the provided "pies and beer", which upon
being taken to the "Fox Inn", a procession was organised in the
following order——

"Two men abreast, carrying two sacks with the pies cut
up.

"Three men abreast, carrying aloft a bottle each; two of these
bottles filled with beer, are ordinary field wood bottles, but without the usual mouth, and are iron-hooped all over, with just a hole
left for drinking from; the third is a 'dummy'.

"Occasionally, when it can be procured, as was the case in 1885,
a hare, in sitting posture, mounted on top of a pole.

"Band of music.

"Procession, which, as may well be imagined, increases greatly
in number as it approaches the 'Hare Pie Bank'. . ."

'Until this year a man followed the band with a basket containing the penny loaves, which were broken up and thrown about
indiscriminately as he went along. On Monday, when the procession neared the bank, the band struck up "See the conquering
hero comes", and, on reaching the bank, the hare-pies were
scrambled for by the spectators, who amused themselves by
throwing the contents at each other.'[1]

AUTUMN

The crops have to die before they can be eaten and at harvest
the symbol of the corn-spirit had to be killed too. Until the nineteenth century, at least, in some parts of Europe where the corn-
spirit was a cock, a live cock was buried up to its neck in the field
and beheaded with the sickle or scythe that cut the last piece of
corn. But in most places a figure of the animal or bird had been

[1] Ibid., pp. 79–80 quoting *Leicester Journal*, 1892.

substituted by then. Frazer describes how an imitation hare was beheaded in Scotland:

'In Galloway, the reaping of the last standing corn is called "cutting the Hare". . . . When the rest of the corn has been reaped, a handful is left standing to form the Hare. It is divided into three parts and plaited, and the ears are tied in a knot. The reapers then retire a few yards and each throws his or her sickle in turn at the Hare to cut it down. It must be cut below the knot, and the reapers continue to throw their sickles at it, one after the other, until one of them succeeds. In the Parish of Minnigaff, when the Hare was cut, the unmarried reapers ran home with all speed, and the one who arrived first was the first to be married. In Germany also one of the names for the last sheaf is the Hare. . . . "He is killing the Hare" is commonly said of the man who cuts the last corn in Germany, Sweden, Holland, France and Italy. In Norway the man who is thus said to "Kill the Hare" must give "hare's blood" in the form of brandy to his fellows to drink.'[1]

Where the reaper-and-binder is still used, the corn is cut in ever narrowing circles as the machine works round and round the field, and the frightened hares or rabbits are driven to the centre. The harvesters, armed with sticks or guns, gather round and kill them as they rush out from the very last piece to be cut. Of course, they are not 'killing the corn-spirit'. They do it for sport and to take home something to eat. But it is another example of how images may be derived from what one sees around one. The hare in the last sheaf was not always visible.

In 1966, a County Roscommon man told us that 'when the people long ago, and even a few years ago, and even like before last year, if you're cutting a field of oats they'll say "you'll hunt down the hare tonight; you'll hunt the old hare this evening". That means you'll finish the oats and there she has to go.'[2] But direct evidence of a symbolic meaning has not been found in Ireland. In replies to a questionnaire about the Last Sheaf, 'people just referred jocosely to the possibility of a hare being in the last sheaf of corn. In Ireland, so far as I can determine, the last

---

[1] Sir James Frazer, op. cit., pp. 452–3.
[2] John Connaughton.

sheaf was not called the Hare; the animal that might be in it would normally be a hare and was so named.'[1]

Yet if one accepts the evidence gathered in other countries, it is tempting to suppose by inference that the notion once had a symbolic meaning in Ireland too. It is misleading to separate the material experience from the spiritual.

Folk stories for example are sometimes analysed and interpreted in an absurd and boring way, and will lend themselves to any argument. Like folk customs, they contain much fantasy and comedy, but this does not mean that they have no depth of meaning. The harvest passage in the famous story 'The King of Liars' may be taken as an example. The whole thing is a fantastic joke, yet the part played by the hare is symbolic.

'The King of Liars' or 'The Great Liar' is one of a large and widespread group of stories of the Baron Munchausen type. The author of Munchausen used many of the same folk themes, ancient themes that have been embellished by successive generations. Most of the Irish liar stories tell of a king who promises a favour, usually his daughter in marriage, to anyone who can get him to say, 'You're a liar'. The hero-liar starts by telling the king about a potato with a haulm as tall as a tree. It had to be rooted out with crowbars, he says, and split in four and it took four men, holding a piece each on a handspike, to carry it home. The King is tempted to call him a liar, but refrains. Then the liar describes a cabbage so large that his bullock stood under its leaves to shelter from the rain; he shook the leaves and the water that fell from them swept the bullock down to a stream where it was drowned. The King is very much tempted, but refrains. The lies increase in absurdity until he can't help shouting, 'You're a liar'. The story of the reaping hare often comes towards the end.

Here are two extracts from Irish versions of 'The Liar', each told by a different story-teller and recorded since 1930. In the first the hero tells the King how he and his father were once planting all of Ireland under oats. When they ran short of oats he took an old horse across to Scotland to fetch more:

'He brought home the old nag and the oats and planted the half-

[1] Seán Ó Súilleabháin, personal communication.

hundredweight of it in the soil. My father had thus planted little Ireland and big Ireland with oats—that's more than you ever had planted, O King! It grew up into fine long oats, and when it ripened in the autumn, there wasn't a man in small Ireland or in big Ireland only my father and myself [to reap it]. Out I went one autumn morning, with my sickle [reaping-hook] to reap it, and my father accompanied me to help. When I stood at the head of the field and looked over the extent of it, I grew angry and ill-tempered, frothing from the mouth, when I saw that I had nobody to reap it except my father and myself . . . and the corn was shedding for want of reaping. I looked around me and saw a hare leaping in the oats. I said to myself that, if I had it, I'd eat it for my dinner, so I threw my sickle as far as I could towards it. It went into its thigh. I ran after the hare to catch it, but as soon as the hare got able to run, off he was, reaping the oats with the sickle in his thigh! I ran on seeing this and sent my father down to the end of the field while I went to the top. We kept urging and hunting the hare from one to the other, and when the evening came, dark and cold and wet, the hare was weakening from all the work, and he fainted at the top of the field. I took my knife out of my pocket and skinned the side of the hare where the sickle was stuck. I put a naggin of buttermilk into his two ears, and up he rose lively and well! His skin was hanging down from his side. He let back his ears and I knew then that he was able to use his muscles. I got an iron crowbar and a ship's cable and sewed the hare's skin around the crowbar and the cable, and spurred him on to work again. To make a long story short, I assure you, O King, that little Ireland and big Ireland were reaped by the hare by night. We stooked every blade he had reaped and make a rick of the sheaves, and when little Ireland and big Ireland were in one large rick, wasn't that rick larger than yours, O King?'[1]

A Mayo version:

'The following morning, as soon as day rose, myself and my mother got up; we tackled [harnessed] an old white garron [horse] for ploughing and started to plough. When the old garron got

[1] *The King of Lies*, extract from oral unpublished version translated by Seán Ó Súilleabháin.

tired, he was failing under the plough. A big eagle came along and stood in the furrow. I caught him and harnessed him to the plough. The big eagle started to plough, with myself guiding it, and to make a long story short, both Big Ireland and Little Ireland were ploughed by the big eagle and myself when my mother brought me my dinner!

'I put the big eagle into the barn, and said to myself that he was worth feeding. Nine barrels of seed-oats that I had for planting were eaten by the big eagle while I was eating my dinner. I tied a sheet about my neck [as a sack] and started to shake out the seed. I put my mother in charge of the big eagle and I had Little Ireland and Big Ireland sown, and my mother and the big eagle had them harrowed by evening.

'I said that I had a good day's work done, and told my mother not to wake me in the morning until she had the breakfast ready on the table. But as the widows of this world are inclined to be more anxious than any other people, she got up at the ring [break] of day, looked out the door, looked back again and said: 'Seán, son, get up quickly, and don't bother with your duds [rags of clothes]. This is our day for real haste, because all the oats you and myself and the big eagle sowed yesterday is full ripe for reaping today.

'I got up, and my mother and myself took two long, slender, sharp sickles and started to reap the oats. We had only a little reaped when up started a hare in front of me in the oats. I threw my hook at him and the tip of it got stuck into the heel of the hare. Off ran the hare west through Ireland and back again, going from side to side, and the hook behind him and he reaping the oats! I started to bind the oats he had reaped, and I set my mother to make stooks of it, and to make a long story short for ye, Little Ireland and Big Ireland were reaped by the hare, tied into sheaves by myself and stooked by my mother by evening!

'I said that indeed we had done a great day's work, and told my mother not to wake me in the morning until she'd have the breakfast ready on the table. But as the widows of this world are inclined to be more anxious than any other people, my mother got up at the ring of day and looked out the door fearing the cattle might be ruining the oats. She returned and said the oats had vanished.'[1]

Everyone will agree that the hare in these stories is a symbol of swiftness. At the risk of being called Great Liars ourselves, we dare to suggest that it was chosen as the reaper also because of its association with fertility. The huge potato and the cabbage are certainly expressions of fertility. All three images can help one to understand primitive art, for art gives form to the abstract and to passing events, and organizes the diffusion of living things and matter that surround us. Folk customs and folk stories fulfil the same need.

[1] Ibid., extract from oral unpublished version translated by Seán Ó Súilleabháin.

13

The Hare as Witch

The hare is linked all over Britain with witches, and there are few people who have not come across this association either in stories written for children or in the tales which are part of the rural tradition. Many of these country tales were still recounted in the remote parts of these islands in an atmosphere of belief or half-belief during recent times. We are including many from Ireland, stories that are believed in today; and they remain as living examples of very ancient belief-patterns. But before we go on to discuss the hare-witch tales it will be necessary to define exactly what is a witch.

This may seem a redundant question. Everyone, even a child—perhaps more particularly a child—knows, what a witch is. Why, therefore, go into one of these pedantic discussions that do nothing more than give us an illuminated panorama of what we already know? There are, however, at least three different ideas or images underlying the word *witch*; and in order to reach an understanding of how the hare became linked with witches it will be necessary to strip the different images one from another. First of all, the image that children have of a witch: this has been stylized by innumerable descriptions and illustrations over the last two or three centuries. She is a long-nosed, nut-cracker chinned old woman with dangerous looking teeth and fingers like talons. She is clad in a black cloak, wears a tall black hat and rides on a broomstick. This image is, like ogres, dragons, unicorns and werewolves, pure fantasy. But even in this fantasy of a witch there is a great deal that could profitably detain a student—the broomstick, for instance—as readers of Margaret Murray's book[1] will know.

[1] M. A. Murray, *The Witch Cult in Western Europe*, Oxford, 1963, pp. 10, 103-6.

The second image is of an old woman living by herself in a country cottage. She may well have a cat; or perhaps more than one cat. She avoids company; she is, in modern terms, an introvert who probably has a highly developed intuitive faculty[1] as many women indeed have; and she may well have a faculty that is something more than intuition and could best be described as extrasensory perception. She is the sort of person who must have been under great risk during the witch persecutions in seventeenth-century England and Scotland, and who has always been under suspicion even up to the present day in remote country places. If she is intelligent and well affected, she may use her high degree of perception to help her neighbours; and often such a woman will have good knowledge of the traditional cures, like wart-charming or old herbal remedies, and become a good, stabilizing influence in the community. She will have the reputation of being a white witch or wise woman. If such a woman is less intelligent, and for some reason embittered, she will use her sensitivity in a negative way, not for the good of the community but for her own private ends; and she will invoke some of the hackneyed trappings of witchcraft to revenge herself upon her neighbours for some real or imagined wrong. Such a lonely old woman in an East Anglian village during the last few years made the traditional clay image and stuck pins into it to revenge herself on a lorry driver who had inadvertently killed one of her cats.

The third image of a witch has come into prominence in recent years; and we have even seen a number of these self-confessed witches on television, or featured in the coloured supplements of the Sunday press. They usually claim that they are members of a coven or assembly of witches, which appears to mean nothing more than a group of people who have become interested in the occult; and have come together to take part in rituals like the Black Mass, ceremonies that have been reconstructed by a reading of some of the more recondite sources of historical witchcraft; and no doubt influenced by experiments made earlier this century by Alesteir Crowley, a well-known pretender to magic.

None of these forms or images of the witch can help us in our

[1] Layard, op. cit., pp. 196–7.

inquiry into the origin of the hare-witch concept. For this we must turn to a much more matter-of-fact image: the witch as a survivor of the priest, priestess, or leading participant in the ceremonies of a very ancient religion. As we have already seen from a previous chapter, man was bound to animals from the very beginning. Animals were an essential part of his religion; and the core of the ritual of this religion was concerned to consecrate the animals and to ensure that they would survive and multiply in order to help man sustain himself on this earth. These early rituals in the cave involving the animals were the germ of religion; and, as we have suggested, they have left their imprint in modern religions in the symbolic role played in these by certain animals. Our thesis is that the hare was one of these consecrated animals; and in the periodic celebration of the rituals connected with this creature, certain members of the group (*witches*, if we are allowed to use the anachronism) assumed the *shape* of the hare as part of the ritual. We know from the cave figures at Le Gabillou and Isturitz that early man was involved with the hare; and we can infer that the people who were taking part in the ceremonies concerning the hare took its skin and the head as part of their dress and simulated the actions of the animals as they had observed them in the wild state. This identification and skilful imitation of the stance and action of animals can clearly be seen from the wall paintings in the caves of Spain and France, for example at Les Trois Freres and Teyjat in the Dordogne, where men are wearing the skin and horns of animals. We do not know of an instance where hare-men are depicted in parietal art—that is, human beings wearing long hare-ears as part of a head-dress to simulate the hare. But we can confidently infer that this was, in fact, a part of the early ceremonies because we have the survival already referred to: the *Saxon Idol of the Moon*.[1] During these rituals the animal-men worked themselves into a trance in which they believed they became, or were changed into, the group or totem animal. This was done, as already suggested, either for religious reasons—for cementing the identity of the group with the animal—or for magical reasons: for ensuring the success of the hunting of the animal that was to follow the

[1] P. 119

144

ceremony. Probably, however, both purposes were implicit in each ritual. But though they *acted* like the animal during the ritual they no more *became* it than did the shaman ascend to heaven, when he 'ascended the pole of the world' by climbing up a high tree; or when he claimed, after being in one of his trances, that he had been 'walk-about in the clouds' and had visited distant places.

This ritual of metamorphosis of man into animal—symbolized and subjectively effected by the donning of the animal's skin and mask, along with the appropriate rhythmical sounds and incantations—and back again into man when the ceremony was over, was one of the earliest ways in which the primitives attempted to control their environment, at the same time inducing in themselves the assurance that by a careful and accurate celebration of the ritual they could do this and survive. Its whole purpose was really practical: to enable early man to take an intractable reality into his own psyche and thus partially to subdue it. But when he came out of the cave and became a settled dweller in the valleys and plains although much of the religious force went out of many of the palaeolithic ceremonies, their shell still remained. That is, the changing of man into animal and back again into man became dissociated from its symbolic role in the context of the ancient ritual; and ordinary people came to assume that a real physical change took place by which a man or a woman could actually take the shape of an animal, a hare for instance.

This belief was kept alive by the survival—centuries after the supposed Christianization of the whole of Europe—of the old religion of the Mother Goddess, with groups of people clandestinely celebrating the old rituals, among them the supposed metamorphosis of man into animal. Margaret Murray has shown convincingly that the witch-groups in medieval and sixteenth to seventeenth-century Europe functioned according to a pattern laid down before the beginnings of history, and still practised in our day by primitive tribes in many parts of the world. The *devil* was the leader of the coven or group: he was the chief priest or medicine man of the old pagan ritual. He and his followers could change themselves into animals by donning the skin of the animal and—like their ancient counterparts—acting and imitating the characteristic movements or gestures of the animal in their secret congregations. As came out in the seventeenty-century Scottish witch trials quoted by Margaret Murray,[1] the method of making the ritual-change into a hare or any other animal was by the recital of an incantation:

> '*I sall goe intill ane haire,*
> *With sorrow, and sych, and meikle caire,*
> *And I sall goe in the Divellis nam,*
> *Ay whill I com hom againe.*'

To become a cat or a crow the same verse was used with an alteration of the second line so as to force a rhyme: instead of 'meikle caire', the words were 'a blak shot' for a cat, and 'a blak thraw' for a crow or craw. To revert again to the human form the words were:

> '*Hare, hare, God send thee care.*
> *I am in an hare's likeness just now,*
> *But I shall be in a woman's likeness even now*'

with the same variations of 'a blak shot' or 'a blak thraw' for a cat or crow.

And the sort of statements that were common in the trials: 'I talked to the Devil: he was in the likeness of a dog', can be explained in the context of the ritual. The devil was not the ecclesiastical Devil but an actual man, the leader or chief witch or priest in the coven who had donned the disguise of an animal and was acting as did his counterpart in the palaeolithic caves, thousands of years before.

But the remarkable thing is that the nearest approach we know in Britain to those ancient witches, whose origins go back to the fertility practices of ancient man, were not called witches at all. They are the old farm-horsemen who performed certain rituals for the purpose of gaining rapport with, and therefore control over, their horses.[2] Like the primitives' magic theirs, too, was

[1] Ibid., pp. 234-5.
[2] See George Ewart Evans, *The Horse in the Furrow*, London, 1960, Section IV. *The Pattern Under the Plough*, London, 1966, Chapters 16-24.

scrupulously *practical*: it had *use*—to ensure the fertility of their animals and their amenability to man's wishes. For the old horsemen there was no question of experimenting with magic or of gaining a gratuitous ecstasy or the satisfaction of wilful curiosity. Here it was all for a purpose, all part of a way of life that was tied to an animal—the horse—in the same way as the primitives' lives were tied to the animals they existed on. The ritual of the Scottish 'Society of the Horseman's Word', in our view, has its origins in these remote ceremonies we have just discussed. The Horseman's Word, that is, the secret word given to an entrant at initiation so we are given to understand, does not pretend to be a magic word or anything fantastic like that (although the initiates, like the Whisperers, may themselves pretend that it is, simply for mystification, purely *ad captandum*). But it is a word that symbolizes the brotherhood of man and animal in a situation where a tight, symbiotic relationship was not a choice but a destiny that had to be sanctified by a solemn and binding ceremony.

To return to the hare-witch theme: most of the tales we have collected can be understood in the light of what has been written above. This will also throw a little light on the kind of tale met with among modern primitives when a man's soul is supposed to be transferred to an animal, of which the following is an example:

'An old man, while staying in a firth to fish for salmon, lost his son, who died some distance up the country. In his grief he could not persuade himself to leave his son's grave, and he therefore put up his winter house on the spot. In this lonely spot they were once surprised by seeing three men entering the house, one of them tall and long-nosed, the other smaller with a flat nose, and the last of very small stature and as white as snow. After passing the evening talking with the host, the short-nosed man asked for a piece of sole-leather, and the white one wanted a piece of walrus-tooth. The old man saw the departing visitors out, but when they left him, stood dumbfounded at seeing them bounding off in the shape of a reindeer, a fox and a hare. It is said that the hare had need of something for a new tooth.'[1]

The Eskimo teller of this story did not say what the long-nosed

[1] Dr. Henry Rink, *Tales and Traditions of the Eskimo*, Edinburgh, 1875, p. 450.

fox wanted, perhaps because he forgot, but the reindeer and the
hare needed to renew parts vital to their lives; reindeer run long
distances between their scanty pastures; a hare without front teeth
or with teeth that have grown too long would die of starvation.
One can guess by analogy with other anthropomorphic stories
that they wanted to renew their lives as human beings too. The
hare was probably the old man's dead son.

In hunting communities, like certain groups of Eskimos, men
and animals get their living in the same way. They share the same
hardships of weather and hunger. Their physical association is
obviously close. A feeling of spiritual kinship naturally goes with
it. The Eskimos of the Ungava region say that the wolves are the
gaunt and hungry children of a mother whose family was too
large for her to feed it properly. The swallows were once wise and
gifted children who played at making toy mud houses on a cliff.
They were changed into birds and have never forgotten how to
build a house of mud. 'They are quite safe, for even the raven does
not molest them and the Eskimo children love to watch them.'
'The hare is really a little child that ran away because of ill-treat-
ment on the part of its elders. He has no tail because, as a child, he
had none; and he lays back his ears when he hears a shout because
he thinks people are talking about him.'[1]

By the time these fables were written down by Europeans they
were perhaps told merely to amuse children, but their source is
religious and is concerned with the immortality of the soul. One
reason for not eating the flesh of certain animals—especially of the
animal that is the totem of your own tribe—is that the soul of a
dead relative is in them. Belief in the transmigration of souls
either into animals or other human beings seems at one time to
have been universal. The thought behind it is familiar to us all and
comes from observation. A parent can often see his dead father or
mother not only in the character but in the gestures and facial expressions of his child and it is natural for anyone who lives among
animals to observe in them traits that belong to people too. They
were and sometimes still are, invested with human souls by

[1] James Hastings, *Encyclopaedia of Religion and Ethics*, Edinburgh, 1908–26, Vol. 3,
pp. 525–6.

imaginative sympathy; the lion has the dignity and courage of a
noble man, the elephant wisdom and the long memory that goes
with it, and so on. Swallows are skilled and spiritual. The hare is
chosen for qualities as varied as its nature and has the soul of the
sufferer, the fecund begetter, creator of arts, inventive dreamer
and, principally, of the man who is gifted with an intuitive
leaping mind.

In some societies it was not everybody's soul that could enter an
animal. Only the chosen—the wise elder or the child that was born
to be a priest or shaman—possessed that power; they possessed it
during their lives as well as after death. Like the witches they
could shift their minds into paraphysical states, rendering themselves 'beside themselves' as we say of people who have tem-
porarily abandoned the controls of reason.

The ritual rhyme of the Scottish witches already given describes
a psychological transformation that went together with dressing
up as a hare. In modern English it means:

> *'I shall go into a hare,*
> *With sorrow and sigh and (probably) mental torment.'*

The word *care*, in its archaic spelling is ambiguous. Until the
eighteenth century it had a much stronger meaning than the present one of *worry* and is defined as *mental suffering*, but in old Scots
to cair meant 'to return to a place where one has been before'.[1] In
either sense it describes one of the states of mind into which a
shaman can go.

The transformation can happen while he or she is awake and
active or in a trance or sleep. The original belief was that the soul
left the body lying passive until its return, but if it entered an
animal never to return it left its human body dead.

This split is familiar to psychiatrists of the modern world. 'The
maladie initiatique is of course a common stage in the career of
shamans, magicians and saints in many parts of the world, and
shamans used often to be described as neurotics by European
writers. With this view of them it is interesting to contrast the
following passage from a discourse on the relations between men

---

[1] Jamieson's *Dictionary of the Scottish Language*, Paisley, 1912.

and Spirits supposed to have been delivered about 500 BC. The shaman, according to this text, is a person upon whom a Bright Spirit has descended, attracted to him because he is "particularly vigorous and lively, staunch in adherence to principle, reverent and just; so wise that in all matters high and low he always takes the right side, so saintly (*shêng*) that he spreads around him a radiance that reaches far and wide. . . ." [1]

Wherever the old rural cultures persist the *maladie initiatique* surprises no one, nor does the concept of transformation which sometimes is part of it. In 1966 an Irish countryman told us of a hare that seemed to be sucking milk from a cow:

'Just as sure as I'm telling you, 'tis somebody that's putting his penance over him . . . yes, yes, the shape of a hare. 'Tis my belief that he was a Christian that was buried, that was bad in this life and that he was putting a penance over him. That's sure.' [2]

The Chippewa Indians made a roof-shaped covering to their graves with a hole at the head of the grave to let the soul in and out. Here is part of a conversation between a U.S. official and one of the Chippewas:

'. . . But you say the soul went at death to the land of happiness. How then can it remain in the body?'

'There are two souls . . . you know that in dreams we pass over wide countries, and see hills and lakes and mountains, and many scenes which pass before our eyes and affect us. Yet at the same time our bodies do not stir; and there is a soul left with the body, else it would be dead. So, you perceive, it must be another soul that accompanies us.' [3]

According to the Thongas of Southern Africa the *noyi* (caster of spells) does not leave his true body on the sleeping-mat when he flies away at night:

'In reality what remains is a *wild* beast, with which the noyi has chosen to identify himself. This fact was disclosed to me by the following striking confession of S. Gana, a very intelligent Nkuna.

[1] Arthur Waley, Introduction to *The Nine Songs*, London, 1955, pp. 9–10.
[2] *The Hare*, BBC Third Programme, 1966.
[3] H. R. Schoolcraft, *History of the Indian Tribes*, Philadelphia, 1853, Vol. 5, p. 79.

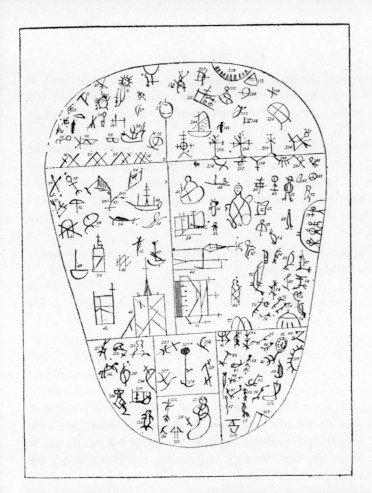

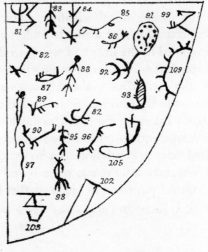

Fig. 5. (*above*) Lapp
Shaman's drumhead with 150
symbols; (*right*) an enlarge-
ment of the lower right-hand
section: number 85 illustrates
a hare, and 86 a fox

"Suppose", he said, "my father is a noyi and I am not. I wish to marry a certain girl whom I love. My father knows that she is a noyi, because they all know each other, and he tells me: 'Don't do that! She is *clever*; you will repent!'

"However, I persist in my idea. He urges me to abandon the plan, and threatens me with great misfortune. I marry her. One night, my father enters my hut and awakens me. He says to me:

'What did I tell you! Look! Your wife has gone!'

"I look at her place and find her sleeping calmly—'No. Here she is.'

'That is not she! She is away! Take this assegai and stab her.'

'No, Father I dare not.'

'Do as I say!'

"And he puts the assegai into my hand and makes me strike her violently in her leg. A cry, the cry of a wild beast, is heard, and a hyena appears in the place of my wife, a hyena which deposits its faeces in its fear, and escapes from the hut, howling. My father gives me some powder to swallow so that I shall be able to recognize the baloyi and their ways and habits. He leaves me—trembling greatly from fear—and goes home. When the sun is about to rise, I hear a noise like that of the wind in the branches, and suddenly something falls down from the top of the hut beside me. It is my wife. She lies sleeping, but her leg shows a wound, the wound that had been made in the hyena!"[1]

It is this concept of the soul leaving the body during dreams while asleep, or hallucinations, which are wakeful dreams, that we must think of if we are to understand any kind of sorcery. It is simplified in the image of witches riding broomsticks or animals through the air or transforming themselves into animals or plants on the earth. But it also expresses a religious truth which was known to the Children of Judah and to those early Christians, the Desert Fathers, who relied so much on visions for their spiritual development; and it has been rediscovered during the past hundred years by psychologists who use the healing power of dreams.

Visionary insight was often found through fasting:

'Daniel purposed in his heart that he would not defile himself

[1] H. A. Junod, *The Life of a South African Tribe*, London, 1927, Vol. 2, p. 508.

with the portion of the King's meat nor with the wine which he drank.... Thus Melzar took away the portion of their meat, and the wine that they should drink; and gave them pulse . . . and Daniel had understanding in all visions and dreams. . . . Then was the secret revealed unto Daniel in a night vision. Then Daniel blessed the God of heaven. . . . He revealeth the deep and secret things: he knoweth what is in the darkness, and the light dwelleth with him.'[1]

The Desert Fathers and the Shamans of Asia, North America and Northern Europe submitted themselves to terrible privations in order to induce dreams which revealed to them the inmost part of their own souls—their unconscious selves—and which also brought inspiration that seemed to come from outside as guidance from God or the Great Spirit. They always remained outside the community morally although after their stay in the wilderness they might live with the others. The shaman's power in the community was stronger than the king's. The chief or king asked him for guidance in all great matters of state, and everyone else relied on him for personal and communal guidance even on practical problems such as which direction to take on the next hunt. He was the mouthpiece of superhuman powers.

In several of the later stories about The Great Hare, when he came to be thought of as a man with magical powers, a shamanistic practice is described. His name in the language from which the following story is translated is Manabozho—literally 'great hare'—and the word lodge is used for any kind of habitation, in this case a hut made of birch-bark and curved branches. It was winter and he had made many vain attempts to get meat. His magical powers had deserted him. He wanted to revive them:

'Manabozho was sitting pensively in his lodge one day, with his head down. He heard the wind whistling around it, and thought, by attentively listening, he could hear the voice of someone speaking to him. It seemed to say to him; Great chief, why are you sorrowful. Am not I your friend—your guardian Spirit? He immediately took up his rattle, and without leaving his sitting pos-

[1] Daniel i, 8 and 16; ii, 19 and 22.

ture, began to sing the chant which at the close of every stanza has the chorus of 'WHAW LAY LE AW.' When he had devoted a long time to this chant, he laid his rattle aside, and determined to fast. For this purpose he went to a cave, and built a very small fire near which he laid down, first telling his wife, that neither she not the children must come near him, till he had finished his fast. At the end of seven days he came back to the lodge, pale and emaciated. His wife in the meantime had dug through the snow, and got a small quantity of the root called truffles. These she boiled and set before him. When he had finished his repast; he took his large bow and bent it. Then placing a strong arrow to the string, he drew it back, and sent the arrow, with the strength of a giant, through the side of his bark lodge. There, said he to his wife, go to the outside, and you will find a large bear, shot through the heart. She did so, and found one as he had predicted.'[1]

It was essential to be alone during the fast, if possible in a place which no one else could find. Manabozho lit a small fire for himself but some of the real priests exposed themselves to extremes of cold or heat, according to the climate of their country, that could and probably often did cause death. For part of the time they became unconscious; they sought a temporary form of death in order to be born again with a mind from which superficialities had been taken away; the ordeal exposed its deeper part and removed the minutiae of day to day life in much the same way that an illness, mental or physical, does. The purification they experienced was visible to many travellers in their eyes and the expression of their faces.

'In one of the texts of Taoism a mechanic is described as fasting, in order to become of concentrated mind, and after several days he has forgotten all about himself.'[2]

The priests and priestesses of the ancient Dianic religion of Europe fasted before rituals such as the eating of first fruits—the harvest celebration—and by what we know of other religions we assume that they fasted for individual inspiration too. They were separated from the communal life of the people who revered

[1] H. R. Schoolcraft, *Algic Researches*, New York, 1839, pp. 223 foll.
[2] James Hastings, op. cit., Vol. 5, p. 762.

them, just as modern priests, parsons or policemen are separated, however often they go into a pub and try to join in. But many of the so-called witches, persecuted relicts of Dianic priestesses, did not wish to join in. Yet they usually went about in ordinary clothes or, if old, dressed in the fashion they liked when they were young and some spoke frequently to other people in the ordinary way. The great majority lived alone with pet animals which were referred to in the law courts as imps or familiars and through whose medium they believed they put their will to practical effect. These domestic familiars were always small animals said to be kept in a box or earthen pot on a bed of wool. 'The witches have their spirits, some hath one, some hath more, as two, three, foure, or five, some in one likenesse, and some in another, as like cats, weasils, toades or mise, whome they nourish with milke or with a chicken, or by letting them suck now and then a drop of bloud.'[1]

The other type of familiar, of which the hare was one, did not belong to the witch. It appeared in the wild as an impersonation of the devil or as his interpreter.

But hares are also described as servants or companions of witches. They were probably tamed by experienced sorcerers or witches and introduced to the house of the initiate where, once accepted, they lived as pets.

About 1645, a young apprentice was on his way home: 'When he came home he laid down to sleep and dreamt that something crept upon his legs and go to his shin, and then he waked and felt it, and it was like a rabbit, and this asked him if he would love it and if he would deny God . . . but he refused, then, but consented to it afterward, when he met it in the field, and it scratched him under his ear and got blood of him, and said now it had what it would have. . . .'[2]

The sucking of blood from any part of the body, or of nipples, was a bond between the sorcerer and the initiate, and from many voluntary statements made in witch-trials it seems to have been a constant bond between familiars and their owners too. No doubt

---

[1] George Giffard, *Discourse of the Subtill Practises of Devilles*, London, 1587, p. 18, quoted by Margaret Murray, *The Witch-Cult in Western Europe*, Oxford, 1962, p. 209.
[2] C. L'Estrange Ewen, *Witch Hunting and Witch Trials*, London, 1929, p. 309.

it was a real bond. Any mammal will suck when young, as calves suck fingers; pet lambs keep the habit all their lives. Sorcerers use sucking, too, both in healing and hurting. In healing they can suck an affected part of the patient's body, to suck away the disease, or another part to extract the evil spirit that is causing the disease. In hurting they are said to drink so much blood that the victim weakens or dies, or even to draw out his entrails and feed on them, but by far the most common hurt of which they are accused is sucking milch cows dry. In parts of Africa the witch does this in his or her human form. In Europe the most usual form is a hare.

The following stories, all recorded between 1930 and 1970, show the persistence of these beliefs. Some, heard from grandparents, are now told for fun, some as events that happened in the old days but not any more; and this is true because most people's imaginations do not work in the old way any more. But most of the people we talked to feel at least as cautious about the hare as they do about walking under ladders or travelling by sea on Friday the 13th. Many believe fully in the hare-witch and told us so without shyness.

'Now this man had only one cow in the poor times and he went out to milk her in the morning and he found that she'd no milk. He did the same the following morning and he found no milk so then in the morning he got up early and found the hare sucking the cow. So he got dogs, borrowed dogs, and he followed the hare until he couldn't catch her, so then he inquired and was told to get a two shilling piece or a florin with a cross . . . chop it up small, put it into a shotgun, and he did and he fired at the hare, wounded her and found this old woman at the old house sitting down, and she was combing her hair and she was bleeding out of one of her feet, so she was a witch sucking the cow.'[1]

That story was told in Ireland, but silver was generally believed to have power over a hare-witch. Perhaps this comes from the association of silver, moon and hare, but a silver coin with a cross on it has the added power of Christianity. The old Scottish groat or fourpenny silver piece had a clearer cross than the florin, and in

[1] *The Hare*, op. cit.

Scottish versions of the story the witch is shot with a groat. (Plate 14).

But sometimes ordinary hunting weapons such as the throwing stick were used:

'A man had ten cows at Buckeragh, and they were missing the milk from these cows; and they wondered. They should be better than this. So they put a man to watch. This is in the summer time. He went down to watch and had two or three of these nice throwing sticks. He said he might keep an eye out to see if he could get a rabbit or a hare. That went on all right, anyhow, and sometime after daylight in the morning wasn't he going round about through the cows and he seen this hare: and, God! he seen this hare, "God," he said, "if he could get a crack at that one now." He watched this hare, anyhow. The next thing didn't he see her going up to a cow and she sitting up, and next thing he seen her putting in her head and took to sucking this cow. Ah, be the Holy! She had sucked that one, anyhow. Begod! she went on to another one; and she done the same. She sucked two or three of them. Whatever she done with all the milk or what she done with it he didn't know. Anyway, he moved about, anyhow, to see if he could get a crack at her; and the cow seen him; didn't she move off, d'ye know. That gave him an open chance, anyhow: and didn't he let fly; and he hit this hare and curled her upside down. And be the Holy, she got up anyhow; and she went off hoppin'. And she got away.

'That went on all right. It come on to the harvest, anyway. That time they used to have to go with the barley; they used to have to go to Kilbeggan with the barley. And Patsy was a young fellow at that time. So I dunno—there was a good few of them starting up; nine or ten cars with the barley; there could be more. And every man had five or six bags of corn, maybe, up on every horse. And they had to go to Kilbeggan with that. And if they didn't start in the middle of the night with that they wouldn't get there in time; and you'd want to get there in time the way you'd get your load, to get your barley off and get home again. And it would be night again; you'd get home in the harvest time maybe, a while after night fall.

'But they were going along, anyway. There were no matches

them times and they had ne'er a . . . it used to be the general
custom, anyhow, for someone to have a coal of the fire in an old
kittle; and they'd have a sod of turf or two in the kettle; but they
must have forgot it this time. For they had ne'er a one. They were
going along, anyway. I think it was somewhere beyond in
Leamonaghan or somewhere along there. But I know it was a
lonesome part of the road; and didn't they see light in a house; and
they proposed, anyhow, for someone to go into the house to get
a light for the pipe and bring out a lump of coal on the pipe; and
they could then get a light from one to the other. So Begob! they
put it on Patsy to go in, anyhow. Patsy went in, anyway; opened
the door and went in. There was two old hags in it. One of them
was sitting in one place and the other was sitting in another. Patsy
said he wanted a coal for his pipe. So he reached down, anyhow,
and he took the tongs and put a coal in the pipe. Of course, it was
a clay pipe them times. And Begod! didn't this one look at him,
anyhow. "Ah", said this one to him, she says, "your soul to
blazes! You are Patsy Kelly," she says, "from Kilcummins", she
says. "Do you remember the morning you hit me with the stick
below in Buckeragh?" And she drew up with the tongs and she
hit him across the back with it; and, Begod! he had to fly out!
She'd kill him, I suppose, if she got another crack at him. That
happened.'

Some of the hare-witches were less vicious. The same speaker
told of a man he knew—John Page:

'It was after John Page had been made a gamekeeper and got a
cottage with a bit of land that he got up one morning to fodder
cattle.

'But this morning he got up; he got up middling early because
he had a couple of animals; and there was about four inches of
snow out; and he got up, and he had a couple o' cattle in the land
down below the house. And he went down with a bit o' hay for
the two cattle. As he was going along he met a hare's track. He
flung the hay to the cattle and he followed the track. Never drew
rein until he went to the steeple of Killrodawn below—a mile and
a half this side of Loch Linn—over from Loch Linn. And the old
wall that was in it—there was an old ivy bush growing on the side

of it. And the hare's track went up this ivy bush that was along
the old wall. And he was going along creeping and the stick ready
to let bang at the hare. And the hare sat up. "Page", he says,
"you're a foolish man to follow me so far!" He drew back his
stick—there's no lie in it!—"Now," says the hare, "don't be
afraid of me," he says, "I'll do you no harm," he says, "you have
a shilling in your pocket; and go to Loch Linn", he says, "and get
two glasses of whiskey", he says, "you want it!" (And you could
get a glass of whiskey for fourpence at the time.) "You can get
two of them," he says, "and that will bring you home to Cloon-
condra. But never follow me again!"

'Divil a hare he ever followed from that day till he died.'[1]

John Page's experience was unusual. In most stories a man cannot approach the witch until she is physically hurt. Only then does
he know her true nature. The idea that the telltale wound persists
after she has reassumed human form occurs not only in contemporary anecdotes but in some of the more stylized narratives that
have been passed by word of mouth from generation to generation, in the Irish language, since the early day of Christianity. It
forms part of the description of Oisín's visit to the Land of Youth.
Oisín, son of Fionn mac Cumhaill, was one of the heroes in the
band of warriors known as the Fianna:

'Long ago the Fianna went out hunting and fowling. They were
going along through hills and glens with their hounds and horses
until a good part of the day had been spent. Then they came upon
a hare, which had one side of gold and the other of silver. The
hounds ran after it and the Fianna after them until they got tired,
and couldn't keep up any longer except Oisín and his own hound.
Oisín followed the hare until evening and the end of the day was
coming on them, and his hound was catching up on the hare, and
he himself on their heels on his slender black steed. When the hare
reached a clump of rushes, the hound pounced on her and took a
bite out of her flank. The hare escaped into the clump.

'When Oisín reached the clump, he got down from his horse,
took hold of the clump and pulled it up. What should he see but
a fine door and a stairs leading from it down under the ground.

[1] John Connaughton.

He went down until he came to a fine palace where there was a fine woman sitting on a silver chair, with a golden chair by her side. She had a hundred thousand welcomes for Oisín, son of the King of the Fianna, and asked him to sit on the golden chair. When he sat down, he noticed the blood dropping from the woman's chair; he asked her why the blood was dripping like that. She told him then that she was the hare that he and the Fianna had been following all day. She stood up and laid a table. The choice of every food and drink was on it, a taste of honey on each bite, and no bite dry. When they had eaten their fill, she pulled down a pack of cards and they played until it was time to sleep.'[1]

Oisín fell in love with her. When he wanted to go back to the world, she told him he had been seven hundred years in the palace with her and that the Fianna were long since dead. He did not believe her, but as soon as his foot touched the earth he became a very old man. Later on he met St. Patrick and, in the story, a famous dialogue takes place between them, Oisín boasting of the strength and prowess of the Fianna, St. Patrick trying to explain the new religion to him.

It is not surprising to find the image of dripping blood in an ancient hero story but it occurs too in the account of an event that is said to have happened within living memory:

[T] 'I will tell you this—they [hares] are a kind of—somewhere or another ... it's not right to be killing them at all. Was I telling you about the man over from the County Galway was out and he had a black greyhound and he rose this hare down not too far from the Shannon? He rose this hare anyway. She ran up across the road at one end. It was not too far from where Sammy Lucas's daughter lived—a few mile from that. Well in fact it was to Sammy Lucas's father that it happened; and he rose this hare, down—maybe a couple of hundred yards down from the road. So she went round-about like—you know the way a hare runs; she goes a certain distance and she'll cut back and up again. Every time she was going she was moving for the house, the whole time. And in the wind-up, the hound was gaining on her middling tidy and there was a

[1] Oral unpublished version from Co. Galway, Ireland, translated from Irish by Seán Ó Súilleabháin.

barred window to the house and she went round the house a couple of times; and the second time anyhow—you know the old-times windows—you know, they were on a hinge. There was a lug like that up in the top and another lug like that in the bottom, do you see? It opened in and out. And I think it were—there was an iron frame to it, an iron frame from small panes; the panes would only be about that size, about six inches to a frame. That sort of window was in it.

'Anyway she come and she lep for the window, and didn't the dog just barely graze her, caught her anyway, going in—and now she went in. The man was coming up along after the hare and the dog was barking—the hound was barking at the man anyhow, and they came up anyhow. They went in after a while to light his pipe. And he had some suspicions anyway. He went in and this old lassie was sitting by the fire and she was fixing up the fire, and he said, "God save all here," you know, like that. And didn't he notice traces of blood on the floor, here and there on the floor—d'ye know what I mean? The dog came in along of him. And she had the tongs in her hand, and she said, "Out you!"—just like that, and she hit the dog sideways, about sideways—like that—and she hit him along the ribs, and the hound—and he yelping—went out the door with him. And devil a day could he ever go after. He died in some short time after. He never ran a day's sport. And I've often heard that that ould lassie—you know the old-times churn ... with a dasher, like that? She'd be churning and it would after be going by itself! She'd be doing jobs round about the house and she have the dasher going by itself. The handle would be going up and down and churning away, and she'd be doing jobs round the house and now and again she'd go and give a look at the milk!'[1]

The hare that is thought to be enchanted is rare and is spoken of as one that is not 'right'. 'It was not a right hare', people will say after a miraculous escape and even if it is killed by the help of magic—the silver coin with a cross on it or the black hound which represents the devil. There is a widespread belief that its flesh is impossible to cook. Alive or dead it avoids destruction by super-natural powers.

[1] John Connaughton.

[T] 'We were going to have a coursing match. We had a certain amount of hares. We hadn't enough of hares. So we went out this day about five o'clock in the evening, and we done a great big portion, d'ye know, where we had a drive before and still we knew there were hares left behind that we didn't get. So I think it was two or three times. We got fourteen hares altogether . . . bring them up and put them into boxes, and the boxes then were carried off and put into a garden [a small field]. Now in the corner of this garden there was about nearly a rood; it was fenced off from the rest of the garden, a square with netting-wire—'twas up to the height of the ceiling there. And there was a door going in and they were fed; they were getting cabbage and turnips and there was water left in there, so they had plenty of feed, anything they wanted to feed as far as feed was concerned. So now, after netting in these hares there was one hare, she gave a bit of a run in along like that; next thing she was up cross back of the wall like this; and she went back a few paces anyhow, and she made a run at this wall. She ran up the wall, up to the top of those wires. She fell back down again. She done that twice. And the third time, she hit the top of the wire and out the far side of it. And the garden was searched high up and low down and the divil a bit of a sight of her they got. Never got her, and she was in the garden somewhere because this gate was shut. Those coming in couldn't get out and they searched the garden, high up and low down, and there were fourteen or fifteen in it at the time—d'ye know what I mean? Myself was there and some of the men were walking on the wall there and they searched the garden high up and low down, and divil the bit of a hope that they got. She wasn't right!

'How could she be right? I mean she was in—she ran to the corner and ran up the wall, and the third time she fell on top of the wire and out the far side of it. Oh, that happened!'

A hare in a graveyard can never be 'right'. The soul of a person who did harm in life may be in it, names must not be mentioned.

'About two miles from here there is a certain village there, and a certain man lived in it about eighty years ago. I knew some of the old people that knew him well, and he was digging—himself and another neighbour of his, they were digging a grave in a cemetery that was quite adjacent to where they were living. They were digging this grave for a neighbour of theirs, and now they had the grave almost finished. And one of the men went down the bottom of the grave patching it up and finishing it. And what do you think? The hare jumped down right into the grave where this man was working. And he looked at it. And he . . . and he given him a blow on the back . . . and he killing him outright. "Be Gor," he says, "I have a fine kitchen for my dinner now," he says, "when I go home." So the two went home then, and he told the Missus when he came in—"You'll have that hare," he says, "cooked in pies for us when we will come back from the funeral."

'The funeral was to take place that same day. Well still, it didn't take them long until he had it skinned and ready for the pot. She put on the water and put a good fire under the pot and she threw in the hare into this pot, and they went off to the funeral then. And of course, naturally enough, it might be three hours in the interval until he came back again himself, and this man that was digging the grave with him. And they thought they'd have a great supper now with the hare. And there the pot was boiling still on the fire. "Why," says he to the Missus, "isn't this hare boiled yet?" "No," she said, "it is not. Now I think", she says, "if it was boiling in the pot", she says, "for three long months that it would not be boiled. Whatever is wrong with him? Examine him yourself now," she says.

'He took the lid off the pot and sure the water was boiling mad in the pot, and there the hare was lying in the water, in the boiling water, and he as cold as the very minute she put it down first in it. "What the devil is wrong with it?" he says—he got a bit vexed over it. "I don't know," she says. "You must leave out that hare." "I think that is the best thing to do," he said, "and let the dogs have him."

'He took him up out of the pot and flung him out in the back yard. They thought there wouldn't be sign nor trace of him in the morning, that the dogs would have him all gone, you know. But in the morning they looked out, the hare was still there and not a dog nor a cat could touch him or go next or near to him.

'And by God, he brought him up and he buried him. Well now,

the most curious thing about it is this: he was . . . that following night he was sitting by the fire: and—God bless his soul—he got a bad pain, so he did, in his chest and around his heart. And the doctor was sent for and, mind you, there was no use. That was now Thursday, and Friday night he died, and he was buried the following Sunday adjacent to the same grave that himself was digging a week only before. And the old people had a suspicion, and there was a wild rumour about too, as well, that it was the hare that brought him. They were thinking that it was the super-natural, you see now, some old hag, the descendant of some breed of some kind, and that he came there purposely to bring this man.

'That's a sure story because some of the old people around here —the Lord have mercy on them—they vouched for the truth of that story. They did.'[1]

Traces of the hare-witch belief are found all over England too, but because the old way of life has long since died out the stories survive as bare anecdotes. An example from Yorkshire is typical:

'One [hare story] was related to me about twenty-five years ago by a Farndale man whose family had resided two hundred and fifty years in that valley. He told of a local witch who turned into a hare and was chased by the hunt to a village called Nawton, a distance of over five miles. There she jumped into a pond and was never seen again, but just before this happened one of the hounds —a black one—pulled a large piece of fur and skin off her haunches. The supposed witch was found to be suffering from a fall that had torn a piece of skin off her thigh.'

But in England, perhaps because it is so rare a sight, a white hare used to be the object of a peculiar fear, an embodiment of tragedy and retribution. Girls who died forsaken by their lovers were said to return in the form of white hares. Only the faithless lover would, in most of these stories, be able to see the hare. In all, it follows him everywhere, sometimes saving him from danger, but invariably causing his death in the end. This version was told in the West of England up till at least the eighteen-eighties:

[1] *The Hare*, op. cit.

'One of the great landowners of the West Country engaged a fine handsome young farmer to manage his farm. The farm was large and rich in land and dairy cattle, and had a good house like a gentleman's house; and soon after the young man had settled in there came to him the daughter of one of the cottagers nearby asking for work in the dairy. He took her on to manage the dairy, and of course she was to live in the house and soon was living there. She was fair and comely and had a pretty figure, but she had no education at all and of course her class was not his.

'Well, of course they fell in love, and being together in the farm-house it wasn't long before he brought her to bed. He was determined to marry her, but his family took against that as hard as they might. They saw to it somehow—very likely by putting in word against her to the landowner—that the dairy-maid was dismissed. And they forced their son to marry a lady they chose for him.

'Word came that the dairy-maid was ill. The old women of the village were saying she was in the family way. And some months after, early one morning, a new-born baby was found strangled in one of her lover's fields. She was accused and taken away, and she was tried before a judge and jury and she was hanged for the murder of her child.

'Now everything went wrong on that fine farm and suddenly the young man left it and went to another part of the country, but even there nothing prospered with him. He took to drinking heavily, and he was more often on the road by night than by day, and everywhere he went a white hare would shine in the dark. Everywhere he went, day or night it would cross his path. Other people often saw it almost under the feet of his horse. Often it would terrify the horse and the horse would run away from it like the wind.

'Well, he carried on this way for some time but whether it was through drink or from the haunting of the white hare—for he and all that knew what had happened understood what the white hare was—whatever the cause of it he grew to look like a ghost himself, a shadow of the fine young man he was a year before. And one night he never got home. He had been out half or most of the night as usual. And early that morning he was found drowned in a forsaken mine. His horse was grazing nearby. Its coat was caked with the lather of fear drying on it. It seemed to the men who took the corpse out from the sunken flooded hollow by the mine-shaft that the horse had suffered great terror. It was clear to them that when the white hare had frightened it at night, it had run away and thrown its rider into that flooded place.'[1]

Another hare-witch story comes from Norfolk, and concerns Ann Boleyn and the church of Salle. This village is a few miles from Blickling, the home of the Boleyn family. Ann had the reputation of being a witch during her lifetime; and there was a local legend which said she still haunted the vicinity on a certain day in the year. It said that after her execution in the Tower of London her headless body was thrown into an old arms-chest and buried in the Tower Chapel; but 'there is a circumstantial account of how her body was disinterred and smuggled out of the Tower by night and taken in a cart among packing cases, under the escort of Thomas Wyatt, to Blickling and then Salle; and there buried in the church as the ancient burial-place of her family'.[2] Historians, however, claim that this story has little truth in it; and the official version[3] maintains that she was buried, and remained buried in the Chapel Royal of the Tower.

But in spite of this, the legend has persisted until the present day. James Clements (1887–1967) was the verger at Salle church for many years; and he told us about the legend and how he came to be involved in it:

'It was back in 1923, and the story about Ann Boleyn being buried in Salle church was in one of the Norwich papers. She and her brother were executed in the Tower: her brother on 18th May 1536, and she herself the next day—Friday, 19th. But later they brought her body—took it from the Tower at dead of night— brought it to Salle. Now this appeared in the paper and it said that on 29th May each year you could see a coach and four horses

[1] Robert Hunt, *Popular Romances of the West of England*, London, 1881, p. 377.

[2] W. C. Parsons, *Salle*, Norwich, 1937, p. 128.

[3] *The Times*, 5th October 1966, has a photograph of Ann Boleyn's tomb in the Chapel Royal. The body was said to have been identified by an extra finger on one hand.

come from Blickling Hall, in the middle of the night, and stop outside Salle Church.'

When James Clements read this story he felt that as church verger it was his concern: no one—man or ghost—should make free of the church without his knowledge. He knew exactly where the Boleyn family vault was supposed to be (in the nave, about half-way up the central aisle) and he had wanted to open it up, knowing that he could identify the remains of Ann Boleyn by the sixth finger that was known to be on one of her hands. But permission to do this was not forthcoming; and as he recorded many years later (August 1966), he was then past the age of doing any digging of that kind. But in the months following the account in the Norwich paper he decided to 'challenge the story', as he told us. On 29th May 1924 he made up his mind to keep vigil in Salle church; and he sat in one of the pews, as he showed us, on the south side of the aisle as near as possible to the supposed place of burial. He went up at 10 o'clock that evening and stayed until 4 o'clock the following morning:

[T] 'I sat in the pew opposite to where she was buried, and there was nothing to see; nothing at all. And I came out of the church—it was bright moonlight and you could see quite plain— and looked along all the old routes, you know, where she was supposed to come (they don't use them now, and they're all grown up). Then I went back and sat down near where she's supposed to lie. Nothing to see. And just before I went to come out [of the church] I stood in the doors, looking down the route again. You could see all round. And then I saw a hare right near me; hopped across and sat within—well, not half-way to that table [about two feet]. It came almost right up to me. I'd got my stick in my hand, and I made a shuffle and it turned and ran by me—ran into the church! Well, of course, I pushed the door to, you see. I could see him going over the church. I could see him because it was clear as could be, like day; the moon was shining so. I chased and chased, and we went round and round. We done two straight tours of the church; and he was done and I was done. And then he went round the font; I followed and tripped up as I was going round it. I fell over, and as I was getting up he got across to the doorway. I thought I'd pushed the door close—if I had done, he'd never have opened it—but it must have been ajar; and he got by somehow and was away.'

It was obvious from the way James Clements related the incident, forty-two years after it happened, that it had made a tremendous impression on him at the time. But when we asked him whether he thought the hare was in any way connected with Ann Boleyn, he replied with typical East Anglian caution, that it might have something to do with her; on the other hand, it might not. But he made one further observation that showed quite plainly his real belief that hare was no ordinary one, and how deeply he was involved in the legend:

'You see I was born during the *Chiming Hours*;[1] and if you are born then you are supposed to have *second sight*, to be able to see things that other people won't see.'

In support of the effectiveness of this *second sight*, he told us of another man in the village who had also been born during the *Chimes Hours*. He had seen the spectral coach with the four horses making for Salle church as he and his brother were returning one Saturday night from Reepham. A commentator might say that this later piece of evidence might be stronger if the incident had occurred on any other night but a Saturday. But there it is, as James Clements related the legend just before his death three years ago.

The pattern of the hare-witch stories in Wales is not very different from those in Ireland; but we are including a selection here because each has an important variation of the essential belief that 'there is some sort of enchantment in the hare', as the Irish farmer put it. The first story comes from north Wales; it was recorded at the end of the last century:[2]

'Beti Ifan was one of the witches of Bedd Gelert. Her fear had fallen upon nearly all the inhabitants, so that she was refused nothing by any one, for she had the reputation of being able to handle ghosts, and to curse people and their possessions. She

---

[1] Or *Chimes Hours*, the canonical hours under the old religion. George Ewart Evans, *Ask the Fellows Who Cut the Hay*, London, 1956, p. 216.

[2] D. E. Jenkins, *Beddgelert: Its Fact, Fairies and Folklore*, 1899, pp. 79-80.

therefore lived in comfort and ease, doing nothing except keeping her house moderately clean, and leaning on the lower half of her front door knitting and watching passers-by. But there was one man in the village, a cobbler and a skilled poacher, who feared neither Beti Ifan nor any other old hag of the kind. His great hobby was to tease and annoy the old woman by showing her a hare or a wild duck, and asking her if she would like to get it. When she replied she would, he used to hand it almost within her reach and then pull it back and walk away. She could not do him much harm, as he had a birth mark above his breast; but she contrived a way by which she could have her revenge on him. She used to transform herself into a wild duck or hare, and continually appear before him on the meadows and among the trees whenever he went out poaching, but took good care to keep outside the reach of the gun. He, being a good shot, and finding himself missing so frequently, began to suspect something to be amiss. He knew of a doctor who was a "skilled man" living not far away, so he went to consult him. The doctor told him:

"Next time you go out, take with you a small branch of mountain ash, and a bit of vervain and place it under the stock of the gun."

'Then giving him a piece of paper with some writing on, he said:

"When you see the hare, or any other creature of which you have some doubt, read this backward; and if it is old Beti you will see her in her own form, though she retain her assumed form. Shoot at her legs; but mind you do not shoot her anywhere else."

'The next day, as he was working his way through a grove near Beti's house, he could see a large hare hopping in front of him. He drew out his paper and read as he was instructed; he then fired at her legs; and the hare ran towards Beti's cottage. He ran after it, and was just in time to see the hare jumping over the lower half of the house door. Going up to the cottage he could hear the old woman groaning. When he went in, she was sitting by the fire with blood streaming from her legs. He was never again troubled with the hare-like appearances of old Beti'r Fedw.'

The duck in this story is invested with the same sinister significance as the hare. In this connection we have seen the foot of a hare nailed, as an apotropaic charm, to the door of a stable or out-house in Lower Machen, south Wales. A Suffolk informant[1] a few years ago saw a duck's mandible nailed to a barn in the village of Great Bricett in that county. The use of vervain and mountain ash, or rowan, as protective devices against witches was very widely known in Britain.

Another interesting variant of the hare-witch or hare-devil motif comes from Nebo, Denbighshire. An old farm-worker[2] told the story to Robin Gwyndaf Jones of the Welsh Folk Museum, St. Fagans, Cardiff:

[T] 'It happened in Maesgwyn. It was a great sin at that time, do you see, to play cards on a Sunday instead of going to religious service. They used to play cards in the loft above a stable at this farm. Farm servants used to congregate—some would come from this farm, and some from another—to play at cards on a Sunday morning; about eight or nine of them. An uncle of mine was there with them. He was only a lad—a fine, polished young blade—at the time.

'Now while they were at it playing cards, in comes a hare through the loft-door—bang! right into the middle of the cards! Well, that was the end of card-playing in Maesgwyn! They used to say that no one would sleep[3] in the loft after that, not if you'd give them anything in the world! There was a spirit there, you see. A spirit. And that loft was closed for many years after that; and it is as a loft that was always shut up, that I can remember it myself. But after Dwalad Owen came to Maesgwyn to farm he said there was no such thing as a ghost there; and he caused the door of this loft to be opened, with proper stairs leading to it. It's a most pleasant loft today, with not a mite nor a murmur of any sort of spirit there—after it had been closed up for so many years. It was one of the beliefs of the old people, do you see.

[1] Cecil Runeckles, born at Needham Market.

[2] John Ellis Jones (1886–1969) Dolglesyn, Nebo, nr. Llanrwst, Denbighshire. Recorded (in Welsh), July 1968. Tape at Welsh Folk Museum, St. Fagans, Cardiff. (Tape: W.F.M., 1948–9.)

[3] It was usual for farm workers in Wales and the north of England, and in Scotland, to 'sleep in', usually in a loft or bothy.

'But those who were playing cards in the loft there really thought the devil had come amongst them; had come *full-pelt* from somewhere. The door must have been ajar, and it shot into the other side of the loft, through the cards and everything. And it went out again after this without anyone there putting a finger on it. I've often heard my uncle imitating—rehearsing exactly how this hare went.'

It is not difficult to reconstruct the circumstances of this card-school and its sequel. Playing with the devil's cards, especially on a Sunday, in a small Welsh village at the end of the last century, when the devil was convincingly conjured up from the pulpit in almost every sermon, was a powerful act against orthodoxy. And when the poor hare blundered into the loft it was inevitable that it should carry away the guilty conscience projected on to it by the alarmed card-players.

Here is another story which reflects the same belief as the Bedd Gelert story: that a hare that cannot be caught or shot is not a *right hare*, in other words a witch. Although in this particular tale the hare's place has been taken by a rabbit, this is not an unusual exchange, as we have already suggested. The man who tells the story was, in his younger days, a farmer in the Pennant district of Cardiganshire:[1] it is about a well-known witch, Mari Berllan Piter who once lived in a cottage near Pennant:

[T] 'A very interesting story. There was a rabbit in the chimney of Berllan Piter, they said; and I can remember a well-known sportsman coming down from London, a crack shot. And he made a special journey down to have a shot at this rabbit that was in the chimney; and he spent all the cartridges he'd bought specially to kill this rabbit—he was shooting with both barrels each time, you see. But it was into the chimney that the rabbit made its escape each time. And the crack shot from London failed completely to kill it.

'Then another man came to shoot it, an old sailor. How I came to hear about the sailor was like this. The morning after I'd been giving a bit of a talk on the BBC about this Mari of Berllan Piter

---

[1] Dan Jones, Pen Pombren, Pennant (Cardiganshire), nr. Aberystwyth. Born 1892 at Ynys Hir, Aberarth. Tape (in Welsh): W.F.M., 1540.

I went into the smithy at Aberaeron; and here comes an old boy into the smithy and he says to the blacksmith:

"Boyo! Did you hear that preacher talking about Mari Berllan Piter last night? *Diawch*, it was good!" he said, "*he* was telling the truth—every word of it!"

"Well, boyo," said the blacksmith, "that was no preacher. This man here was the preacher!"

'And the old sailor turned to me and said:

"Boyo! Boyo! You knew about Mari?"

"I've heard about her," I said, "in fact, plenty. Do you believe in witchery then?"

"Believe!" he said. "You'd believe, too, if you had seen what I saw!"

"Well, what did you see?"

"It was like this: I'd been at sea for a good spell," he said, "as a lad, you see; and I'd come on to about eighteen years of age. And one day after I came home I was sent by my mother to take a message, from the back of Aberaeron there to Mynachty—to take a message to Plas Mynachty. And I had a good partner with me," he said; "and we were both very fond of shooting; and we each had a gun with us. And as we had heard about this rabbit of Berllan Piter, down we went to the old house. And there was the rabbit—on the hillocks on the hillside at the back of the house. She was there, just as if she was sitting on her backside, like, playing with her feet and her whiskers—exactly as if she was making sport of us!" he said. "Then all of a sudden she got up and made for the chimney. And our two guns blazed out at her through the trees. But they didn't stop her from getting to the chimney!"

'That's the old boy's story; and there's no doubt at all that some of the old people actually believed that she, Mari, was the rabbit; she was in the form of a rabbit, you see. That's an indication of the strength you can hear and feel in their recital that it was impossible to shoot the creature simply because Mari herself was the rabbit.'

The device of using a silver bullet to wound or kill a hare-witch is common to the four countries of Britain. But an unusual variant of the myth comes from Trefdraeth (Newport) in Pembrokeshire. The informant is a retired farmer[1] who has lived all his life in Trefdraeth; and he talked about the wise- or cunning-man, or conjurer (*dyn hysbys*), who lived in the parish of Nanhyfer (Nevern) in Pembrokeshire during the nineteenth century. It was reported that he could cause snakes to appear in the sky; he could prevent farmers' wives from successfully churning their butter; and he could also find any animal that had gone astray:

[T] 'This man, Lefi Salmon, could make animals appear at will —hares, for instance. A man was once walking along the road near Plas y Ffynnon there; and about a dozen hares started to follow him. And when he turned and tried to drive them away, they vanished completely. He [Lefi Salmon] did it by some trick or other. But these hares appeared at other places as well as Plas y Ffynnon—alongside the road on certain occasions. I have a story of someone who tried to shoot one of these hares and nothing happened. The hare didn't run or disappear: it just stayed on the spot! They shot at it with an old muzzle-loader gun. I heard another story about a man—what was his name? Let me think— Morris from . . . But it doesn't matter! We'll call him *Morris y Llysten Bach* (I'm going back now to the middle of the last century, mind you). An old man by the name of Samuel Thomas who'd been brought up here in Trefdraeth, a very able man, told me the story. He was telling me that this man Morris had taken four shots at a hare, and the thing didn't stir! He went home with all the power he had in his legs—after getting the fright of his life!

'No, I've not heard of anyone shooting a hare with a round piece of silver. But there was the root of some plant—I just can't remember—the root of some plant. I've heard they used to shoot hares with it. Was it wood-nightshade? A kind of root—*wood*-nightshade, not the deadly nightshade. The Welsh name is *erfinen Fair*.

'Samuel Thomas told me all this. And he was a good man with a gun himself. And they used to say that if some creature was in the power of the *dyn hysbys* or witch—he was the man, he was the

---

[1] Joseph Thomas (born 1880; farmer, craftsman, and self-trained vet.). Tape: W.F.M. 2905.

man to kill it. But he failed to kill these hares with anything, except when he used this root *erfinen Fair*. The root he used is about the size of my finger, or perhaps a little bigger. He'd put powder into the barrel, and a piece of this root—press it down with a ramrod, just like when you're firing a shot. And they say you could cut a hole through a door using this root. Undoubtedly, there was some supernatural power in the plant, the same sort of power they say there is in certain other plants.

'I've often used this plant, *erfinen Fair*, to cure a stiff joint, my knee, oftentimes! There's plenty of it in Glanduad, where I used to farm. You got to have a wooded piece of ground for it to grow. It was in common use once.'

The plant that the old farmer refers to is not wood-nightshade but black bryony. Like white bryony it was called *big-root* by many East Anglian farm horsemen; and they used it, after it had been scraped into shreds, to put into their horses' bait. It was one of the conditioning herbs, and was much prized for bringing up a gloss on a horse's coat.[1] But it also appears to have been associated with some of the horsemen's magical practices; and one horseman mentioned it alongside mandrake, apparently assuming that from their bifurcated or branched roots they were related plants. It was in fact used as a substitute for the mandrake, and some horsemen believed that 'it had aphrodisiac qualities for both man and horse.'[2] There are, of course, many superstitions linked with the mandrake, most of them arising out of its anthropomorphic shape; and the Welsh name for black bryony—*erfinen Fair* or the Virgin Mary's root—suggests that this plant, too, had qualities that were thought to go far beyond the physical.

Witchcraft itself goes far beyond the physical. Animal disguises, wax figures stuck with pins, roots, herbs and so on are merely its outward manifestations. The cures and calamities it brings to the body begin in the mind, by a process that is acknowledged by modern doctors. The terms in which its suggestive powers are put seem remote from modern ways of thinking, but it is possible even in our society to curse a sensitive person to death by suggest-

[1] George Ewart Evans, *The Horse in the Furrow*, pp. 26, 235.
[2] Margaret Baker, *Discovering the Folklore of Plants*, 1969, pp. 18, 42.

ing he is unwanted, incurably ill or chased by inescapable doom. 'The chilling breath of moral disapproval' can stunt a child's development. Ostracism in factory life and the emotions of anger, envy and fear everywhere else can send people into a decline, to use an old and accurate phrase. The converse is perhaps more commonly known and applies equally to witchcraft. Faith often leads to recovery from illness. The diffident and trodden down can be made happy and confident by love. By inspiring a backward or neurotic child a teacher can nurture hidden excellence.

So much nonsense is written by and of the so-called witches of modern Europe, whom we mentioned earlier in this chapter, that both history and contemporary truth is obscured. The subject is shrouded in whimsicality of a noxious kind. Also, 'historians, in our enlightened centuries, have tended to concentrate on the absurdity of these beliefs and to ask why they were taken seriously for so long.'[1] But to understand what witchcraft meant in Europe in the not so distant past one has only to examine the way it now works in most of the countries of the world. For example, 'The Nyakusa believe that a witch has a python in his belly, and that at night he flies through the air, either in the form of a python or on its back, and in this guise sucks the internal substance from people as they lie asleep, or the milk from their cattle.'[2] In Africa, too, there is a belief that it is possible to enchant food so that it becomes uncookable. 'A "sister's son" who is ill-treated can curse his "mother's brother" so that food will never again cook on his fire.'[3]

And the reason for the existence of witchcraft is the same as it always was: 'in a world where there are few assured techniques for dealing with everyday crises, notably sickness, a belief in witches, or the equivalent of one, is not only not foolish, it is indispensable. To this argument one might add that, although some people in the technically sophisticated world really understand the natural sciences, the majority do not; all most of us know is where to go for explanations, particularly in the commonest form of disaster, sickness. We accept the doctor's advice as we might once have

[1] Lucy Mair, *Witchcraft*, London, 1969, p. 7.   [2] Ibid., p. 20.
[3] Ibid., p. 14.

accepted that of the diviner who told us whether we were suffering through the anger of an ancestor's spirit or the hatred of a witch.'[1]

Witchcraft only works among people who believe in it. The secret of its power is psychological and in its milder forms it merely gives or takes away self-confidence.

Belief in oneself has a strong and easily recognizable influence on sport. A quarrel before a game of golf, or the evil eye of a bad-tempered partner or opponent during it, will put the best player off his game. Any emotion that dispels concentration will spoil a marksman's day. A man who visits Scotland every year to stalk deer gave the following account of an incident in the Highlands:

'I was walking along the crest of a high hill with the stalker—it was on the border of Argyllshire and Inverness-shire—and we met a hare, a blue mountain hare. There it was sitting in front of us. We stopped; and the hare hopped towards us. It came very close, a matter of a few feet. Then it hopped round us, in part of a circle; and we stood watching it. I was fascinated. We didn't move. But finally the hare hopped away.

'As soon as this happened, the stalker said, "That's the old witch of Beinn A'Bhric. We shall do no good today!"

'Apparently this hill is linked with a witch, and it has a peculiarly shaped stone in the form of an armchair. This is called the *Witch's Seat*.

'But we had a disastrous day after that—whatever the reason. Now the crowning disaster on a deer-stalk is to wound a stag and not get it. If this happens you go home with the tail between your legs, and you have your dinner with the dogs. I don't think there was a major disaster like this on that particular day. It's a long time ago and I can't remember the exact details. But whatever happened was bad enough; and we didn't have a successful day.'

It was undoubtedly the hare-witch that gave them a bad day or, in other words, the thought of failure made them fail. But the story, like the others we have quoted, is remarkable not only apropos witches but because it combines fact and fantasy in a way that is characteristic of the old writers on natural history and of pre-literate culture all over the world. A deer stalker ghillie is a

[1] Ibid., pp. 8–9.

13. A cupid catching a hare, from an Ancient Greek vase (*British Museum*)

14. (*left*) Tail side of florin with cross, 1921 (*Mansell Collection*); (*right*) Scottish silver groat of David II, son of Robert the Bruce (*British Museum*)

15. Luxuria. Drawing by Pisanello, now in the Albertina, Vienna

practical man with a superb knowledge of nature. If he were not he could never keep his job. This one must have known that the curious movements of the hare were perfectly natural, yet at the same time he believed he was watching a witch.

It is this quality that makes traditional stories so much richer that most newly contrived inventions of writers who use magical themes. Although the hare-witch stories are mainly fantasy they are set in a context of exactly observed detail. As a conclusion to this chapter we shall give one instance of this.

One of the most accurate writers on natural history included in his chapters on the hare several first-hand reports from observers of their habits:

'The thoroughly authenticated manoeuvres of a hunted hare include doubling back on its tracks, and then leaping off at right angles to start in another direction, entering an outhouse or other building, or lying down in the herbage or ivy on top of a wall; and Mr. J. S. Gibbons has known one to run along the top of a wall so as to throw hounds off the scent.'[1]

These ways of escape are described in the stories of the hare-witch. The hare-witch very often takes refuge in a house; its arts of escape are not exaggerated. The one that told its pursuer to go and buy himself two glasses of whiskey had tried to get away by hiding in the ivy on top of an old wall (p. 159).

[1] G. E. H. Barrett-Hamilton, op. cit., Vol. 2, pp. 274-5.

14

The Hare as Trickster

The ancient myths in which animals were gods were gradually transformed until nothing was left but an anecdote or superstition which had lost much of its meaning, and the stages of this transformation seem to coincide with the development of society. Nomadic peoples, hunting or herding in small groups, have preserved the most ancient forms of mysticism. As people settled down to farming and the group became larger, its life more complex, the stories became complex too and began to lose their religious meaning. This progression can be seen most clearly in the history of the myth of The Great Hare: god to hero or terrestrial giant, hero to unusual specimen of animal or man, unusual specimen to clever fellow who plays tricks on other animals or men. The Hare that kept men and women in a bag until he had made the world fit for them to live in, remained their benefactor. 'He taught men how to make *aqakwuts* (axes), lances and arrow-points, and all implements of bone and stone, and also how to make snares, and traps, and nets, to take animals, and birds, and fishes. . . . He killed the ancient monsters whose bones we now see under the earth.'[1]

That reference to dinosaurs was noted down by Schoolcraft about 1840. The Algonquin Indians told him 'that the animals at first had the rule on Earth'. Most of their mythical animals were huge monsters. Only the Great Hare had the strength to put them down. If he could do that, and invent all kinds of small things indispensable to life, it is no surprise to find that later generations to whom a fishing-net was no longer a miracle, seized upon his gift

[1] H. R. Schoolcraft, *History of the Indian Tribes*, Philadelphia, 1853, Vol. 1, p. 18.

of cleverness and made him put it to hundreds of different uses. In the following stories he retains his divine nature but uses his powers in a human way. Among the North Eastern Algonquins the name for the Great Hare was Glooskap.

'In the long ago time when people lived always in the early red morning, before sunrise, before the *Squid-to-neck* was peopled as to-day, Glooskap went very far north, where all was ice.

'He came to a wigwam. Herein he found a giant, a great giant, for he was Winter. Glooskap entered; he sat down. Then Winter gave him a pipe; he smoked, and the giant told tales of the old times.

'The charm was on him; it was the Frost. The giant talked on and froze, and Glooskap fell asleep. He slept for six months, like a toad. Then the charm fled, and he awoke. He went his way home; he went to the south, and at every step it grew warmer, and the flowers began to come up and talk to him.

'He came to where there were many little ones dancing in the forest; their queen was Summer. I am singing the truth: it was Summer, the most beautiful one ever born. He caught her up; he kept her by a crafty trick. The Master cut a moose-hide into a long cord; as he ran away with Summer he let the end trail behind him.

'They, the fairies of Light, pulled at the cord, but as Glooskap ran, the cord ran out, and though they pulled he left them far away. So he came to the lodge of Winter, but now he had Summer in his bosom; and Winter welcomed him, for he hoped to freeze him again to sleep. I am singing the song of Summer.

'But this time the Master did the talking. This time his *m'téoulin* was the strongest. And ere long the sweat ran down Winter's face, and then he melted more and quite away, as did the wigwam. Then every thing awoke; the grass grew, the fairies came out, and the snow ran down the rivers, carrying away the dead leaves. Then Glooskap left Summer with them, and went home.'[1]

In that early poem, here translated into prose, he defeats his opponents by talk. Even the moose-hide cord is thought to be a

---

[1] C. G. Leland, *Algonquin Legends of New England*, Boston, U.S.A., 1884, pp. 134-5.

simile for deceptive talk, like the old saying 'to talk like paying out rope'.

A large number of stories, which are for the most part comic, are certainly more recent than that in style, but Leland who collected many of them points out that they are often old in theme. Of the Mighty Wasis he wrote: 'A real Indian tale, may always be assumed to be ancient when it is told to set forth an *origin*. This gives the origin of a baby's crowing.'

'Now it came to pass when Glooskap had conquered all his enemies, even the *Kewahqu'*, who were giants and sorcerers, and the *m'téoulin*, who were magicians, and the *Pamola*, who is the evil spirit of the night air, and all manner of ghosts, witches, devils, cannibals, and goblins, that he thought upon what he had done, and wondered if his work was at an end.

'And he said this to a certain woman. But she replied, "Not so fast, Master, for there yet remains One whom no one has ever conquered or got the better of in any way, and who will remain unconquered to the end of time."

"And who is he?" inquired the Master.

"It is the mighty Wasis," she replied, "and there he sits; and I warn you that if you meddle with him you will be in sore trouble."

'Now Wasis was the Baby. And he sat on the floor sucking a piece of maple-sugar, greatly contented, troubling no one.

'As the Lord of Men and Beasts had never married or had a child, he knew naught of the way of managing children. Therefore he was quite certain, as is the wont of such people, that he knew all about it. So he turned to Baby with a bewitching smile and bade him come to him.

'Then Baby smiled again, but did not budge. And the Master spake sweetly and made his voice like that of the summer bird, but it was of no avail, for Wasis sat still and sucked his maple-sugar.

'Then the Master frowned and spoke terribly, and ordered Wasis to come crawling to him immediately. And Baby burst out into crying and yelling, but did not move for all that.

'Then, since he could do but one thing more, the Master had recourse to magic. He used his most awful spells, and sang the songs which raise the dead and scare the devils. And Wasis sat and looked on admiringly, and seemed to find it very interesting, but all the same he never moved an inch.

'So Glooskap gave it up in despair, and Wasis, sitting on the floor in the sunshine, went goo! goo! and crowed.

'And to this day when you see a babe well contented going goo! goo! and crowing, and no one can tell why, know that it is because he remembers the time when he overcame the Master who had conquered all the world. For of all the beings that have ever been since the beginning, Baby is alone the only invincible one.'[1]

Fig. 6.   The Great Hare brought down from a
god to a trickster

In another group of stories, better known because some have been retold for children, the Great Hare has become an ordinary hare. He is distinguished from the other animals both by his cleverness and his unique stupidity—qualities which have always gone together, as in the ancient roles of king's jester or the *amadán* (fool) of Irish folk stories. In pre- or non-industrial societies such as Ireland and large parts of Russia the idiot, whether mentally deficient or separated from other people merely by his innocence and ignorance of the practical ways of the world, is revered almost

[1] Ibid., pp. 120-2.

as a saint. In Ireland he or she is called *Duine le Dia*—one who belongs to God—and it is said that the word of an idiot 'is like a thorn in mud'; in other words he is soft in the head as mud is soft to walk on, but suddenly sharp when you least expect it.

The Great Hare's instinctive aim with an arrow, described in our previous chapter, by which he killed a bear he could not see, is an example of the thorn in the mud. It comes at the end of a long account of his idiotic attempts to get food:

'The Great Hare was living alone with his grandmother and in mid-winter, when they could get nothing to eat he saw the Otter plunge into the lake and come out with a bunch of eels. The Otter invited him to share the meal and he was so impressed by the easy way of living, that he moved with his grandmother near to the lake and told her to get ready to cook. "But what shall I cook, my grandson?" "I'll see to that," he said and plunged deep into the lake. He came out shivering and spluttering without any fish. The otter and the grandmother were watching. "What on earth is wrong with him?" said the otter. "He has seen someone do something and is trying to do the same," the grandmother said as they saw him limping home frozen. She had to nurse him then. But the otter plunged into the water and made them a present of a load of fish.

'He saw the woodpecker making a hole in a tree with his beak and finding creatures to eat, so he fixed a long bone into his nose and pecked at the tree until his nose bled and he fell down senseless to the ground.'[1] And so on, until he is persuaded to fast and meditate alone. Then comes the sudden inspiration, the blind and accurate shot, the thorn in the mud.

Frequently he tries to help but often gets the worst of it:

'He was once large and stout and had a long tail and his upper lip was like the lip of other animals. And one day in the old times, as he sat on a rock, with his fine long tail trailing afar into the bushes an old man came by who asked the way. He showed him the way but leapt ahead so fast that he was soon out of sight, and the old man in his hurry to catch up fell into a deep pit. The hare turned back and found him in it but could not get him out. He

[1] Ibid., p. 223, abridged and partly summarized.

said, "Catch hold of my tail!" The old man caught it and jumped
but the tail broke off short. Then the hare said, "Catch hold of me
by the waist," but the man was heavy and almost broke his back.
That is how the hare got his short tail and slender waist.

'The old man was on his way to marry a young girl. But she
was in love with Mikumwess, the forest fairy. The old man married her in spite of that and invited the hare to the wedding dance.
Hares dance on their tip-toes, so he put ear-rings on his heels and
danced with the bride. Now this bride had on only a very short
skirt, and in crossing a brook it had got wet. So that, as she
danced, it began to shrink and shrink until he, pitying the poor
girl, ran out and got a deerskin and hastily twisted a cord to tie it
with. He held one end of the cord in his teeth and twisted it so
rapidly that he cut his upper lip through to the nose, for which
reason his descendants all have hare-lips to this day.

'The bride danced with him all night and the old man was
angry. He walked away and left her. She and the hare lived happily
together after that, until the day when she ran away with the forest
fairy, and if she has not run away again, she is living with the
forest fairy now.'[1]

He is still a benefactor and is rewarded by love. Often his
attempts to help others are absurdly foolish and he is left humi-
liated, but sometimes he is wholly wise and clever, as in this
international tale still told in Ireland:

'Long ago, there were wild animals on the hills and they were
all able to talk, they say.

'There was a big lion there, and he was killing every animal he
could find on the hills. The king of the animals said that the lion
wouldn't leave one of them alive in a week's time, unless they held
a meeting to see what they should do. When they came together,
they didn't know how to stop the lion from his bad work. So the
king of the animals went to the lion and told him that, if he stayed
inside in his den, that one of the animals would go to him every
day to be eaten. "Very well," said the lion, very proud of himself.

'So the animals used to throw a ball up into the air and whichever of them the ball fell on would have to go to the lion to be

eaten. Where should the ball fall but on the hare, and he had to go to the lion. He was slow to go, the creature, for he knew it was to his death he was going. He went to drink from a well of water and he saw his shadow in the well. When he reached the lion, the lion gave an ugly grunt that it was only a hare that came to him—a small hare, at that. He wouldn't make much of a breakfast!

"Hold your tongue," said the hare. "I got here as quick as I could, and I'm out of breath trying to get here to you, and something delayed me." He told the lion about what he saw in the well. "Come along with me and I'll show him to you," says the hare. The hare went on ahead of the lion, fearing the lion would eat him, till they came to the well. "Look down there now," says the hare, "And see what's there." When the lion looked down he saw his own reflection—an animal as big as himself. When the lion gave a snarl, the lion in the well did the same, and what did the lion do but plunge into the well! He couldn't rise up out of it again, so he started to call on the hare to get him out. "You can stay there now until I help you out," says the hare, with a laugh. The hare went and told the other animals about what he had done, and they all came with him to the well to see the drowned lion. They were all very happy then.'[1]

Similar stories are told in many parts of the world. The trickster is sometimes a man, often a fool who occasionally outwits his tormentors, often a cunning animal—fox, jackal, baboon, frog, etc. In Africa the jackal plays much the same part as the fox in Europe, but stories of the hare as trickster seem to be more numerous and varied. Here he is usually destructive, but in a mysterious story heard in the Sudan his magical powers are linked with creation:

'The hare travelled into the town of the king and he found beans, plenty of beans. And he sat down to eat. When he had finished . . . he filled a bag with the rest. He loaded it on to a camel, but the camel fell down, then on to a horse, but the horse began to fall down, then on to a cow, but the cow refused because it was too heavy. Then he asked his friend the lion to help him.

[1] Oral, unpublished version recorded in Achill, Co. Mayo; translated by Seán Ó Súilleabháin.

The lion refused when he heard the beans were stolen. But the hare said, "I am small, you are big." So the lion went. He found the bag very heavy; he refused and went away. The hare went too.

'He fetched a cock; he told him, "You cock! all kinds of people were fetched by me, but they have refused. But now come and help me, and I shall give you part of the beans to eat." The cock went, the hare put the bag on the cock, and it carried it home. When they came near the house, it threw it down. The cock's back was bruised from carrying the bag. The hare said, "What is to be done with the back of the cock?" He crushed leaves of a tree and placed them on the sore place of the cock's back.

'And there sprang up a large tree on the sore place of the cock's back, some seeds having got into the wound by putting the leaves on it. The hare saw the tree was very high on the back of the cock. The tree bore fruit; when the fruit was seen by the hare, he said, "Dear me! by what (how) are they to be thrown down?" He took a stone and threw it at them. The stone fell into the middle of a river and became an island.

'The hare went to plant some vegetables on the island, and he planted melon seeds. Then there came a traveller, he said, "Give me something to eat" (the traveller saw the melons, which in the meantime had ripened!). But the hare refused saying, "Cousin, I have come in this very moment so I am not prepared to give you food." The hare looked back; he saw there were many melons. The hare arose, he took a knife and split a melon. The knife went into the middle of the melon, the hare was perplexed, he said to himself, "Where has the knife gone?" Suddenly the knife cut his (the hare's) head off. He, the hare, went into the melon and found there many people, who were alive. When he was tired, he came out; he found his head carrying firewood. He called it, "You head, come!" But the head refused. He called it again, but it refused. Then he struck it with the flat hand. The head came and returned to its place.'[1]

The 'Hare and Tapero' has a mystical significance even more obscure to us. It is interesting to compare it with the Algonquin story of the hare at the wedding dance.

[1] Diedrich Westermann, *The Shilluk People*, Berlin, 1912, pp. 195 foll.

Among the Shilluk people it is the girls who select their dancing partners, not the men:

'The hare went up (into the air) to find a drum; he and his uncle Tapero. And the hare danced to the drum, he danced up in the air. But Tapero remained outside (the ring of the dancers), he was not selected (for dancing) by a girl. But the hare was selected by the girls, and he danced with them. Again Tapero remained outside, he was not selected by a girl, but the hare was again selected, and danced. At last the dancers scattered. Then the hare called, "Uncle Tapero, shall we not go?" Tapero remained silent, he was angry because the hare had been selected. Tapero went down, but the hare remained above. Some time after the hare also came; he fastened his foot with a rope, and said (to Tapero?), "I am going down, I will return to our country." Again he said, "As soon as I come down to the ground and (I) pull the rope, I shall arrive in my country (at once)." But he pulled the rope too early, before he had reached the ground. So the hare fell down and was dashed to pieces.'[1]

Sometimes the hare is appealed to for wise judgement:

A Tibetan story, perhaps a satire on bureaucracy, tells of a ewe who asked a hare to save her and her lamb from a wolf. The hare dressed himself in a new robe and hat with a long ear-ring in his left ear, and rode her, holding pen and paper in his paws, towards the wolf. He told the wolf that he had been commissioned to bring ten wolfskins to the King of India, and wrote down 'one' on his paper. The wolf was so frightened when he saw the hare write that, that he ran away.[1]

But a large majority are simple tales of the deceiver and the deceiver deceived:

'Once there was a Lion, who came to a town and said, "I want this man to be my brother and by and bye I will take him to my house." The Man said, "Very well," so every day the Lion came to visit him. By and bye the Hare came in and saw this, so he went away and put on nice clothes and came back, saying, "I want this man to be my brother." The Men said, "No, he is the Lion's

---

[1] Ibid., p. 190.
[2] Capt. W. F. O'Connor, *Folk Tales from Tibet*, London, 1907, pp. 56 foll.

brother." He said, "The Lion is of no importance; he is my horse." The Men laughed but the Hare repeated it. He went home and the Men told the Lion what the Hare had said. The Lion was very angry and said he would go and get the Hare and make him tell them that he had spoken falsely. He went to the Hare and told him what the Men had said. The Hare denied it and said if he were not feeling so ill he would go and tell the Men themselves that they had said what was not true. The Lion wanted him to come and say so; but the Hare said he was too ill to walk. The Lion said, "Very well, I will carry you." The Hare said, "Very well, because I want to tell them it is a lie." So the Lion took him on his back. By and bye the Hare says he is so weak that he will fall off unless the Lion will let him put a bridle in his mouth (a rope made of bark from a tree). The Lion submits and goes on with the rope in his mouth. By and bye the Hare says the flies bother him so that he cannot hold on and asks the Lion to give him a little stick to drive them away. The Lion says, "Very well," and gives him a switch. Then they come near to the town and all the Men come out and see the Hare riding on the Lion's back and beating him with a switch. He says, "Hi! hi! didn't I say you were my horse?" '[1]

Often he plays less subtle tricks and narrowly escapes:

'Elephant prepared beer and sent word to all animals with horns, saying: "I have prepared beer, let all animals with horns come and drink!" He fixed a day and all animals with horns were notified: Reed bucks, elands, koedoes, wild oxen, buffaloes, and all kinds of buck.

'Hare heard about it, he thought for a while. Then he went home and called his wife, saying, "Let us find horns!" They went and found the bones of an old buck which had died long ago. Hare took the horns, then he went home and said to his wife: "Put these horns on me, place my ears into them, and fix them tight with beeswax." Hare's wife did so and fixed the horns on Hare's head with great care.

'The day came and all animals with horns went to the Ele-

[1] Madeleine Holland, *Folk-lore of the Banyanja*, 'Folk-lore', London, 1916, pp. 162-3.

phant's beer party. Hare also went with his horns, and began to
sing:

> *"I am the buck—the buck of the valley.*
> *I am the buck—the buck of the valley."*

'They received him well and he sat down. Beer was brought and
all animals with horns began to drink. Hare also drank, he went
on drinking, he began to feel half-drunk, stumbled, *dederere*, and
fell asleep.

'Hare was completely unconscious. The sun began to shine, and
its warm rays began to melt the beeswax with which Hare's wife
had fixed his horns. Hare did not notice anything. The horns began to fall from his ears. The others saw it and said: "Look, the
buck-of-the-valley. It seems to be Master Hare! They went and
told Elephant about it. So Elephant said, "Keep good guard!
When he wakes up, bring him to me!"

'They began their watch. Hare was still asleep, but he was beginning to wake up a little, drunk as he was. He was startled in
his heart, and thought, "Well, I am finished!"

'He prepared to escape. Suddenly he jumped: *Gèdlèdlè-gèdlèlè,
psiii-psiii!* Hare was gone'.[1]

When he challenges the Elephant to a tug-of-war the hare is
testing wits against brute strength:

'Hare met Elephant and said: "Grandpa Elephant, let me tie you
with this rope. I will beat you in a test of strength; if we both pull,
you towards the forest, I towards the river, I can beat you!" Elephant replied, "Are you a man to challenge my strength? Could
you even carry the weight of my leg?" To which the Hare
answered, saying, "I do not want to use my mouth in vain speech.
Come and be tied!" Elephant agreed and Hare tied him with his
rope. Hare went then to the river, where he found the Hippo and
said: "Grandpa Hippo, I challenge your strength. I will tie you
with this rope of mine and afterwards tie myself with it, you pull-
ing towards the river, I towards the forest." Hippo laughed like
Elephant, but Hare shouted: "You old Father Hippo, here is the
rope, come and be tied! When I say 'go' you must pull towards

[1] H. A. Junod, *Bantu Heritage*, Johannesburg, 1938, p. 72, abbreviated.

the river and I towards the forest!" Elephant was also waiting for
the Hare to say, "Go!" When both were well tied, Hare went to
the middle of the rope and shouted, "Go!" Elephant heard and
Hippo heard also. So the first pulled towards the forest and the
second towards the river. Elephant, feeling the strength of the
Hippo, was surprised as he felt sure he was fighting Hare. . . .
Ohooo! He began to overpower Hippo, who was forced out of
the water and began crying, "You have beaten me, you Hare!"
Elephant heard the noise and came. . . . Ha! He found he was
struggling with Hippo and said, "How is it that I am struggling
against you?" Hippo answered, saying, "I thought I was struggling against Hare." So said Elephant. They untied each other and
ran for Hare to kill him. But he had gone long ago!

'On his way Hare met Tortoise and began laughing: "You
Tortoise, you are going ahead laboriously, *khwanya-khwanya*, do
you think that you could race me?" Tortoise said, "Come along
you Hare. I challenge you." When he heard this Hare laughed,
laughed so much that he fell on his back laughing and said, "Are
you a witch, you Tortoise, to challenge me, one of the people-of-
the Hare?" He added: "All right, I will come tomorrow. We will
start here, then go to the little mafureira tree, then to the terebinth
further on, and we will see who will be first!" Tortoise agreed,
saying, "All right, Hare! I will see you on the morrow!" Hare
went away to sleep. Meanwhile, Tortoise went and called other
tortoises, putting them at the resting places which Hare had
pointed out.

'The following morning Hare came and said, "Tortoise, when
I say 'Go' we will start running!" He said "Go!" and started to
run speedily. Tortoise began to walk laboriously, then stopped.
Hare nearly killed himself running, and looking back he did not
see Tortoise at all. He began laughing and said to himself, "I have
left Tortoise far behind!" He ran again and came to the mafureira
tree, only to find that Tortoise had arrived long ago. Tortoise
said, "Where are you going, you Hare? I arrived a long time ago
and have been going here and there, waiting for you!" Hare
stopped, wondering, and said, "How did you run over here, you
Tortoise?" They began again, running towards the little terebinth,

and again Hare found that Tortoise had arrived long before. He began to lose heart. He said, "Let us start the race back."

'So they did, and it was just the same on the return journey.

'Hare said: "You have not yet got me! I will prepare beer, and we will see if you can still challenge me and drink it to the end!" "All right," said Tortoise. Hare began to brew beer. Tortoise went and called hundreds of other tortoises to that place. When the beer was ready, Hare came and called Tortoise. He said, "Come and drink my beer to the end!" Tortoise came and when satisfied said, "Let me go out for a while to urinate!" Another tortoise came back; when satisfied he also said, "Let me go out for a while to urinate!" In that way Tortoise drank Hare's beer to the very end! Hare was more than startled, he went: "Gooo!" (expression of defeat).

'A deceiver is deceived. Hare deceived Elephant and Hippo, but he himself was deceived by Tortoise.'[1]

As in Judo, the squat and seemingly awkward, or the frail and light in body, can usually win. Only such can vanquish the hare. In the Japanese scrolls of animal caricatures from the temple of Kozanji the hare is tossed by a frog in a wrestling match. There is no text but the defeat of the hare by the frog is apparent in the illustration. (Plate 19.)[2]

In another African story the hare is tricked to death by a swallow:

'The hare and the swallow were good friends and when the swallow went to call on him, he saw a pot of vegetables on the fire; it was gourd seasoned with almonds. The hare's wife served them with this dish and they had dinner together.

'Then the swallow said, "Tell me. How is this cooked?"

"It's cooked in water and flavoured with almonds."

"I didn't like to push my helping away," the swallow said, "because you might have been offended. But at home we don't cook gourd with water. It's cooked in my own sweat. When we've fetched the gourds from the fields, we clean out the pot

[1] Ibid., pp. 73–4.
[2] R. T. Paine and A. Soper, *The Art and Architecture of Japan* (Pelican History of Art), London, 1955, pp. 68–9.

and I get in. Then the pieces of gourd are put on top of me. I perspire and that's the water we use; it's that that makes the gourd boil."

"How is it it doesn't kill you?" said the hare.

"Of course it doesn't!"

"You're lying."

"I'm not. Come to us tomorrow and you'll see."

'The swallow went home and told his wife to get some maize and gourd ready for the hare's meal next day. He told her to give the hare an upturned mortar to sit on by the door of their hut. "If he asks where I am, tell him I am in the cooking pot. But really I shall be perching on top of the door. Give him some maize to eat while he is waiting and when the gourd is ready bring a dish and lay it on the threshold. Then carry the pot from the fire and empty it on to the dish."

'The hare arrived in good time and the swallow's wife did as she had been told. He sat by the door eating his maize, waiting for the swallow to come out of the pot. At last, when the gourd was ready, the swallow's wife lifted the pot from the fire and came running with it to the doorway.

"Now you'll see your friend come out," she said, and emptied the pot on to the dish. The steam billowed out and rose in thick mist to the top of the doorway where the swallow was perching. Then the swallow flew down from his hiding place. The hare could hear the sound of his wings flapping—*pa-pa-pa*. He was covered with sweat from the steam.

"Oh, he really did tell the truth," said the hare.

"Have you been here long?" said the swallow.

"A good long time."

'The swallow went to bathe and came back clean. The swallow's wife laid a mat on the ground. They sat on it and she gave them their dinner.

"How is it?" (It was flavoured with almonds.)

"Exquisite," said the hare. "We can cook it this way too, at home. Come to us tomorrow. I'll tell my wife to cook me in the pot, just like you."

'He went home and told his wife what a delicious meal he had

had with the swallows. "Boil me with the gourd tomorrow," he said.

"But that would kill you!"

"Not at all."

'Next day, he squeezed himself into the cooking pot laying back his ears flat over his neck and shoulders. His wife placed the pieces of gourd on top of him, but put in no water. Then she put the pot on the fire. When it got hot, he began to scream but he could not get out because the gourd was on top of him and she had covered the pot with a plate. She stoked the fire but did not hear his cries.

'While this was going on the swallow arrived and said, "Where's my friend?"

"He's here," said the hare's wife. "I've put him in the pot to cook with the gourd."

"What! But why on earth. . . ?"

"He told me that the gourd must be boiled in his sweat. He said he'd eaten it like that at your house."

'The swallow pretended to be astonished. "But, but, but . . ." he said, "I was joking yesterday. I wasn't in the pot. I was perching on top of the door."

'The hare's wife took the pot off the fire and carried it outside. She tipped it up to empty it. There was the hare, burnt up. Dead.

'The swallow said, "This is a day of sorrow in the house of the hare. My friend is dead. He was put into the pot to be cooked with the gourd. But it is not his fault, poor hare." '[1]

The best-known stories of the hare as a trickster are preserved in the *Uncle Remus* books, which show a kindly humour not found in the African originals. Joel Chandler Harris, their author, had a wide and exact knowledge of American Negro oral tradition. He was an accurate listener and said of these books, 'There is nothing here but an old Negro man, a little boy, and a dull reporter.'[2] Some of the old African versions of the stories were recorded and translated during his life time, and may be compared with *Uncle*

[1] H. A. Junod, *Les Chants et les Contes des Ba-Rongaes de la Baie de Delagoa*, Lausanne, 1897, pp. 131 foll.; translated by David Thomson.

[2] Quoted by Stella Brewer Brookes, Introduction to *Uncle Remus*, New York, 1965, p. viii.

16. Hare with watermark beneath it. Hieroglyph from inner coffin of Sennbui. Middle Kingdom, about 2000 B.C. (*British Museum*)

17. A cupid with a hare seated on his left hand, from an Ancient Greek vase (*British Museum*)

18. The Holy Family with three hares. Woodcut by Albrecht Dürer (1471–1528)

Remus as an example of how ancient themes are adapted to a different time and place.

A picture of life on a plantation in Georgia emerges incidentally from Uncle Remus's stories and the exploits of the animals are mischievous rather than wicked. In Africa the same adventures seem like grim parables of the people's everyday lives. Brer Fox makes the Tar Baby merely to pay off an old score. Here is a version from South-East Africa. It was a common practice there to kill animals in order to obtain their horns or bones.

We have summarized the first part and given the Tar-Baby episode in full:

'The Hare put a pot of water on the fire and told the Gazelle to get in. The Gazelle said, "All right. But you try it first." The Hare sat down in the pot while the water was still cool and the Gazelle put the lid on over him. After a while he asked her to let him out. He jumped out and said, "It is your turn now." He put the lid on over her. He made the fire big and the water began to boil. She cried out but he would not open the lid. "I need those little horns that you have on your head," he said. When she was dead he took her horns and made them into trumpets. He called many animals by blowing on the horns. [Presumably by imitating their voices, cf. pp. 80–2.] He tricked them one by one and killed them. He tricked people too. He went to a place where there were many people.

'Then he began to steal. He took his horn and climbed a hill and sounded it—*nté, nté, nté*—and shouted, "An army is approaching. Flee!"

'As soon as they heard that, the women who were harvesting the peas and groundnuts in the fields ran away. They were in fear of enemy warriors. They hid far off in the marshes. The Hare came down and stole their peas and groundnuts. He even made a store for himself which he put on one side.

'When he had eaten the last pea, he sounded the horn again—*nté, nté, nté*—and shouted, "An army is approaching. Flee!"

'They ran away again. He took all he wanted and made a hidden store.

'Then the people began to say to each other, "The Hare is de-

ceiving us. Let us go and find some black bird-lime." They collected a lot of it, plenty. They then went to the fields, and made an
image with hands, feet, nose, ears, eyes, hair: the image of a
woman.

'The Hare began again to sound the horn—*nté, nté, nté*—and
shouted, "An army is approaching! Flee!"

'They fled. He came down into the fields. The image was still
there. It had not moved. He came nearer and shouted, "Woman!
Get out!" The woman said nothing. She stood still. He said, "Get
out or I'll thrash you!" He came close and struck her with his fist.
His fist sank deep into the bird-lime and was caught there. "Let
me go or I'll kill you," he cried. Then he hit her with his other fist
and that stuck too. He jabbed her with his leg. It stuck to her. He
jabbed her with his other leg. That stuck too. Then he cried, "I'll
bite you with my teeth!" He was caught by the teeth too, and there
he was dangling on the image of a woman, swinging this way,
swinging that way.

'The makers of the image came back and found him swinging
there: "So it is you, Mr. Hare, who has been cheating us!"

"Set me free," said the Hare.

'They extricated him and said, "We are going to kill you."
"Listen," he said. "Don't kill me here on the ground. Kill me on the
back of the Chief." They returned to the village and spread a mat
on the ground. The Chief lay down on it and the Hare crouched
on his back.

'A warrior, one of the most powerful of body, took up an
assegai intending to transfix the Hare. But the Hare leaped high
and far into the air and ran away. And the man saw that he had
killed the Chief. And the people of the village slaughtered the
man who had killed their chief.'[1]

As a last example, in this chapter, we have chosen 'The Hare
and the Tree-frog'. It is typical of many that remain only in bits,
as anecdotes. But this one is complete.

'There was once a King called Maçingué-ona-Ndjao (probably
the lion, King of animals, though the storyteller does not say so).

[1] H. A. Junod, op. cit., p. 90 foll. (obtenu de Kouézou); translated by David
Thomson.

He ordered all the animals to come and clean out his well. (The wells in this country are usually mere holes in the sand dug down to the level of the underground water.)

'The Hare was called with the others, but Mister Hare refused to go.

'When they had finished cleaning the well, they said to the Hare, "You did not want to help us. You cannot draw your water from this well." He answered, "I don't want to. I'll go for my water to another place."

'They put the Gazelle there and said, "Watch out! If the Hare comes for water, catch him and keep him prisoner." The Gazelle stood on guard.

'The Hare came with two calabashes in his hands—one full of honey, the other empty. He meant to fill the empty one with water. The Gazelle said to him, "What are you looking for about here?" "Oh, beautiful lady, I bow to you," said the Hare.

"Don't try to deceive me," she said. "You have come here for the Chief's water. But you would not help us."

'The Hare dipped a hen's feather in the honey and smeared her mouth with it. She cried out, "It's good. Give me some more!"

'Mister Hare said, "Yes. If you let me get my water."

'The Gazelle said, "No." The Hare said, "All right, then. If you let me tie your legs together, I'll give you some more." She let him tie her legs together. He gave her no more honey. He filled his calabash with water. Then he took up a stick and beat her. Then he ran away.

'The Antelope came there and said, "Who tied you up like that?"

"The Hare tied me up."

"The Hare! A little nothing of an animal and he conquers you!"

'The Gazelle said, "He is not so little. He will also know how to tie you up."

'The Antelope let loose the Gazelle and stayed on guard by the well.

'A few days later Mister Hare came back and greeted the Antelope: "Oh beautiful lady, I bow to you."

'The Antelope answered, "Don't deceive me as you deceived the Gazelle you tied up here the other day."

'The Hare said, "I would never think of playing a trick on you, oh beautiful lady. I have only come to ask for water."

'The Antelope tried to butt him with her horns. He dipped his feather in the honey and smeared her mouth. "Give me more!" she cried. "Yes, but if I don't tie your legs together, the honey will not satisfy you." She held out her legs. He gave her not a drop more honey, but beat her and said, "Now I have knocked some sense into you! I shall treat the rest of you in the same way, one after the other."

'The Buffalo came. Mister Hare greeted him. "Oh my lord with the glittering horns, you whose face excels in beauty the faces of all the lords in the world, I bow to you."

'While the Buffalo was trying to stab him with his horns, he stood up on his legs, reaching high, and smeared his mouth with honey. By this ruse he managed to tie him up too.

'He conquered all the animals in the same way. To the Hippopotamus he gave a double thrashing. He hit him in the face with a dogberry stick and then went to look for a mangrove branch. He gave him a sound and weighty beating.

'When all this was over the Tree-frog[1] went to the Chief and said, "How is it that you have not succeeded in catching the Hare? I should very much like to catch him myself."

'She plunged into the water. Mister Hare came to the well and saw no one there. "I was right all along," he said to himself. "There is no one any more who can stop me from getting my water at this well." He filled his calabash. Then he went back to wash himself. After he had bathed in the well he began to stir the water up and muddy it.

'The Tree-frog seized him by one of his hind paws. He tried to

---

[1] Tree Frogs (family *Hylidae*), are often credited with magical powers. One of the smallest of the species, about 1⅜ in. long, can jump 36 times its own length. Others build dams with forelegs. All can leap to catch insects in the air, and use their webbed hindfeet as parachutes as they fall. The rather wide ends of their toes are fitted with strong suckers for clinging. They can walk upside down on the backs of leaves. Their shape, from the front, is strikingly altered when they blow out their throats to croak.

See Purnell's *Encyclopedia of Animal Life*, Vol. 6, p. 2,450–2.

free it. She took one of his front paws and held it and grasped it together with the hind one. He tried and tried to get away, but the Tree-frog caught his other hind leg and grasped it against the front one.

'That is how she made the Hare a prisoner. She took him, and his calabashes, and went back to the Chief.

'All the beasts of the fields gathered then to execute the Hare. He said to them, "It will not work like that. You must put me on the back of the Chief's son."

'But when they set out to kill him, he escaped with a leap and ran away. They found they had killed the Chief's son.'[1]

So far as we have been able to find out large animals never play the part of trickster, though some, like the elephant, may succeed in outwitting him from time to time. His cleverest opponent is usually smaller than himself, a reptile, insect or little bird. The theme is mind over matter, the power of lightness over weight, and is developed beautifully in *Monkey*,[2] the greatest trickster story of the world. Monkey can fly. In life the gibbon's graceful leaping from branch to branch is near to flight. The trickster hare can leap so high and far that no one sees him. He vanishes in the second that the warrior takes to strike. The life of the spirit, both in magical cults and in the higher religions, has been released from the Earth. The genie emerges from flame or smoke, the Will-o-the-Wisp from dark misty places. The witch and the lunatic both can fly. Hermes or Mercury, the winged messenger of the gods, is often depicted as flying. He and the hare have much in common. We have seen the association of ideas that connects hare-gods and goddesses with the moon. Hermes was identified with the moon-god Thoth, and Hermopolis (city of Thoth) was also named Unnu—the city of Un or Un-nefer (beautiful Un), the hare-headed god, and his female equivalent, the goddess Unnut.[3]

Hermes has all the qualities of a trickster too. In the early Greek tradition he is famed for eloquence. He was also the inventor of

---

[1] H. A. Junod, op. cit., p. 127 seq.; translated by David Thomson.

[2] by Wu Ch'êng-ên, a sixteenth-century work translated by Arthur Waley, The Penguin Classics, London, 1961.

[3] See E. A. Wallis Budge, *The Gods of the Egyptians*, London, 1904, Vol. 1, pp. 426–7.

writing and other arts. Later, the Romans under their name for him, Mercurius, valued him as god of trade, profit making, slippery talk and fast travel which was then an essential part of trade.

Hermes was a god of thieving too. His trickster exploits are as ingenious as the hare's. A few hours after his birth—and infancy is the state of the brilliant fool—he escaped from the cave where his cradle was, climbed the mountains of Pieria and stole fifty heifers from Apollo's herd of cattle. He made them walk backwards to disguise their footmarks and put on huge peculiar sandals to disguise his own. After he had hidden the heifers he got back into his cave through the keyhole 'like a vapour or breath of autumn'.[1]

He also, as would naturally follow, presided over games of chance and because 'the art of the trader is to overcome the buyer's hesitation by subtle and persuasive words'[2] belief in his eloquence was confirmed.

The name Mercury was given in the thirteenth century to quicksilver, a metal that slips away in pieces when you try to handle it and can only be controlled in a cage.

All these qualities suit the trickster hare. The symbol is the same—mind and spirit in control of physical force.

When the Nordic gods tried to bind Fenris, the wolf, with stronger and stronger iron fetters he broke free again and again. At last they 'let there be wrought the fetter that is called the supple fetter'. It was made of 'footfall of cat, breath of fish, spittle of bird' and other things that do not exist, and was 'smooth and soft as a silken string'.[3] They laid it on the wolf and the harder he strained against it the more firmly he was held.

When the Great Hare went to fight his father he asked him what missile he feared most. His father answered 'the Black Rock'—a rock of gigantic size and weight. Then the father asked the hare what he feared most. The Great Hare, trembling at the thought of it, said he feared the root of the bullrush more than any other missile.[4]

---

[1] Larousse, *Encyclopedia of Mythology*, London, 1964, p. 135. [2] Ibid., p. 133.
[3] Snorri Sturlason (attributed to), *The Prose or Younger Edda*, translated by D. W. Dasent, Stockholm, 1842, p. 35.
[4] Cornelius Matthews, *The Enchanted Moccasins*, New York, 1877, pp. 220 seq.

A root holds the spirit of life, an unseen force, and is itself unseen when living. Like the supple fetter it contains the Chinese concept of *Jang*: yieldingness, the strength of water, which gives way in one place only to force itself forward elsewhere.[1] In the cruder forms of the trickster story this concept is barely perceptible. In the most primitive myths and in the highly developed literature of China it is apparent.

[1] See Joseph Needham, *Science and Civilisation in China*, Cambridge, 1962, Vol. II, p. 61.

15

The Names of the Hare

$\mathbb{B}$efore discussing other beliefs about the hare we are transcribing a Middle English poem which has a bearing both on these and on the many attributes of the hare that have been noted in the previous pages. The poem is written in a late thirteenth-century hand; and there is evidence that it comes from a Welsh border (Shropshire) family. It has been published along with copious notes by Alan S. C. Ross.[1] The poem was apparently designed as a ritual to be recited by the hunter on his first encountering a hare; and the seventy-seven different names given to the hare in the poem were supposed, on their recital, to deliver it into the hunter's power. Most of the names are abusive; and many of them appear to be proper names applied to the hare, just as today East Anglian countrymen refer affectionately to the hare as *Owd Sarah* or *Owd Sally*. But there is this difference in the poem: most of the names are pejorative; and just as we sometimes call a person *Old Neddy*, thus transposing one of the donkey's less desirable attributes to the man, here in the poem *turpin* (line 14) means a rascal (O.F., a soldier or highwayman? Lat. *turpis*); and has all his failings transferred to the creature.

Professor Ross draws an interesting parallel for this 'calling of names', and points out that the epithetical or descriptive style (*dyfalu*) is very much like that used in Welsh verse at the time. He also demonstrates the great similarity in purpose and content between this poem and a *cywydd*[2] by the Welsh poet Dafydd ap

---

[1] Bodleian MS Digby 86, f. 168 v. See A. S. C. Ross, *Proceedings of Leeds Philosophical Society, Literary and Historical Section*, Section 3, 1935, pp. 347–77.

[2] Thomas Parry, *Gwaith Dafydd ap Gwilym*, Cardiff, 1952; pp. 124–7, 481–2.

Gwilym, a contemporary of Chaucer. In his poem Dafydd describes how he had arranged to meet his girl of the moment in a nearby grove; but on going to the trysting place he saw her coming out from the trees in a fright. She had been startled by a hare suddenly jumping out of its cover; and interpreting this as a bad omen for her affair with the poet she had immediately run home. This left the poet angry and disappointed, and to draw off his emotions he had written an abusive poem with the unlucky hare as its target. The Middle English poem is shown overleaf:

There is no need to comment on many of the descriptive names in the poem as the meaning of most of them is plain. But *þe eueleImet* in line 19—the one it's ill-luck to meet—is, as already suggested, probably the poem's justification. It was presumably written to cancel out the misfortune that is bound to follow if anyone meets a hare as he goes out on a particular mission. Therefore, the purpose of this uncharming charm was to make the hare itself as vulnerable in the hunt as any ordinary creature. The ill-luck associated with the hare was deep-rooted, and Sir Thomas Browne later noted[1] in the seventeenth century that most older people feared meeting a hare on the highroad. The same dread of the hare as a creature of ill-omen is implicit in the epithet *make-agrise* in line 43: the thing that makes people shudder; in *make-fare*, line 48: the one that makes people flee; and in line 54 where *þe der þat no-mon ne-dar nemnen* refers to the hare as a creature that is taboo to such an extent that no man dare call it by its right name.

There are, however, many epithets in the poem that deserve mention; and in the following we are indebted to Professor Ross whose notes we have used to supplement our observations on the hare's behaviour. His interest in the poem is mainly philological; but he wrote[2] that he intended publishing an article on its folklore aspects. He did not write this article, and we have attempted to supply comments on the folklore in this and the following chapter. Professor Ross's observation that modern English dialect enabled him to throw light on many of the obscure words in the old manuscript is worth repeating here; and though his statement

---

[1] *Pseudodoxia Epidemica* (edition, London, 1928), p. 384.
[2] Op. cit., p. 348.

The Names of the Hare

Les nouns de vn leure en engleis

Þe mon þat þe hare Imet,
Ne shal him neuere be þe bet,
Bote if he lei doun on londe
Þat he bereþ in his honde,
5 (Be hit staf be hit bouwe),
And blesce him wiþ his helbowe.
And mid wel goed devosioun
He shal saien on oreisoun
In þe worshipe of þe hare;
10 Þenne mai he wel fare:
'Þe hare, þe scotart,
Þe bigge, þe bouchart,
Þe scotewine, þe skikart,
Þe turpin, þe tirart,
15 Þe wei-betere, þe ballart,
Þe gobidich, þe soillart,
Þe wimount, þe babbart,
Þe stele-awai, þe momelart,
Þe eueleImet, þe babbart,
20 Þe scot, þe deubert,
Þe gras-bitere, þe goibert,
Þe late-at-hom, þe swikebert,
Þe frendlese, þe wodecat,
Þe brodlokere, þe bromkat,
25 Þe purblinde, þe fursecat,
Þe louting, þe westlokere,
Þe waldeneie, þe sid-lokere,
And eke þe roulekere;
Þe stobhert, þe long-here,
30 Þe strauder, þe lekere,
Þe wilde der, þe lepere,
Þe shorte der, þe lorkere,
Þe wint-swifft, þe sculkere,
Þe hare-serd, þe hegroukere,

202

The Names of the Hare

The Names of the Hare in English

The man who encounters the hare
Will never get the better of him,
Except he lay down on ground
The weapon he bears in his hand
5   (Be it hunting-staff or bow),
And bless him with his elbow.
And with sincere devotion
Utter this one prayer
In praise of the hare—
10 Then will he better fare:
'The hare, the hare-kin,
Old Big-bum, Old Bouchart,
The hare-ling, the frisky one,
Old Turpin, the fast traveller,
15 The way-beater, the white-spotted one,
The lurker in ditches, the filthy beast,
Old Wimount, the coward,
The slink-away, the nibbler,
The one it's bad luck to meet, the white-livered,
20 The scutter, the fellow in the dew,
The grass nibbler, Old Goibert,
The one who doesn't go straight home, the traitor,
The friendless one, the cat of the wood,
The starer with wide eyes, the cat that lurks in the broom,
25 The purblind one, the furze-cat,
The clumsy one, the blear-eyed one,
The wall-eyed one, the looker to the side,
And also the hedge-frisker,
The stag of the stubble, long-eared,
30 The animal of the stubble, the springer,
The wild animal, the jumper,
The short animal, the lurker,
The swift-as-wind, the skulker,
The shagger, the squatter in the hedge,

35 Þe deudinge, þe deuhoppere,
   Þe sittere, þe gras-hoppere,
   Þe ffitelfot, þe foldsittere,
   Þe liȝtt-fot, þe fernsittere,
   Þe cawelhert, þe wortcroppere,
40 Þe gobigrounde, þe sittestille,
   Þe pintail, þe toure-tohulle;
   Þe coue-arise,
   Þe make-agrise,
   Þe wite-wombe,
45 Þe go-mit-lombe,
   Þe choumbe, þe chaulart,
   Þe chiche, þe couart,
   Þe make-fare, þe brekefforewart,
   Þe ffnattart, þe pollart,
50 (His hei nome is srewart);
   Þe hert wiþ þe leþerene hornes,
   Þe der þa woneþ in þe cornes,
   Þe der þat alle men scornes,
   Þe der þat no-mon ne-dar nemnem.'
55 Wen þou hauest al þis I-said,
   Þenne is þe hare miȝtte alaid.
   Þenne miȝtt þou wenden forþ,
   Est and west and souþ and norþ,
   Wedrewardes so mon wile—
60 Þe mon þat con ani skile.
   Haue nou godnedai, sir hare!
   God þe lete so wel fare,
   Þat þou come to me ded,
   Oþer in ciue, oþer in bred!

                              Amen.

35   *The dew-beater, the dew-hopper,*
The sitter on its form, the hopper in the grass,
The fidgety-footed one, the sitter on the ground,
The light-foot, the sitter in the bracken,
The stag of the cabbages, the cropper of herbage,

40   *The low creeper, the sitter-still,*
The small-tailed one, the one who turns to the hills,
The get-up quickly,
The one who makes you shudder,
The white-bellied one,

45   *The one that takes refuge with the lambs,*
The numbskull, the food mumbler,
The niggard, the flincher,
The one who makes people flee, the covenant-breaker,
The snuffler, the cropped head

50   *(His chief name is Scoundrel),*
The stag with the leathery hornes,
The animal that dwells in the corn,
The animal that all men scorns,
The animal that no one dare name.'

55   *When you have said all this,*
Then is the hare's strength put down.
Then you might go out
East, west, north, and south,
Wherever a man will—

60   *A man that has any skill.*
And now, good day to you, Sir Hare!
God let you in such wise fare
As will bring you to me dead,
Either in onion broth or just in bread!

                                 Amen.

that the dialect is 'a much neglected source of philological commentary' was made over thirty-five years ago, the position has not changed to any great extent since that time—at least in some regions of England.

Þe ballart (line 15), the white-spotted one, refers to the spots that some hares have on their face and forehead. There is a 'fanciful notion' that these spots are connected with the number of young in a litter. Evan William Davies,[1] one of our informants, lives on the Glamorgan-Brecon border not many miles from the supposed provenance of the poem. He told us:

[T] 'Yes, I've seen a hare carrying one of her young in her mouth. When the doe brings young she brings them out in the open now, don't she? She brings generally two or three. If she gets three, there's a star on one of them.'

Þe deubert (line 20) as *Þe duedinge, pe deuhoppere* (line 35), the fellow in the dew, the dew-beater, the dew-hopper, point to the hare's habit of feeding in the early morning and late evening. A hare's tricks or *mazes* are often visible in the dew in the early morning. *Dinge* in the second phrase is the fairly common dialect word *ding* to strike or beat. In Suffolk, for instance, *a ding o' the skull* is a blow on the head. Here, then, a knocker off of the dew.

Þe late-at-hom (line 22), the one that doesn't go home straight, refers to the doubling back of the hare when it makes its mazes and its seldom returning direct to its form. Many of our informants, including those in Wales, have emphasized this trick of the hare:[2]

Two further notes are relevant here. Hares that feed on grass that is heavy with dew occasionally eat too much and get *blown*. H. F. Bloomfield (born 1888), an Ipswich man, remembered walking near the river with some other boys when he discovered a hare lying on the side of the road. Its stomach was swollen and it was so helpless that they were able to pick it up. They placed it in a hollow tree, expecting to claim it when they returned from the river. But when they came back the hare had gone: it had probably recovered and made off to safety.

---

[1] Coelbren, Neath, Glamorgan.
[2] See p. 78.

The Names of the Hare

The hare's mazes, its purposeful twistings and turnings, have been much admired. Their best celebration is by the poet Christopher Smart in his *Jubilate Agno* (verse 23):

> *Let Jehoiada bless God with an Hare,*
> *Whose mazes are determined for the health of the body*
> *and to parry the adversary.*

Another poet[1] accurately described the ingenuity with which a hare constructs its mazes, and the caution it uses in returning to its seat—all confirming the observation of the countryman:

> *With steps reversed*
> *She forms the doubling maze; then ere the morn*
> *Peeps thro' the clouds, leaps to her close recess.*

Þe *wodecat*, Þe *bromkat* and Þe *fursecat* (lines 23–5) also confirm the Welsh influence in the poem: they appear to be renderings of *cath-y-coed* and *cath-eithin*: wood cat, and cat of the broom and furze. *Puss* is a nickname for the hare in parts of England even today. (See also the poet Cowper's account of the treatment of his tame hares in Appendix One.)

Brodlokere (line 24) refers to the popular belief that the hare always sleeps with its eyes open (*brod*—with a stare, with eyes wide open). It would be impossible to prove or disprove this statement because it is unlikely that anyone could approach near enough to a hare in the wild state without disturbing it from its sleep. Its sense of smell and its hearing are so delicately tuned to its one method of self-preservation—speed combined with a quick getaway—that even a sight of the hare from a fair distance always apprehends it with its eyes wide open. It has been observed[2] that leverets in captivity close their eyes while asleep; but their reactions are entirely different from those of the hare in the wild state: being tame and in a secure environment they would have little fear of being surprised with their eyes closed, the necessity for immediate alertness at anyone's approach having been removed. Þe *sid-lokere* (line 27) is a natural phrase for the hare since its eyes

[1] William Somerville (1692–1743), *The Chase*, Book 2.
[2] H. G. Lloyd. Personal communication.

are set so much on the side of its head that it can see behind it—
a great advantage when it is being pursued by any animal; but
also a disadvantage which shows itself in a hare's running straight
into an obstacle immediately in front of it (see p. 230).

Þe *sculkere* (line 34) is a good adjective for a hare after it has been
frightened:[1] 'The demeanour of a hare when startled in the open
is strikingly different from the low, crouching attitude which it
generally adopts when in its form. On hearing an unusual sound,
its first impulse is to sit upright with erected ears and reconnoitre;
afterwards it may endeavour to conceal itself by squatting close to
the ground, by skulking away with depressed ears, or it may at
once take to flight.'

The stag of the cabbages, *Pe cawelhert* (line 39) is a blown-up
description of the hare in the manner of the poem. But many of
our informants have told us about the hare's habit of raiding
kitchen-gardens in the winter-time when its food is scarce or
covered with snow. An informant from Pembrokeshire:

[T] 'The hares used to come to Llanfyrnach rectory. If there
was a bit of snow or frosty weather there was one guaranteed to
be in their garden there every day.'

Þe *toure-tohulle* (line 41), the one who turns to the hills, refers to
the hare's making by instinct for the hills whenever it is chased.
Its long hind-legs put it at a great advantage when travelling uphill and it can easily out-distance a fast greyhound when going in
this direction. Travelling downhill is a different matter (see p.
33).

Þe *go-mit lombe* (line 45): the one that takes refuge with the
lambs, is a phrase that can be quoted when anyone impugns the
hare's intelligence. It has often been recorded that a hare, when it
is hard pressed, will seek out a flock of sheep and conceal itself
amongst them, making it difficult for it to be sighted or for its
pursuers to pick up its scent. The following account illustrates
this: it also provides an additional note on the once common
method of hunting rabbits and hares, with hawks:[2] 'Captain

[1] Barrett-Hamilton, op. cit., Vol. 2, p. 272.
[2] James Edmund Harting, *Hints on the Management of Hawks*, London, 1898, pp.
138–9.

F. D. Bland, of Draycott, near Stoke-on-Trent, thus relates his experience with the Goshawk:

"A relation of mine having given me permission to hawk rabbits on his estate in Yorkshire, I made a fresh start with two hawks—an untrained eyas female, which I obtained from Mr. Henri Lefebvre of Paris, and an adult female, which I bought from Sir Ralph Payne-Gallwey. I soon got the former into working order, and killed a lot of rabbits with her, but unfortunately she died during her first moult; and with the old hawk of Sir Ralph's I have had grand sport. Last year, besides a heavy bag of rabbits, I killed two hares with her. I slipped her at six hares altogether, and she flew at each one with great determination, and caught them all; but four of them, after a splendid 'rough and tumble', managed to get the best of it, and kicked themselves free before I could get up to her assistance. One was a really magnificent struggle. I let her go at a big hare which jumped up some forty yards ahead in a large pasture; on her first 'binding' to it, hare and hawk went twice head over heels, and then, the hawk slipping her hold, puss went on alone, leaving her on the ground; but she was not yet defeated, for she picked herself up, and again overtook and struck the hare, only to be kicked off again after another struggle. A third time did this plucky Goshawk make off after the hare, which by this time had managed to reach the shelter of a small flock of sheep and very cleverly ran under them and escaped. The hawk, dead beat, 'took stand' in a small fir tree." '

Line 51, *Þe hert wiþ þe leperene hornes,*[1] the stag with the leathery horns, is worth noting for two reasons. There was an ancient belief that horned hares actually existed, and this belief has some basis in fact. For the disease which attacks the Jack Rabbits of North America (true hares, as we have seen) causes growths on the head that often look exactly like a pair of horns. It could, however, be argued that the hare's long ears look exactly like horns when they are erect. Secondly, the hare is referred to again

---

[1] Cf. a riddle about the hare from South Antrim:
A hopper of ditches,
A cropper of corn;
A wee brown cow,
And a pair of leather horns.

in the poem as a stag or deer. An old Irish countryman told us:

[T] 'It [the hare] just leaps and bounds; this . . . the very same as the deer does. So it goes to tell us that he is somewhat a species of the deer.'

The countryman was not, in fact, being just fanciful: he was merely transmitting an ancient tradition; for the Irish name for a hare is *gearrfhia* or small deer.

Finally, the last line of the poem: Howell Jeffreys, a countryman from Dyffryn Cellwen, Glamorgan, told us while we were discussing the hare as food:

[T] 'Hare's meat is drier than rabbit's meat. Some people don't like it, but with plenty of onions it's lovely!'

That is exactly how the thirteenth-century hunter, presumably operating not far away from Dyffryn Cellwen, prayed to have his hare after he had caught it:

Oper in ciue, oper in bred!

that is, 'either in onion broth or just in bread!' before he said *Amen* to a quarry well pursued and a meal fully enjoyed.

While discussing names connected with the hare we should add a cautionary note. As often with names, they are not always what they seem. For instance, the *Harepath*,[1] the great trackway across Exmoor, has nothing to do with the hare. This track was the main route of the Saxon invaders of this part of England. It was known to them as the *here paeth* or army road. The hare also has a strange namesake, the sea-hare[2]—another apparent misnomer—a popular name for a large mollusc of the *gastropoda* class, at least since Pliny's time. In European waters they are usually only about three inches long, but on the Pacific coast of North America they grow to a foot or more in length, and are about the same weight as a real hare—seven or eight pounds, and sometimes more. They are brown, olive-coloured or reddish, and often have black mottled markings. They sit in the sand in a round, hunched position, like a hare in its form; and their long brown feelers, similar to a snail's horns, resemble a hare's ears. They are hermaphrodites—that is to

---

[1] Charles Whybrow, *Antiquary's Exmoor*, Dulverton, Somerset, 1970, p. 40.
[2] Purnell's *Encyclopedia of Animal Life*, Paulton, Somerset, 1970, p. 2,065.

say, each one has both male and female organs; and from ancient times they have been credited, like the hare on land, with satanic powers.

We have already given many of the traditional local names bestowed on the hare in Britain; but this is a good place to recapitulate and to add to those names already written down. The sex names[1] are jack or buck for the male, and jill (or gill) and doe for the female. East Anglia appears to be very rich in local names, as we would perhaps expect from a region which is traditionally plentiful in hares. The most common are:Sarah, or Sally, Owd [Old] Sarah or Owd Sally, Aunt Sally or Owd Aunt. Baud or bawd has also been listed for Norfolk: this is supposed to be a shortened form of bawdrons or baudrons which means cat; and, as the frequency of the name puss for the hare suggests, the links between the cat and the hare in popular tradition are many.

Norfolk, and also Cornwall,[2] had—and perhaps still have—Wat for the hare's name, one that Shakespeare uses in *Venus and Adonis*:

> *By this, poor Wat, far off upon a hill,*
> *Stands on his hinder legs with list'ning ear,*
> *To hearken if his foes pursue him still:*

Wat is probably a variant of Walt or Walter which are also known. In Suffolk bandy or bowen, referring to the curvature of the hare's hind legs, were also used by the older generation. Scotland and the north of England have bautie, bawtie, bawty, betty and bun; the Gaelic name for hare is *gearr*, and *gearrog* for a young hare. Cumberland has Katie; and Northumberland and Northern Ireland have laverock or lavrock which are apparently mishearings for leveret. Malkin, maulkin, mawkin or maudkin, which are used in Scotland and north Yorkshire are all said to be derived from familiar cat-names: Maud, Matilda, Mall, Moll (for Mary) (see p. 34). Grimalkin (grey-malkin) is a cat's name; and it is significant that this is the name of one of the witches in *Macbeth*. In the Suffolk dialect a mawkin is a scarecrow or an unkempt girl or woman.

---

[1] Barrett-Hamilton, op. cit., Part 12, pp. 251 seq.
[2] E. M. Wright, *Rustic Speech and Folklore*, p. 340.

From Wales *cath-eithin* and *cath-y-coed* (furze-cat and wood-cat) have already been mentioned. The Dafydd ap Gwilym poem also has *cath-hirdaeth*, the cat that makes a long journey; *cath-ynfyd*, the stupid cat, and *esgair cath*, cat-legged. The usual names for the hare in Wales, however, are *sgwarnog* and *ysgyfarnog*, literally, the eared animal—from *ysgyfar*, an ear: *ysgyfarn*, an ear of wheat. *Ceinach* is also used; and in south Wales *pryf* or *pryf mawr*. All these names have a long history, and it is worth mentioning that one of our Welsh informants used the same name for the hare's form—*gwâl*, as his countryman Dafydd ap Gwilym did six hundred years before.

16
Other Beliefs and Customs

A true superstition is something that stands over (*superstat*)—a remnant of an ancient and complex body of belief. An example of this is the taboo on the hare's name which is often found amongst Scottish fishermen.[1] If a fisherman was baiting a line no one dare mention a hare in his hearing. For him to see a hare was worse: 'None will go down to the sea that day when they see a maukin [hare].'[2] And, as we mentioned earlier, there was an absolute taboo against speaking of a hare or a rabbit when the fishermen were on board their vessel. If circumstances made it necessary for them to refer to the hare they would invent a descriptive name as in the poem we have just discussed: 'The furry creature with the long ears.' The same superstitious awe for the hare was also common among English fishermen until recent years.

In many cultures everybody has a forbidden name. A man has an ordinary name for daily use and a real name which only he and his parents know. This name is never pronounced and he when young is enjoined to keep it secret all his life. In some countries the real name is whispered into the baby's ear on the day he is born and he never knows it. The real names of gods and lesser spirits were kept secret too. Only the priests knew them. 'The mysteries of these secret names of the classical gods have been very often so carefully preserved by the depositories of this treasure that even today we do not know the real personal names of most of the great figures of past religions.'[3]

---

[1] P. F. Anson, *Fisher Folklore*, London, 1905, pp. 101, 104.
[2] Ibid., p. 65.
[3] James Hastings, op. cit., Vol. 9, pp. 132 foll.

If the real name of a person was pronounced—usually by de-clamation or chanting—it was thought to draw the person into the power of the speaker, and of course power by suggestion is effec-tive when the victim or patient believes. The name became the person. But the power to summon a god or devil in the same way, by speaking his name, was naturally much feared, and 'when pic-ture writing acquired the magical power of the voice' the names of gods or lesser spirits could not even be written down. In *The Secrets of Enoch*,[1] 'Wisdom', not God, is commanded to create man. The name Jehovah is a mistaken rendering of four Hebrew vowels—IHUH or JHVH—that made up the Tetragrammaton which was too sacred to be uttered.[2] It was simply 'a direction to the reader to substitute ADONAI for the 'ineffable name'.[3] The name was regarded as a manifestation of God. To speak or write it was not only profane but perilous, for no man could face His awful presence.

'Talk of an angel and you'll hear the fluttering of its wings.' 'Talk of the devil and he's sure to appear.' In Christian countries the hare, like many other symbols of the old religion, was thought of as an evil spirit. It always portended bad luck. But originally it could be a good or bad omen according to the way it moved. It was one of the creatures used for divination. In some parts of England to this day, 'it is lucky to meet a hare, and a wish should be made as soon as it has passed. In others it is only the white hare which is unlucky. To see a black one is a sign of good fortune.'[4]

But to see a white hare near a Cornish seaport meant that a storm was coming. Indeed, the kind of hare met, the circum-stances, and even the time were often important as the following account[5] from north Wales shows. It also demonstrates how seriously a chance meeting with a hare was regarded in com-paratively recent times: 'Another man, middle aged, well-informed and studious since his youth, arose early to go to market at

---

[1] Apocrypha, *Secrets of Enoch*, xxx, 8.
[2] E. Cobham Brewer, op. cit.
[3] *Shorter Oxford English Dictionary*.
[4] E. & M. A. Radford, op. cit., p. 181.
[5] J. Jones (*Myrddin Fardd*), *LLen Gwerin Sir Caernarfon*, Caernarfon, 1908, pp. 133-4.

Caernarfon. But shortly after he started it happened that a hare ran across the road. He saw it and immediately became downcast, and considered turning back. He decided, however, to continue although much dispirited. When the market was over a neighbour asked him what sort of a day's trading he'd had:

"Oh," he said, "I knew perfectly well, as soon as I saw that hare in the road this morning, that today would be a bad one for me at the market."

In the opinion of the old people, a hare crossing the road in front of you or coming to meet you before breakfast means a woman who is your enemy. But if you meet a hare in the evening it means a queen. That is, misfortune in the morning, good fortune in the evening. If a farmer sees three or four hares playing together in the month of March, it will be bad luck for him. These would really be the witches of the neighbourhood rejoicing together in the form of hares; and no greyhound could catch them except one which is completely black—without a single white hair on its body.'

'But,' someone will object, 'this is understandable. It happened in the country seventy or eighty years ago. It wouldn't happen here today.' Perhaps not exactly in this form. Here is a story, told by a Norfolk farmer's wife, of an incident that happened two or three years ago:

'I was talking about hares to a friend who is agricultural editor of a newspaper. He told me: "I was driving out with a man the other day when a hare crossed the road:

"Had that been my old father driving he'd have turned back and gone straight home," said the car driver. He didn't. But I noticed that he drove with special care the rest of the way; though he's a Cambridge B.A. and so on, and supposed to be above mere superstition." '

Such notions seem whimsical, as though they were conceived at random. It is difficult to trace them back to their origins but easy to recognize the human need they served, which is one of the hungers of imagination. Formal education has only recently begun to pay proper attention to the imaginative needs of children. The rules of fact, reason and logic have long played an overriding, instead of a complementary part, yet no one, child or adult, can safely dispense with the illogical. Its exclusion causes neurosis and part of the cure for such neurosis is found by some psychologists in the use of oracular methods.

The need for the illogical survives, as strong as it ever was, in the technological societies of Europe and America and is satisfied to some extent by modern adaptations of the ancient arts of divination—palmistry, what the stars foretell, personality testing, marriage bureaux and so on. These often bring peace of mind to the anxious; they guide people towards a decision in matters where reasoning alone cannot help.

In the societies of Ancient Greece and Rome, augury—the art of interpretating omens or the will of a god by observing animals, especially birds—was often performed with the help of geometrical shapes, rectangles for example, which are still used by the Dogon tribe in the Sudan. In Rome, at the inauguration of a king, the Augur, after a prayer, sat on the top of a hill, with the king to-be at his left (the side of instinct), fixed on a landmark in front of him and 'marked out the *regiones* from East to West, the North being to the left, the South to the right. . . . He said aloud what auspices he sought for (i.e. whether birds, lightning or what).'[1] The historian describing this ritual says, 'As I write on this December day I recall the fact that I have myself during the past week foretold a spell of cold after observing a great arrival of winter thrushes from the north.'[2] He refers to Livy's statement that a study of the flight of birds gave information about mountain passes and the course of great rivers (presumably to an army entering a strange country).

But highly developed forms of augury are the reverse of rational. By providing a framework within which the imagination of the diviner must work, by setting limits to a complex problem, they encourage intuition and help people to make decisions in cases where no amount of reasoning will help. Mary Douglas has reminded us 'that every creative worker knows the sudden feeling of receiving a new idea out of the blue. Fred Hoyle's best setting

[1] W. W. Fowler, *Religious Experience of the Roman People*, London, 1911, p. 175.
[2] Ibid., p. 294.

for revolutionary ideas is a fishing trip, away from it all—and especially away from the laboratory. . . . Other people have solved theoretical problems after finding the answer in a dream. It seems to be no accident that Archimedes shouted *Eureka!* in his bath. . . .'[1] But as she points out there are thousands of occasions when creative workers lie passive in a bath or relax while fishing without a glimmer of a revelation. The revelation if it comes appears to come by chance, and most of us recognize this seeming chance when we forget a familiar name. Thinking about it, trying consciously to remember it, is useless. It comes up from the depths of the mind at an unexpected moment hours later. It is these depths, below the power of reason, that can sometimes be tapped through the formal convention of an oracle.

The Dogon people make what Mary Douglas calls a question-naire. 'They draw three long rectangles in the sand. One represents God (who stands for order and reason), one Man and one the Fox (who is the obverse of order— not a sinister obverse but a richly creative one). . . . The questioner soon fills in the framework with little symbols: a stone, a stick, a wisp of straw.' He scatters food around and goes to bed. 'In the night the white foxes that live in the Sudan will have come, taken the food and left their little tracks over the questionnaire.'[2]

A personal or tribal problem is not solved by the foxes' foot-marks or the displacement of symbols. It can only be solved by an imaginative interpretation of them. The mind of the diviner need no longer search a limitless space unguided by signs. He has a framework to help him to look at everything anew. His imagina-tion, like an artist's, needs a form to work within. His memory aroused by what may seem irrelevant throws light on the present. A leaf falling or a blade of grass may bring Walt Whitman's name back into one's mind.

We cite these suggestions only as hints of what the omens of the hare meant to Europeans long ago. It is difficult enough to under-stand a present day culture so far removed from one's own as the Dogons', and far more difficult to know the emotional effect of

[1] Mary Douglas, *Nommo and the Fox*, London, 1968, *The Listener*, Vol. 80, p. 328.
[2] Ibid.

divination by interpreting the movements of hares, a form of oracle which probably has not been used in Europe for hundreds of years. But the hare and the fox have much in common. They are both active by night, both symbols of the irrational, the intuitive, of cunning and the fickleness of the moon. Except in dew or in a sandy or snowy place it would be impossible to trace the footsteps of a hare. Augury by the flight of birds may be a firmer clue, for the diviners must have watched the actual movements of the hare, as they watched birds, and its prodigious leaping, its wide circles and sudden turns have often been compared to flight.

We guess, for want of evidence, that the diviner before interpreting these movements marked out the land in his mind as the Roman augur did. But, although fish, insects, reptiles and many kinds of quadruped mammals, and the gestures and other instinctive actions of men, were used by the Roman augurs, only bird augury has been fully documented. About the hare, we have not been able to discover any details. The Boadicea incident which numerous authors have quoted throws little light on the method, but it contains the only description we know. It tells of 'a remarkable way of divining related of Bouduca or Boadicea Queen of the Iceni—when she had harangued her soldiers to spirit them up against the Romans, she opened her bosom and let go a hare, which she had there concealed, that the augurs might thence proceed to divine. The frighted animal made such turnings and windings in her course, as, according to the then rules of judging, prognosticated happy success. The joyful multitude made loud huzzas, Boadicea seized the opportunity, approved their ardour, led them straight to their enemies, and gained the victory.'[1]

It may have been that the 'turnings and windings' of this hare were mostly with the sun, from left to right. To see a hare circle anti-clockwise is still thought unlucky:

'If one sees a hare going around one's house widdershins—that is against the sun—then look out. Some disaster is about to befall you.'[2]

---

[1] William Borlase, *Cornish Antiquities*, p. 135, quoted by C. Carew Hazlitt, *Faiths and Folklore*, Vol. 1, p. 305.
[2] Norman Halkett speaking in *The Hare*, op. cit.

As I was beating on the Forest Ground,

Up starts a Hare before my two Grey Hounds;

The Dogs being light of foot, did fairly run

Unto her fifteen Rods just twenty one

The Distance that she started up before

Was fourscore sixteen Rods just and no more

Now this I'd have you unto me declare

How far they run before they caught the Hare

4 score sixteen = 96 Rds

Rds
21
15
‒6   Dogs gain'd in running

Rd   Rd   Rds
6   21   96
        96
        126
        189
6)2016
     336 Dogs run
Ans } 96 Hare run
     240 Hare run

Fig. 7.   From the copybook of a Suffolk schoolboy: 'Master William
Aldous, *Eius Liber*, A.D. 1805'

But where faith changes into superstition, its vestiges are explained away:

'If an hare cross the highway, there are a few above three score years that are not perplexed thereat, which, notwithstanding, is but an augurial terror, according to that received expression *Inauspicatum dat iter oblatus lepus.* [If you meet a hare as you set out, it's a bad journey for you.] And the ground of the conceit was probably no greater than this, that a fearful animal, passing by us, portended unto us something to be feared.'[1]

The idea is the same as one of the interpretations of the taboo against eating hare flesh—that to eat a timid animal makes one timid, and it is part of a much stronger power, the belief in sympathetic magic, a parallel in its psychological effect to homeopathy in physical medicine, the use of an element of the ill to cure the ill, the hair of the dog, vaccination and so on.

In the seventeenth century Home wrote of the belief that if a pregnant woman saw a hare her child would be born with a hare-lip:

'In so much as some in company with a woman great with childe have upon the crossing of such creatures, cut or torn some of the clothes off that woman, with childe to prevent (as they imagined) the ill luck that might befall her. I know I tell you most true; and I hope in such a subject as this, touching these superstitions, I shall not offend in acquainting you with these particulars.'[2]

And recently we heard:

'A. McC. of Co. Antrim was a shoemaker. He was visiting his father some time after he married, and he had his wife with him. And when they were passing this spot a hare "spooted" [rushed out] and run across the way they were going—this isn't such a long time ago, and 'tis all true, every word. What did A. McC. do? He whipped out his knife and lifted up her clothes and he split her shift from the shoulders down. The reason of that was: she was in the family-way, and if he hadn't done that, the child would be born with a "hare-scaart" [hare-lip]—a split in the lip.'[3]

Also:

---

[1] Sir Thomas Browne, *Pseudodoxia Epidemica*, London, 1928, Vol. 3, pp. 141–2.
[2] Quoted by Carew Hazlitt, op. cit., Vol. 1, p. 305.
[3] Anonymous, oral, unpublished.

'And it was down here he was living. He bought it from Tommy Lynch. £900 I think he paid to Tommy Lynch for the place, for the big house in Lent. And anyway this son, he got married to a lady. And this time anyway, there was a child to be born in it. And Old Johnnie Quinn went . . . he was walking somewhere and he met a fellow that had a hare. And he bought the hare. And be Gor, he brought in the hare and she came out of the room and looked at the hare and when this child was born, when he was born there was no arch to his mouth. There was no arch in his mouth. Now there was big bits out of his lip too. And if it is a thing that he knew, but he didn't know anything about it —to cut the hare's ear, going into the house—if he knew, don't you see, but he didn't know anything about it, if he cuts his ear with a knife she could be looking at him [the hare], there for a week. And he [her son] had a hare-lip and don't you see it was very hard to understand his talk. But they didn't go to such bother with doctors as now and don't you see; you couldn't understand his talk. That's how it happened. If the ear was cut and the hare going into the house, when Quinn's mother was carrying him, see, there'd be no harm.'[1]

But most folklore material connected with the hare, whether informed by sympathetic magic or not, appears to support its connection with an ancient religion: the worship of the Mother Goddess, the deity that Robert Graves has characterized as the White Goddess. The whole of the complex witch-connections of the hare can, in fact, be regarded from one angle as the vestiges of the worship of the White Goddess. Both the hare and the cat were sacred to her, and in the superstitions, which are the squandered legacy of the old religious beliefs, the hare and the cat have become the witches' familiars. We have confirmation of this link from an ancient pagan custom that survived in Britain into recent times. This is the enclosing of a sacrificial victim during the building of a new house. Primitive peoples have practised this up to the present day; and there can be little doubt that the animals that are usually sacrificed in the present ceremony are surrogates for human victims. It is recorded that when St. Columba was building

---

[1] Anonymous, oral, unpublished.

his church at Iona he asked his disciples which of them would submit to be buried in the foundations to propitiate the spirits of the soil who, apparently, demolished during the night that part of the structure they had built during the day. St. Oran stepped forward and he was buried under the church.

The remains of a cat have frequently been discovered in the footings of buildings and also—but less often—of the hare. Here, however, is one outstanding and strangely recent example of a hare-sacrifice.[1] It comes from Cornwall: 'About 1890, an addition was being made to a cottage near Falmouth. One day the work stopped; upon enquiry the builders revealed that a sacrifice would have to be made, to the "outside gods", of a virgin hare trapped by a virgin boy. Seeing that the building would never get finished otherwise, the sacrifice was agreed to, provided that no cruelty was involved. Some years afterwards, during repairs to the roof, the remains of a rabbit were found in a beautifully made coffin near the top of the wall.'

The rabbit evidently 'stood in' for the hare; but it is worth noting that it was buried nearer the roof than the foundations. Some sacrifices were made on the roof itself—rooftree sacrifices—and these were designed to propitiate the Goddess in her aspect of the huntress or wood-deity (Diana). An animal was slaughtered on the rooftree, and its blood allowed to run down; and—as has been pointed out[2]—the East German custom of the *Richtfest*, the tying of a garland to the roof, is undoubtedly a substitute for the sacrifice of a live cock or other animal in this way. The throwing of horse-bones on to the roof, also a German custom, and their inclusion in the structure of the building aimed at propitiating the Goddess in her form of Epona, *The Mare*.[3]

The hare, too, is connected with the Christian church; and this link could well have been forged deliberately, as part of the purposeful transference of many of the symbols and much of the content of the old pagan religion into a Christian context. For it is difficult to root out immemorial symbols because they are

---

[1] M. M. Howard, 'Dried Cats', *Man*, 1951, pp. 252 foll.
[2] Ibid.
[3] George Ewart Evans, *The Pattern Under the Plough*, p. 200.

buried so deeply in the unconscious of the race: indeed, the evidence we have of their having lasted for so many thousands of years argues that this would be impossible. The symbols are there without our being aware of them: our response to them is not voluntary; and the last thing we can do is to invent symbols that have an universal significance. But symbols can be transposed, reconsecrated, negotiating a difficult consent in an entirely different setting. Whether it was deliberate policy or not, the hare has assuredly been brought into the Christian dominion, and has come under the protection of at least two saints, one English and one Welsh, or to be more exact, Welsh-Irish.

In her collection of stories[1] written from the fourth to the end of the twelfth century, Helen Waddell included the story of St. Godric and the hare. The saint planted vegetables in his garden to feed the poor but a thief began to steal them. One day the saint came upon the thief in the garden. It was a hare. 'The saint caught it and struck it with his rod; and binding a bundle of vegetables on its shoulders sent it off with these words: "See to it that neither thyself nor any of thy acquaintance come to the place again; nor dare encroach on what was meant for the need of the poor." And so it befel.' Thereafter the hare, presumably in a state of grace, came under the saint's protection; and if a hare was caught in a snare the saint would release it; and if a hare was fleeing from the huntsman he would take it into his house and protect it until the hunt had gone away.

There is a district in Wales where hares are called *wyn bach Melangell* (Melangell's little lambs) to this day.[2] The phrase is a clue to an attractive legend of a very early saint: Monacella or Melangell. She became the patron saint of hares; and for centuries no one in her parish—Pennant Melangell in Montgomeryshire—would kill a hare. If by chance a hare was pursued by dogs, one had only to cry out: 'God and St. Monacella be with thee!' for the hare to escape from its pursuers. Melangell, according to one version of the legend, was a daughter of an Irish king. Her father had chosen a nobleman of the court for her husband: she refused him;

[1] *Beasts and Saints*, London, 1934, pp. 87–9.
[2] *Archaeologia Cambrensis*, Series 1, Vol. 3 (1848), pp. 137–42, 224–8.

fled the kingdom and settled in Powys in Wales. But one historian wrote:[1] 'Melangell, the daughter of Tudwal Tudglyd, of the
line of Macsen Wledig, was the foundress of Pennant Melangell,
Montgomeryshire. She was sister to Rhydderch Hael ap Stratt
Clyde; and her mother was Ethni, surnamed *Wyddeles* or the Irish-
woman. Festival May 27.'

The genealogy of the saint indicates the age of the legend; and
according to a seventeenth-century manuscript[2] the incident upon
which it was founded took place in A.D. 604: 'Brochwel Ysgythrog, Prince and Earl of Chester, dwelt at that time in Pengwern
Powys (Shrewsbury). One day the Prince was out hunting near
Pennant within the principality of Powys when his hounds put up
a hare. The hare took refuge in a nearby thicket of bramble; and
the Prince following his dogs into the thicket found a maiden of
great beauty, praying devoutly, her thoughts entirely on God; and
the hare was lying outstretched under the edge of her garment, its
face turned boldly and fearlessly towards the dogs. The Prince
shouted: "*Prendite, caniculi, prendite!*" [Seize her, little dogs, seize
her]. But the more he shouted and urged the dogs forward the
faster they retreated, howling, from the little creature. At last the
Prince addressed the maiden, and asked her how she had fled
from her native soil and had been guided to this spot. The Prince,
greatly impressed thereupon granted this part of her land for a
perpetual and inviolate sanctuary for any man or woman. Melangell lived for thirty-seven years in her retreat; and the wild hares
were about her like tame animals throughout the whole of her
life.'

The incident concerning the Prince, and Melangell and the
hare, was carved on a fifteenth-century rood-screen, a portion of
which forms a part of the west gallery of Pennant-Melangell
church. 'The fragments of the twelfth-century shrine of the saint
were extracted from the lychgate and south wall of the church in
1958, and have been incorporated in a reconstruction of the
shrine in the *Cell-y-bedd*, a structure attached to the east end of the
church. The churchyard has been used in the past for cock-fight-

---

[1] Professor Rees, *Welsh Saints*, p. 269.
[2] *Archaeologia Cambrensis*, ibid., pp. 139–40 (paraphrase of a Latin MS).

19. From the twelfth-century scrolls of frolicking animals, Kozanji,
Kyoto, said to be a religious satire by a buddhist monk. *Above:* hare
and frog wrestling, *below:* hare thrown by frog

20. Hare-headed divinity of Ancient Egypt. From the coffin of Bakenmut, divine father of Amum. Thebes, twenty-first dynasty *(British Museum)*

ing, as it was thought that the sacred precincts would protect the birds from spells which might be cast upon them by other owners.'[1]

Fig. 8.   The Tinners' Rabbits as they appear
on Widecombe church roof

The hare has also been consecrated by getting into the fabric of other churches. The area where this occurs most frequently is in the south-west of England; and it is in a very unusual form: three hares, having only three ears between them, are joined in a kind of animated Catherine-wheel. The device is carved on the roof bosses of several churches in and around Dartmoor.[2] It is called *The Tinners' Rabbits*, although the long ears in the device obviously intended them to be taken for hares. The device was the emblem or craft-sign of the tinners whose mining of tin on Dartmoor was the source of the wealth that built many of these churches. This is another instance of a pre-Christian symbol being adopted by the church; for we know from some of the other craft guilds—the Saddlers, the Hammermen, the Society of the Horseman's Word, in Scotland, and the masons' guild, as taken over by

[1] David Verey, *Mid Wales* (Shell Guide), London, 1960, p. 77.
[2] Ruth St. Leger-Gordon, *The Witchcraft and Folklore of Dartmoor*, London, 1965, pp. 45–6.

the Freemasons[1]—that their ritual and signs have their origins in the ancient religion of the Mother Goddess. And although the hare is again masquerading as a rabbit, we should not be surprised: as a rabbit he would be divested of his sinister overtones, purposefully invested on him as a symbol of a discredited religion, and would cause no offence under the name, at least, of the harmless rabbit: it is probable also that for this reason the *Easter Hare*, a classic fertility symbol, is sometimes dressed up as the *Easter Bunny*. The Tinners' Rabbits also appear on the other side of England, in a window in Long Melford church in Suffolk. It is called the *Rabbit Window*; but here, just as clearly as in the carving on Widecombe church roof, the rabbits are lusty hares.

To illustrate the age of this sinister light in which the hare was regarded we are including two stories from Wales, each taken from either end of an historical period or span of fourteen or fifteen centuries. The earlier one is the first known reference in Welsh literature and folklore to a hare transformation. It comes from the Taliesin tale in the collection of old Welsh myths and legends, *Y Mabinogi*. A prince called Tegid Foel and his wife Ceridwen had a son called Morfran. Although his sister Creirwy was the fairest maiden in the kingdom, Morfran had the reputation of being the ugliest creature ever born. He had—so a Welsh Triad recorded—remained unhurt in the battle of Camlan:[2] 'No one dare attack him because they thought he was a devil that had come to help the other side. His skin was covered with hair like a stag's.' His mother decided to remedy this by transforming him through her magic arts: even if he were the ugliest man in the world, he could still be made acceptable if he became the wisest. She decided to boil the Cauldron of Inspiration on her son's behalf. It had to boil continuously for a year and a day. By that time the three blessed drops of Inspiration would have been distilled from the various plants and substances that Ceridwen fed into it. She put Gwion Back to stir the cauldron, and a blind man, Morda, to keep the fire going under it. She charged them to keep the cauldron boiling continuously. Unfortunately, just before the end of the year the

[1] George Ewart Evans, *The Pattern Under the Plough*, Chapter 23.
[2] Professor Ifor Williams, *Chwedl Taliesin*, University of Wales Press, Cardiff, 1957.

three vital drops of the elixir flew out of the cauldron and alighted on the finger of the diminutive Gwion. They were, of course, hot; and instinctively he put his finger into his mouth. Immediately, he had knowledge of everything that was to come; and instantly he knew that his chief worry would be to escape the anger of the frustrated Ceridwen. She came after him without delay; and he saw her and changed himself into a hare. But she changed herself into a greyhound and headed him off from his course. He ran towards the river and changed into a fish: she took the form of an otter-bitch; and so on. . . . Gwion's transformations were many before he escaped from Ceridwen; but it is significant that the hare was the first of his changes.'

The second story illustrates how the hare has the habit of turning up in a 'magical' setting; it also demonstrates how an ancient and widely diffused myth can attach itself to an historical figure. Guto Morgan (1700–37) of the parish of Llanwynno in Glamorgan was called Guto Nythbrân (Guto of Crow's Nest) from the farm on the hills where he was born and brought up. He had a great reputation as a long distance runner; and some of his contests and feats are recorded. But since his day he has become the focus of legends. The hare story is one of them: it is recorded in a nineteenth-century history of the parish:[1]

'There is a story and a tradition that he was once asked by his father to gather up the sheep on the mountain and bring them down to the yard at Nythbrân.

"Go," said his father, "and take the dogs with you, and bring the sheep down as quickly as you can."

'Guto answered:

"Keep the dogs here. I'll do better without them," and away he went. He brought the flock into the yard in a very short time, without aid of man or dog.

"Did you have any trouble with the sheep, Guto?" asked the old man.

"No," said Guto, "except with that reddish-grey one over there, but I caught her and broke her leg."

[1] Glanffrwd, *Hanes Plwyf Llanwynno* (History of the Parish of Llanwynno), 1888; translated by Thomas Evans, Merthyr Tudful, 1950, p. 91.

"Listen, boy," said the father, "that's a hare! What on earth are you thinking of? Where did you find her?"

'Guto replied:

"She rose from the ferns on Llwyncelyn mountain, and before she reached the Hafod I caught her, and then she had a nap with the flock." '

This is almost identical with the Manx legend of the *feno-dyree* or brownie who once felt well-disposed towards a certain farmer:

'. . . and once upon a time he undertook to bring down for the farmer his wethers from Snaefell. When the feno-dyree had safely put them in an outhouse, he said that he had trouble with a little ram, as it had run three times round Snaefell that morning. The farmer did not quite understand him, but on going to look at the sheep, he found to his surprise that the little ram was no other than a hare, which, poor creature, was dying of fright and fatigue.'

Sir John Rhys, who recorded the above,[1] pointed out how similar it is to the story of Peredur in the *Mabinogi*. Peredur was brought up in unfrequented places:

'And the youth went daily to divert himself in the forest, by flinging sticks and staves. And one day he saw his mother's flock of goats, and near the goats two hinds were standing. And he marvelled greatly that these two should be without horns while the others had them. And he thought they had long run wild, and on that account they had lost their horns. And by activity and swiftness of foot, he drove the hinds and the goats together into the house which there was for the goats at the extremity of the forest. Then Peredur returned to his mother:

"Ah, Mother," said he, "a marvellous thing have I seen in the wood: two of thy goats have run wild and lost their horns, through their having been so long missing in the wood. And no man had ever more trouble than I had to drive them in."

'And they all arose and went to see. And when they beheld the hinds they were greatly astonished.'[2]

It is worth comparing the hare-deer variant in the above myth

[1] *Celtic Folklore*, Oxford, 1901; Vol. 1, pp. 286-7.
[2] *The Mabinogion*, London, 1906, pp. 126-7.

with the old Irish belief, already mentioned (p. 210), of the close link between the hare and the deer.

But this theme or story-motif has a much wider spread than Celtic Britain. It is also to be found in the *Saga of Sassoun*,[1] the Armenian folk-epic, where David—son of Mehair the Great— once herded the town's cattle. On their straying off during the course of the day, he went after them over hill and through forest and rounded them up; and all the wild animals—wolves, bears, lions and tigers—with them! And he brought them home much to the townspeople's dismay.

Another facet of hare folklore is noticeable particularly in the Celtic countries—the *tall story*. There is a common type of story both in Ireland (see pp. 138 foll.) and Wales; and it is not told in an attempt to hoodwink the listener or to induce him to believe in the literal truth of the story. It is more of a story told to show the ingenuity and range of subject of an inveterate story-teller whose ancestors in their day might well have been professionals. It may be said in passing that it is probably a misunderstanding of this type of story that has persuaded the more literal-minded Anglo-Saxons that many, if not all, Celts are liars!

In Wales these tales are known as *storiäu celwydd goleu* (stories based on white lies). The Welsh Folk Museum at St. Fagans, Cardiff, has a collection of them recorded in recent years. Here are two of them about the hare. They are told by Robert Williams, Uwchmynydd, Caernarvonshire, a noted white-lie expert:

'A man was making for Cwtrhian chasing a hare: and it went down a narrow little lane. And who was coming towards them but an old woman. She took up the hem of her apron and the old hare jumped into it. That man was looking for the hare all the day long after this. But the old lady had taken it home to eat it.'

'A man was setting a net at Brychestyn mountain to catch a hare. But this old hare hit his brother right in the chest so that he lay there almost dead—lying still for hours, perfectly still. He couldn't move after the old hare hit him.'

In Glamorgan Howell Jeffreys told us a tall story about a hare, with a theme that is quite widespread:

[1] Mischa Kudian, *The Saga of Sassoun*, London, 1970.

[T] 'I've heard old poachers bragging and making the thing amusing—about putting a bill-hook where the hare was running out. And the hare was split in two. But so was his dog!'

In Pembrokeshire[1] they went one better. A greyhound was split in two by running on to a scythe-blade. Its skilful owner rejoined it; but he made the mistake of putting the two halves together the wrong way round. It turned out, however, to be the finest greyhound in the district for coursing hares: it could see both in front and behind! Another greyhound in Anglesey ran at such a fantastic speed after two hares that he cut a heavy gate clean in two. Not far away from this—in Caernarvonshire—there were two fantastic hares. One of them doubled back and ran right through the body of a greyhound; the other had his four legs cut off but still kept running.[2]

An interesting commentary on the above story about the hunter's brother being laid out by a running hare comes from the Norfolk farmer, Albert Hupton. This confirms that a hare running at full speed, and more-or-less 'blind' with its eyes concentrated on the following dog so that its front vision is momentarily masked, can in fact do some damage by the force of its impact:

[T] 'It happened at Bloomfield. My uncle was a-walking on the path, and his dog put up a hare. And the hare came down the footpath, the dog behind it. And the hare hit my uncle, went right into his legs and knocked him clean over; and he laid there!'

Percy Muttit, the Suffolk gamekeeper, also knows from his own experience, as we have seen (pp. 51–2) that a running hare can strike a man with considerable force.

Another tall story comes from Arthur Harmer, the Norfolk farmer:

'A boy had to take a live hare in a hamper and deliver it at a certain house at Christmas time. About half-way on his journey he put the hamper down to have a rest. Being curious he lifted the lid a little to see how the hare was getting on. The hare saw its

---

[1] Welsh Folk Museum. Tapes 2586 and 2606.
[2] Antti Aarne and Stith Thompson, *The Types of Folktale*, 1089L: 'Lie, the Split Dog'.

chance and was away in one bound. The boy followed him a short distance across the field, but he soon gave up.

"Never mind," he say, "you don't want to worry. I got your address right here!" '

As well as its place in story the hare is a figure in the proverbs and sayings of many lands. Here are some from Ireland:

> *It is easier to catch a sleeping hare than two awake.*
> *'Wait a while till you marry a woman,' as the man said to the hare.*
> *The weariness of my heart on the hares and the young women who won't be satisfied.*
> *A hare or a clump of ferns* (for two things that are indistinguishable).
> *A blind man can find his mouth but it's not everyday he catches a hare.*
> *It's hard to put a grain of salt on a hare's tail.*
> *A blind man often caught a hare.*
> *Rabbit meat and hare soup* (see p. 99).
> *Every second year the hare is male and female* (cf. old Welsh laws referred to on p. 25).

From Wales:

> *When there are plenty of hares the woodcock has a chance.* (*Ysgyfarnog ymhob lle, cyffylog mewn cyfle.*) Presumably, the hares engage all the hunters' attention.
> *The hare is on her form.* (*Mae'r ysgyfarnog ar ei gŵal.*)
> *A hare is a hare.* (*Sgwarnog yw sgwarnog.*)
> *Witch* [misfortune] *in the morning. Success in the afternoon.*
> (*Witch yn y bore, Llwyddes brydnawn.*)
> (A proverb from the Rhondda valley about meeting a hare.)[1]

From China:

> *When the hare dies the fox mourns.*
> (There but for the grace of God. . . .)
> *When the hare rises the falcon swoops.*
> (To describe rapidity of action.)

[1] W.F.M. MS 95.

Hare horns, tortoise hairs.
(Impossible or very rare.)
Watch the tree and await the hare.
(An injunction to those in difficulty not to wait for luck to change but to do something to improve their situation.)[1]

Don't loose the falcon until you see the hare.
William Barnes in his *Glossary of the Dorset Dialect*[2] includes a phrase, *hic a'ter hock*, or *hicker to hacker*. His note to this is of interest. 'The pursued seemingly pursuing the pursuer. If a dog were running round in a broad ring after a hare, and the hare were farther than half of the ring before the dog, he would seem to be the catcher. A man, telling of seeing such a case of hounds and hare, said: "There they went hicker to hacker all auver; John's hounds avore and the heare a'ter." '
Some English proverbs are:

Hold with the hare and run with the hounds.
Mad as a marsh hare.

(Erasmus, the sixteenth-century scholar observed: 'Hares as wilder in the marshes because of the absence of hedges and cover.')

To kiss the harefoot.
(To be late for anything, to be a day after the fair. The hare has gone by and left its footprint for you to salute.)

He that will have a hare for breakfast must hunt overnight.
Who hunteth two hares loses the one and leaveth the other.
God send you readier meat than running hares.
Men mytten as well haue huntyd an hare with a tabre.

(A tabor or tabour is a small drum. There are numerous later versions of this old saying. All refer to the impossible.)[3]
And a quotation from Shakespeare:[4]

[1] Personal communication: J. H. C. Gerson.
[2] Reprint, 1970, Guernsey, p. 71.
[3] E. C. Brewer, *Dictionary of Phrase and Fable*, London, 1904; and Burton Stevenson, *Book of Proverbs*.
[4] *Henry IV*, I, i, 3.

Other Beliefs and Customs

O! the blood more stirs
To rouse a lion than to start a hare

has at least a proverbial quality if not actually itself a proverb. But it is likely that the nineteenth-century German author, Heinrich Hoffman, was quoting a proverb or common saying when he wrote:[1]

'*Help! Fire! Help! The Hare! The Hare!*'

because, as we have seen, the identification of the hare with fire was world-wide.

Linked with the proverbs and sayings are the occasions when the hare enters ritually, as it were, into the games and language of children:

'*If you see a white hare you are unlucky, but if you see a black hare you will have luck.*'[2]

Hares are sometimes mentioned in the *spell* or *charm* children repeat for luck at the first day of the month. A Claydon (Suffolk) woman told us she used to say *Hares, Hares* before going to bed on the last day of the month, and *Rabbits, Rabbits*, when she got up in the morning. But this is a very common custom. The connection of the hare with the moon and therefore with the monthly cycle needs no further comment; nor does the *hare-and-hounds* game played by children.

A game children play all over the world of flashing reflected sunlight from a piece of glass or broken mirror is called in Russia *zaichiki*, little hares. The children sit together and hold the pieces of glass towards the sun, then direct the beam of reflected light into each other's faces. Because the beams move from place to place so quickly, they are called 'little hares'. In similar senses the Russian word for hare is used for 'white horses', the foaming crests of waves, for the foam on beer and the flickering flames of a fire.

One further aspect of hare folklore which we should mention is

[1] *The Man Who Went Out Shooting.*
[2] Iona and Peter Opie, *The Language and Lore of Children*, Oxford, 1959, pp. 215, 300.

the use of the hare's paw or foot as a charm. We have mentioned
the hare's foot nailed to an outhouse in a rural part of Glamorgan,
in exactly the same way as a horseshoe is nailed, and for the same
reason. It was also carried in the pocket for the same purpose, 'for
luck' or to save a man from being touched by 'ill-luck'. In
America card-players carried a rabbit's (hare's) foot in their
pocket; and dice-players often muttered *rabbit's foot, rabbit's foot*
before they threw. Here is an account by Harold Jenner, the
Suffolk naturalist:

[T] 'Oh, there are charms in this part of the world. My old
poaching pal, old Billy, he always carried a hare's foot in his
pocket. He was a countryman, a poacher. He was a professional
poacher: he never did anything else. Always a hare's foot. He gave
me one: "You keep that, boy, and you'll be all right." When I
came down to see him, just before I went off into the Navy at the
outbreak of war; came to say *Cheerio* to him (it was the last time I
saw him because he died while I was away), he say: "Boy, got
you hare's foot?" I said, "Yes, I have."

'I used to carry it and show it to him to keep him happy. I'm
completely without any superstition whatever. I used to carry it
to please the old boy. He'd say:

' "Boy! you carry that and you'll come out of this lot all right!"
And I carried it, and came out all right. But I don't associate it
with the hare's foot at all. But this pleased the old boy, and this
was the hare's foot he gave me:

' "Here you are, boy! Now I've given you that, that'll keep you
all right. That's good luck, that is. You keep hold o' that!" And
I did. But that's all there was to it. I don't believe in the superstition.'

A hare's foot was also kept in the pocket for another reason: as
a cure for bodily ailments. Pepys the diarist carried one:[1]

'Dec. 31st, 1664: So ends the old yeare, I bless God, with great
joy to me, and not only from my having made so good a yeare of
profit . . . but I bless God I have never been in so good plight as
to my health in so very cold weather as this is, nor indeed in any

---

[1] *Diary of Samuel Pepys*, ed. Henry B. Wheatley, London, 1904, Vol. IV, pp. 298
314-15.

hot weather, these ten years, as I am at this day. . . . But I am at a great losse to know whether it be my hare's foote, or taking every morning a pill of turpentine, or my having left off the wearing of a gowne.'

But before he had got half-way through the following month Pepys had a bad attack of the colic against which the hare's foot was thought to be an effective charm. Two entries in the diary will tell the story:

'Jan. 19th, 1664–65: *Memorandum*. This day and yesterday, I think it is the change of the weather, I have a great deal of pain, but nothing like I used to have. I can hardly keep myself loose, but on the contrary am forced to drive away my pain.

'Jan. 20th, 1664–65: So homeward, in my way buying a hare and taking it home, which upon my discourse today with Mr. Batten in Westminster Hall, who showed me my mistake that my hare's foote hath not the joynt to it; and assures me he never had his cholique since he carried it about him: and it is a strange thing how fancy works, for I no sooner almost handled his foote but my belly began to be loose and to break wind, and whereas I was in some pain yesterday and tother [sic] day and in fear of more today, I became very well, and so continue.'

Certain tradesmen and craftsmen, however, used the hare's foot for severely practical reasons. Goldsmiths[1] in Germany used it for carefully sweeping up the gold dust that was left on the bench after they had been working. A dentist's son[2] remembers that his father used a hare's foot in his workshop for sprinkling French chalk during the making of artificial dentures. A Norfolk woman still uses a hare's foot for removing dust from any difficult corner of a piece of furniture or a room. In effect, the foot is used as a brush which is exactly one of the uses the hare himself made of it on occasion, as the poet Cowper noted while observing his own pet hares (see Appendix One, p. 247).

Mention of the hare's foot brings to mind an observation gathered from two countrymen in the midlands of Ireland. One said: 'Sometimes the hare, when being chased, will lift one leg

[1] Dr. Berthold Wolpe, Royal College of Art.
[2] Dr. J. C. B. Bone, Brooke, Norfolk.

and run on three. This is to decoy the hunters away from the leverets.'

The other:

'It does it to limber itself up and make itself more supple. It would be a good dog that would catch that one. It is the hind leg, right or left, she lifts under the body. And she goes on three legs for about fifty yards.'

We are satisfied that this is a sound, factual observation; but there is a folklore aspect to it as well. A writer on Manx folklore stated:[1] 'Three-legged hares of sinister potency, as known in Wales, Lincolnshire, Scandinavia and Teutonic countries, ought to have been expected to thrive on Manx soil; but if they do, they have eluded me hitherto.'

A coda to this chapter comes from Suffolk. George Garrard, born in 1891 at Stowupland, recalls that a Highland regiment was stationed nearby during the First World War. A few days after they arrived the regiment paraded complete with bagpipes. All the hares in the district immediately took to their heels; and not one was to be seen in the vicinity during the period the regiment remained there.

---

[1] W. Walter Gill, *A Second Manx Scrapbook*, London, 1932, p. 274.

17

And Now Good Day to You, Sir Hare

At the beginning of this book we suggested that the hare had not been studied enough; and at the end of our search, after listening to dozens of experts, it still appears that owing to its shyness and lonely habits and, at times, its inaccessibility it has not been sufficiently and precisely observed in its natural setting. What the hare deserves is the kind of understanding Barrett-Hamilton showed in his section on the hare in *A History of British Mammals*;[1] or the skill and imagination Julian Huxley brought to the observation and documenting of the great-crested grebe.[2] There is still many a gap in our catalogue of the hare's behaviour; and filling in each of them would not be an easy undertaking. Yet it might be possible, after the various kinds of hares had been observed systematically over a long period, to clear up the contradictions and ambiguities that still exist in the various interpretations of its behaviour.

But perhaps the most striking aspect of Huxley's study of the grebe is not his findings but that a full documentation of the behaviour of these birds had to wait until half a century ago. But this is perhaps understandable. People like Gilbert White were rare; and until this century, in any case, most naturalists were wide-ranging in their observations, seldom concentrating on one particular bird or creature. Moreover, it probably needs someone with a scientific training, someone with the necessary objectivity,

[1] 'This was perhaps the first really systematic study, plus natural-history reportage, plus traditional lore modern view of the subject.' Ivor Montagu, *The Youngest Son*, London, 1970, p. 335.
[2] Julian Huxley, *The Courtship Habits of the Great Crested Grebe*, London, 1968 (reprinted from *Proceedings of Zoological Society*, 1914).

attention to detail, a single-minded persistence, and—most of all—
the time to carry through the exacting task of concentrating on
one animal. Traditional observation has not been evidence of a
sufficiently full kind simply because there was not enough of it and
by its very nature it was sporadic: neither the gamekeeper nor the
ordinary countryman had the leisure or the incentive to make a
detailed observation, over a long period, of any one animal, much
less of such a difficult creature as the hare. A great deal of field
work has been done by professional scientists on the distribution,
fluctuation in numbers, feeding habits and so on of wild hares,
but, as we said before, the most startling scientific discoveries—
the moulting process, resorption of the embryo, superfoetation—
have been made by post-mortem examination. Observing the hare
in captivity may appear an answer to many of the questions we
posed; but though this may seem an obvious way out it could not
be a completely satisfactory answer and would certainly be no
adequate substitute for the devoted observation that many people
—amateurs and professionals—give to birds. For a hare in captivity,
as we learn from Cowper's account (Appendix One) and other
writings on this subject, is an entirely different animal from the
hare in the wild state. A hare in a cage or hutch, or even about the
house, is like a fish in a tank, a man-trapped specimen rather than
the creature it was proposed to study in the round, that is, in its
natural habitat and in its social context in myth, story and superstition. For there is a close link between observation and myth and
popular beliefs—observation that in the past has been both precise
and faulty, and the direct cause of long-standing 'superstitions'
which we would prefer to call wrong beliefs, reserving *superstitions*, as we have already stated, for those remnants of belief that
survive from a former religion.

It was not long ago that many people, the countryman among
them, believed that swallows hibernated in the mud at the bottom
of ponds. They thought this because it seemed to them the only
possible explanation for the sudden disappearance of these birds.
There they were on an autumn day flying low, skimming over
ponds, broads and rivers; and the next day they were gone.
Similarly, we heard a hill-farmer in Wales less than fifty years ago,

saying (and believing) that the cuckoo at the end of summer changes into a magpie. How else could we explain its disappearance? It was inconceivable to the farmer that a bird could fly hundreds of miles over the sea to a different climate.

But faulty and insufficient observation by no means explains all the old beliefs about the hare. The remark of one of our Irish informants is to the point here: '*Still*', he said, 'isn't it funny that superstition is there from old time and cannot be knocked down!' Even fragmentary superstition is much more than inaccurate perception. Beliefs about the hare go very deep, and we must beware of euhemerizing and taking reason further than it can justifiably go, even when we are discussing superstition; how much more so when we are dealing with myth. For although some of the myths can be partially explained by pointing to their origin in the hare's natural behaviour—as we tried to do in the moon- and fire-myths —it would be wrong to push this much further than the myth's periphery. And for this reason: myth is not concerned primarily with the manifest subject—the hare, in our study—but with man himself. He is the real subject of myth, and animals play chiefly an interpretative role, being as it were mirrors wherein he sees his own appetites, his own moods, his own virtues and his own vices. Myths, in other words, were man's first 'scientific language'. With myths he chronicled his internal and external history—the history of his own mind or soul as well of his society. And just as in dreams we are given visual data-images that only later can be translated into words, so in myth we construct, or are given, certain images about ourselves that only later can be rationalized into a rounded narrative; and only then when we make use of *imagination*, the very process we started with—admittedly, however, for a now different and more conscious purpose.

The hare was one of these original image-nuclei or archetypes used by man before he developed his reasoning power, his latest acquired instrument of knowing and understanding. Many of these images have lost their force because we have found out how that part of reality for which they stood *works*: we have reasoned it out, and many of the former images and symbols have become obsolete. Yet the old form of thinking has not been entirely superseded, if only because we have not yet *reasoned out* every-thing, and many of our most vital intuitions are not capable of being put into words: we have to find a symbol for them because although we *know* them intuitively we do not yet know them in the commonly accepted meaning of the word. We can hardly ver-balize this kind of knowledge, much less give a reasoned account of it; and where we cannot make a clear-cut distinctive formula-tion we have to fall back on mythical images, poetical intimations, call them by whatever name we will.

A Welsh farmer made a remark that in one sense is a kind of final comment on this attempt to get to the bottom of the strange-ness that is about the hare:

'A hare, as someone has said, is a hare.'

Over a period of five years we have been interested in the hare, first in the stories and myths about it and then with its natural habits. But we have not been able to hold the creature completely. It has always been able to turn suddenly, to execute its *mazes*, to accelerate or swerve out of the neat grid of classification, to dis-appear through an opening, its *smile* or *meuse*, that the classifier has neither noticed nor suspected. Just as so often happens in the field, the hare still escapes if it is given the slenderest chance to reach a larger environment. We are not, for instance, sure that we have fully explained its apparently suicidal attraction to aero-dromes: nor for that matter can we really determine even now whether the hare is by nature a bold or timid creature.

But how do people in general regard the hare today? Few in our present, urban-dominated culture in these islands will now openly link it with the supernatural. Within the last two genera-tions the temper of belief, even in the rural areas, has changed more than it has in the last two thousand years. An observation like this is already a truism. But it does remind us that both myth and religious beliefs existed more-or-less intact for centuries in the old country communities; and belief remained unchanged pre-cisely because the material conditions that were its matrix were themselves comparatively static. But during this century, these historic communities have also been brought into the orbit of

21. Graffito from Lacock Abbey, Wiltshire

22. Graffito from Cathedral and Abbey Church of St. Alban

23. The stag of the cabbages, the cropper of herbage (from Hoffman's *Atlas*, 'The Common Hare')

24. Where Scottish mountain hares are plentiful their footprints often make criss-cross patterns in the snow. The tracks leading vertically out of the picture were made by two hares loping slowly in that direction. *(See pp 217–18)*

industrial change that had reached the town very much earlier; and the country beliefs soon lost those invisible moorings that tied them firmly to the ancient processes and customs.

Today, most of the primitive communities even in New Guinea, one of the most undeveloped areas of the world and up to now the anthropologists' paradise, have been drawn into the present rapid changes. Soon there will be few 'copy-book' areas left in the world to study the beliefs and customs that demonstrate the historical understructure of much of modern man's thinking. We are fortunate, therefore, to have been able to gather here, in the four countries, a little evidence of the old mythology from those survivors of the former culture.

Yet, although there will be few left who believe in the myths about the hare, our wonder at its curious behaviour will still remain. And as long as we ourselves possess some of the hare's apparent attributes—its unpredictableness, its occasional jumping right over the head of reason, its sharpness, its seasonal abandon, and its frequent stupidity—the myth of the hare will not be entirely dead. The hare will always be at hand for us to externalize some of these qualities, both good and bad, either in the stories we make for our children or in dreams, those intricate stories we make—or which are made—for ourselves. It was a conviction of the value and permanence of myth that set us off to record this material about the hare. What we have tried to do is not simply to go in pursuit of the merely curious, but to suggest that the study of old beliefs is not only of historical interest but of direct value to the culture and changes of our time.

Appendix One

Tame Hares

A vivid description of hares in captivity was written by the poet William Cowper during one of his long periods of sanity. The pets had been given him ten years earlier, a few months after he had tried to hang himself for the second time. He had been able at last to do odd jobs about the garden for some weeks. 'Yesterday, as he was feeding the chickens,' wrote a friend, 'some incident made him smile. I am pretty sure it is the first smile that has been seen on his face for sixteen months.'[1]

He seems to have chosen his first leveret out of kindness, to rescue it from the children it belonged to. But in those days, as now, hares were unusual pets. There must have been many more rabbits, puppies, kittens to choose from. We never read of adult hares as pets in ordinary households. They die or escape within the first few months. In the eighteenth century they were the 'companions and servants of witches',[2] of people who were often spoken of as mad and who, like Cowper during his bouts of madness, kept away from society. It was chance perhaps, but perhaps not, that he who had spent so long in Dr. Cotton's Home for Madmen at St. Alban's kept hares as his favourite pets for nearly twelve years.

William Cowper's form of madness would now be called 'manic-depression'. Part of its modern cure is 'occupational therapy'. The hares became companions. His love of them, and the practical work it demanded of him, is said to have hastened his recovery.

[1] John Newton, quoted by David Cecil in *The Stricken Deer* (Fontana Library), London, 1965, p. 146.
[2] Barrett-Hamilton, op. cit.

IN the year 1774, being much indisposed both in mind and body, incapable of diverting myself either with company or books, and yet in a condition that made some diversion necessary, I was glad of any thing that would engage my attention, without fatiguing it. The children of a neighbour of mine had a leveret given them for a plaything; it was at that time about three months old. Understanding better how to tease the poor creature than to feed it, and soon becoming weary of their charge, they readily consented that their father, who saw it pining and growing leaner every day, should offer it to my acceptance. I was willing enough to take the prisoner under my protection, perceiving that, in the management of such an animal, and in the attempt to tame it, I should find just that sort of employment which my case required. It was soon known among the neighbours that I was pleased with the present, and the consequence was, that in a short time I had as many leverets offered to me as would have stocked a paddock. I undertook the care of three, which it is necessary that I should here distinguish by the names I gave them—Puss, Tiney, and Bess. Notwithstanding the two feminine appellatives, I must inform you, that they were all males. Immediately commencing carpenter, I built them houses to sleep in; each had a separate apartment, so contrived that their ordure would pass through the bottom of it; an earthen pan placed under each received whatsoever fell which being duly emptied and washed, they were thus kept perfectly sweet and clean. In the daytime they had the range of a hall, and at night retired each to his own bed, never intruding into that of another.

'Puss grew presently familiar, would leap into my lap, raise himself upon his hinder feet, and bite the hair from my temples. He would suffer me to take him up, and to carry him about in my arms, and has more than once fallen fast asleep upon my knee. He was ill three days, during which time I nursed him, kept him apart from his fellows, that they might not molest him, (for, like many other wild animals, they persecute one of their own species that is sick), and by constant care, and trying him with a variety of herbs, restored him to perfect health. No creature could be more grateful than my patient after his recovery; a sentiment which he most significantly expressed by licking my hand, first the back of it, then the palm, then every finger separately, then between all the fingers, as if anxious to leave no part of it unsaluted; a ceremony which he never performed but once again upon a similar occasion. Finding him extremely tractable, I made it my custom to carry him always after breakfast into the garden, where he hid himself generally under the leaves of a cucumber vine, sleeping or chewing the cud[1] till evening; in the leaves also of that vine he found a favourite repast. I had not long habituated him to this taste of liberty, before he began to be impatient for the return of the time when he might enjoy it. He would invite me to the garden by drumming upon my knee, and by a look of such expression, as it was not possible to misinterpret. If this rhetoric did not immediately succeed, he would take the skirt of my coat between his teeth, and pull it with all his force. Thus Puss might be said to be perfectly tamed, the shyness of his nature was done away, and on the whole it was visible by many symptoms, which I have not room to enumerate, that he was happier in human society than when shut up with his natural companions.

'Not so Tiney; upon him the kindest treatment had not the least effect. He too was sick, and in his sickness had an equal share of my attention; but if after his recovery I took the liberty to stroke him, he would grunt, strike with his fore feet, spring forward, and bite. He was however very entertaining in his way; even his surliness was a matter of mirth, and in his play he preserved such an air of gravity, and performed his feats with such a solemnity of manner, that in him too I had an agreeable companion.

'Bess, who died soon after he was full grown, and whose death was occasioned by his being turned into his box, which had been washed, while it was yet damp, was a hare of great humour and

---

[1] On hares 'chewing the cud', see p. 26.

drollery. Puss was tamed by gentle usage; Tiney was not to be tamed at all; and Bess had a courage and confidence that made him tame from the beginning. I always admitted them into the parlour after supper, when the carpet affording their feet a firm hold, they would frisk, and bound, and play a thousand gambols, in which Bess, being remarkably strong and fearless, was always superior to the rest, and proved himself the Vestris of the party. One evening the cat, being in the room, had the hardiness to pat Bess upon the cheek, an indignity which he resented by drumming upon her back with such violence that the cat was happy to escape from under his paws, and hide herself.

'I describe these animals as having each a character of his own. Such they were in fact, and their countenances were so expressive of that character, that, when I looked only on the face of either, I immediately knew which it was. It is said that a shepherd, however numerous his flock, soon becomes so familiar with their features, that he can, by that indication only, distinguish each from all the rest; and yet, to a common observer, the difference is hardly perceptible. I doubt not that the same discrimination in the cast of countenances would be discoverable in hares, and am persuaded that among a thousand of them no two could be found exactly similar; a circumstance little suspected by those who have not had opportunity to observe it. These creatures have a singular sagacity in discovering the minutest alteration that is made in the place to which they are accustomed, and instantly apply their nose to the examination of a new object. A small hole being burnt in the carpet, it was mended with a patch, and that patch in a moment underwent the strictest scrutiny. They seem too to be very much directed by the smell in the choice of their favourites: to some persons, though they saw them daily, they could never be reconciled, and would even scream when they attempted to touch them; but a miller coming in engaged their affections at once; his powdered coat had charms that were irresistible. It is no wonder that my intimate acquaintance with these specimens of the kind has taught me to hold the sportsman's amusement in abhorrence; he little knows what amiable creatures he persecutes, of what gratitude they are capable, how cheerful they are in their spirits, what enjoyment they have of life, and that, impressed as they seem with a peculiar dread of man, it is only because man gives them peculiar cause for it.

'That I may not be tedious, I will just give a short summary of those articles of diet that suit them best.

'I take it to be a general opinion that they graze, but it is an erroneous one, at least grass is not their staple; they seem rather to use it medicinally, soon quitting it for leaves of almost any kind. Sowthistle, dandelion, and lettuce, are their favourite vegetables, especially the last. I discovered by accident that fine white sand is in great estimation with them; I suppose as a digestive. It happened, that I was cleaning a birdcage when the hares were with me; I placed a pot filled with such sand upon the floor, which being at once directed to by a strong instinct, they devoured voraciously; since that time I have generally taken care to see them well supplied with it. They account green corn a delicacy, both blade and stalk, but the ear they seldom eat: straw of any kind, especially wheat-straw, is another of their dainties; they will feed greedily upon oats, but if furnished with clean straw never want them; it serves them also for a bed, and, if shaken up daily, will be kept sweet and dry for a considerable time. They do not indeed require aromatic herbs, but will eat a small quantity of them with great relish, and are particularly fond of the plant called musk; they seem to resemble sheep in this, that, if their pasture be too succulent, they are very subject to the rot; to prevent which, I always made bread their principal nourishment, and, filling a pan with it cut into small squares, placed it every evening in their chambers, for they feed only at evening and in the night; during the winter, when vegetables were not to be got, I mingled this mess of bread with shreds of carrot, adding to it the rind of apples cut extremely thin; for, though they are fond of the paring, the apple itself disgusts them. These however not being a sufficient substitute for the juice of summer herbs, they must at this time be supplied with water; but so placed, that they cannot overset it into their beds. I must not omit, that occasionally they are much pleased with twigs of hawthorn, and of the common brier, eating even the very wood when it is of considerable thickness.

'Bess, I have said, died young; Tiney lived to be nine years old, and died at last, I have reason to think, of some hurt in his loins by a fall; Puss is still living, and has just completed his tenth year, discovering no signs of decay, nor even of age, except that he has grown more discreet and less frolicsome than he was. I cannot conclude without observing, that I have lately introduced a dog to his acquaintance, a spaniel that had never seen a hare to a hare that had never seen a spaniel. I did it with great caution, but there was no real need of it. Puss discovered no token of fear, nor Marquis the least symptom of hostility. There is therefore, it should seem, no natural antipathy between dog and hare, but the pursuit of the one occasions the flight of the other, and the dog pursues because he is trained to it; they eat bread at the same time out of the same hand, and are in all respects sociable and friendly.

'I should not do complete justice to my subject, did I not add, that they have no ill scent belonging to them, that they are in-defatigably nice in keeping themselves clean, for which purpose nature has furnished them with a brush under each foot: and that they are never infested by any vermin.

May 28, 1784.

'MEMORANDUM FOUND AMONG MR. COWPER'S PAPERS.

Tuesday, March 9, 1786.

THIS day died poor Puss, aged eleven years eleven months. He died between twelve and one at noon, of mere old age, and apparently without pain.'

Appendix Two

An Early Poem About the Hare[1]

By a forest as I gan fare,
  Walking all myself alone,
I heard a mourning of a hare,
  Ruefully she made her moan.
'Dearworth God! how shall I live,
  And lead my life in land?
From dale to down I am ydrive!
  I not where I may sit, or stand!
I may neither rest, nor sleep,
  By no valley that is so derne;
Nor no covert may me keep,
  But ever I run from herne to herne!

'Hunters will not hear their Mass,
  In hope of hunting for to wend;
They couple their hounds more and less,
  And bring them to the fieldès end.
Raches run on every side,
  In furrows they hope me to find;
Hunters take their horses and ride,
  And cast the country by the wind.
Anon, as they come me behind,
  I look a-low, and sit full still and low.
The first man that me doth find
  Anon he crieth, "So ho! So ho!"
"Lo!" he saith, "where sitteth a hare!
  Arise up, Wat! and go forth belive!"

[1] From *The Dunbar Anthology* (ed. Prof. E. Arber), London, 1901.

With sorrow and with much care,
I 'scape away with my life!

'*At Winter, in the deep snow,*
Men will me seek for to trace;
And by my steps I am yknow,
And follow me from place to place.

'*And if I to the town come, or turn,*
Be it in worts or in leeks,
Then will the Wives also ye run,
Fear me with their dogs heyke.
And if I sit and crop the cole,
And the Wife be in the way,
Anon she will swear, "By cock's soul!
There is a hare in my hay!"[1]
Anon she will clepe forth her knave,
And look right well where I sit.
Behind she will, with a stave,
Full well purpose me to hit.
"Go forth, Wat! with CHRIST'*s curse!*
And if I live, thou shalt be take!
I have a hare-pipe in my purse;
It shall be set, all for thy sake!"
Then hath this Wife two dogs great,
On me she biddeth them go;
And as a shrew she will me threat,
And ever she crieth, "Go, dog! go!"
But always thus must I go!
By no bank I may abide!
Lord God! that me is woe!
Many a hap hath me betide!
There is no beast in the world, I ween,

---

[1] The hare's confession (three lines before) that he is nibbling in a field of cabbages appears to conflict with the wife's cry that he is in her hay. The probable explanation is that *hay* here is from the *O.E. haga* meaning a hedge (the medieval manorial officer the *hayward* or hedge-keeper was responsible for preventing animals from straying). *My hay* then is metonymy for my *yard*, my *enclosure* or *field*.

Hart, hind, buck, ne doe,
That suffers half so much teen
    As doth the silly Wat, go where he go!

'*If a Gentleman will have any game,*
    And find me in form, where I sit,
For dread of losing of his name,
    I wot well, he will not me hit!
For an acre's breadth, he will me see,
    Or he will let his hounds run.
Of all the men that be alive,
    I am most beholden to Gentlemen!

'*As soon as I can run to the Lay,*
    Anon the greyhounds will me have!
My bowels be ythrown away.
    And I am borne home on a staff.
As soon as I am coming home,
    I am yhung high up on a pin;
With leeks, worts, I am eat anon,
    And whelps play with my skin!
        Amen, &c.'

Anonymous

The Hare, to the Hunter[1]

Are mindes of men, become so voyde of sense,
That they can joye to hurte a harmelesse thing?
A sillie beast, whiche cannot make defence?
A wretche? a worme that can not bite, nor sting?
If that be so, I thanke my Maker than,
For makyng me, a Beast and not a Man.

The Lyon lickes the sores of wounded Sheepe,

---
[1] From *The Booke of Hunting.*

He spares to pray, whiche yeeldes and craveth grace:
The dead mans corps hath made some Serpentes weepe,
Such rewth may ryse in beasts of bloudie race:
And yet can man, (whiche bragges aboue the rest)
Vse wracke for rewth? can murder like him best?

   This song I sing, in moane and mourneful notes,
(Which fayne would blase, the bloudie minde of Man)
Who not content with Hartes, Hindes, Buckes, Rowes, Gotes,
Bores, Beares, and all, that hunting conquere can,
Must yet seeke out, me silly harmelesse Hare,
To hunte with houndes, and course sometimes with care.

   The Harte doth hurte (I must a trueth confesse)
He spoyleth Corne, and beares the hedge adowne:
So doth the Bucke, and though the Rowe seeme lesse,
Yet doth he harme in many a field and Towne:
The clyming Gote doth pill both plant and vine,
The pleasant meades are rowted up with Swine.

   But I poor Beast, whose feeding is not seene,
Who breake no hedge, who pill no pleasant plant:
Who stroye no fruite, who can turne up no greene,
Who spoyle no corne, to make the Plowman want:
Am yet pursewed with hounde, horse, might and mayne
By murdring men, untill they have me slayne.

   Sa how *sayeth one, as soone as he me spies,*
Another cries Now, Now, *that sees me starte,*
The houndes call on, with hydeous noyse and cryes,
The spurgalde Jade must gallop out his parte:
The horne is blowen, and many a voyce full shryll,
Do whoup and crie, me wretched Beast to kyll.

   What meanest thou man, me so for to pursew?
For first my skinne is scarcely worth a placke,
My fleshe is drie, and harde for to endew,

My greace (God knoweth) not great upon my backe,
My selfe, and all, that is within me founde,
Is neyther, good, great, ritche, fatte, sweete, nor sounde.

So that thou shewest thy vauntes to be but vayne,
That bragst of witte, above all other beasts,
And yet by me, thou neyther gettest gayne
Nor findest foode, to serve thy gluttons feasts:
Some sporte perhaps: yet Grevous is the glee
Which endes in Bloud, *that lesson learne of me.*

Anonymous

Glossary to the Poems

Belive: quickly.

Blase: (*Fr. blaser*) to dull or blunt the senses.

By cock: By God.

Clepe forth: call, summon.

Cole: name for various kinds of brassica.

Dearworth: dear, beloved.

Derne: secret.

Endew: (endue or endow) portion.

Gan: did.

Hare-pipe: a snare for catching hares.

Hay: here probably means hedge (i.e. 'in my field'), O.E. *haga*.

Herne: nook, hiding place.

Heyke (n): spring or leap; *heyke* (vb): pester (?).

Jade: a broken-down horse.

Lay: lair, couch, *form* or *seat* (of the hare).

Ne: nor.

Pill: rob or plunder.

Placke: a small copper coin formerly current in Scotland; worth about a third of an English penny.

Raches: (ratches) dogs that hunt by scent.

Rewth: (ruth) pity, compassion.

Rowes: (1) small, almost tailless deer found in the north of England and Scotland; (2) the female of the hart (roe).

Spurgalde: wounded or galled by the spur.

Stroye: destroy.

Teen: vexation, grief.

Than: then.

Ween: know.

Worts: vegetables, any plant of the cabbage kind.
Wracke: wreck, destruction.
Ydrive: driven.
Yhung: hung.
Yknow: known.
Ythrown: thrown.

Index

Page references to illustrations in the text are given in italic

Aberdeenshire, 34–5, 57
Aelianus, Claudius, 24
aerodromes, 28–32
Africa, 111, 150, 156, 175, 184, 190–3
Aldergrove, 28–9
Aldous, Master William, copybook of, *219*
Algonquin Indians, 15, 130, 178–9, *185*
America, North, 15, 111, 118, 129–30
Anatomy of Melancholy, The, 91
Anne, Queen, 81
Anson, P. F., 213
Antrim, 209, 220
Are mindes of men, become so voide of sense, 250
Argyllshire, 176
Aristotle, 24
Arminghall, 62
Arne, Antti, 230
Athlone, 83, 88
autumn, 136–41

Baker, Margaret, 174
Ballinahown, 44
Bannermore, 45
Barnes, William, 232
Barrett-Hamilton, G. E. H., 43, 45, 46, 48, 59, 60, 81, 177, 208, 211, 237, 242
baud, 34, 211
Bedd Gelert, 168, 171
Bede, Venerable, 132
Beeton, Mrs., 91, 93

Beinn A'Bhric, 176
Berllan Piter, Mari, 171–2
Bible, 26, 128–9, 152–3
Biddell, Herman, 73
Billson, C. J., 135
Bishop, R. H., 125
Blackwell, T. S., 45
Blake, William, plate 4
Bland, F. D., 209
Bleek, W. H. I., 117
Blickling, 166–7
Bloch, Von S., 24
Bloomfield, 230
Bloomfield, H. F., 206
blue hare, *see* mountain hare
Blythburgh, 23, 52, 80, 124
Boadicea, Queen, 97, 218
bogs, 46–7
Boke of St. Alban's, The, 61
Boleyn, Anne, 166–8
Bone, J. C. B. 235
Borlase, William, 218
boxing, 30, 47, 51–4
Bradley, George, 72
Brecknock Beacons, 40
Breconshire, 78, 84, 206
Bredon, Juliet, 115
breeding, 27, 53–4, 57–8
Brer Rabbit, 19, 192–3
Brewer, E. Cobham, 132, 214, 232
Brochwel Ysgythrog, 224
Brooke, 69, 235
Brookes, Stella Brewer, 192
brown hare, *see* common hare
Browne, Sir Thomas, 25, 100, 201, 220

Buckeragh, 157
Buddhism, 115–17, 121
Budge, E. A. Wallis, 197
Bunbury, Sir H., 74
Burton, Robert, 91–2
Butts, Mrs. Thomas, plate 4
By a forest as a I gan fare, 248

Caenarvonshire, 230
Caernarfon, 215
Caithness, 34–5
Callan, Pat, 90
calling hares, 80–1
Cambridgeshire, 57
Campbell, Joseph, 25
Cardiganshire, 171
catching hares, methods of, 80–
 90; *see also* hunting
Cato, 100
cave paintings, 18, 33, *59*, 60,
 104, 105–8, 144
Cawston, Mr., 67
Cecil, David, 242
Cefn Coed y Cymer, 84
Ceridwen, 226–7
charms, 170, 234–5
Chaturdanta, 114
Chesham, Lord, 74
Chillesford Lodge, 73
Chiming Hours (or *Chimes H*), 168
China, 14, 19, 111, 115–17, 231
Chippewa Indians, 150
circles, hares running in, 47–8;
 hares sitting in, 53–4
Claydon, 233
Clements, James, 166–8
Cobbett, William, 71–3, 75
Coelbren, 78, 206
colour variations, 20–1, 36–40, 49,
 50
Columba, Saint, 221–2
common hare, 20, 50–8; plate 3
Connaughton, John, 47, 86–8, 90,
 99–100, 137, 159, 161

Connemara, 48
cooking, 91–102, 210
Cornwall, 211, 214, 222
Cowper, William, 30, 207, 235,
 242–7
cows, hares milking, 150, 156–7
Cox, Harding, 48
Creirwy, 226
Crisp, Mr., 73
Crowley, Alesteir, 143
Cumberland, 211
Curraghboy, 97

Dafydd ap Gwilym, 200–1, 212
Dartmoor, 225
David II, coin of, plate 14
Davies, Evan William, 78–9, 206
Davies, Lynn, 84
Davies, Mansel, 40, 77–8
defence, 51–2
Delaney, James, 98
Déné Hareskins, 118, 121
Dent, Anthony A., 96
Devery, 87
Diana, 119, 154–5, 222
Dogon, 216, 217
dogs, hunting with, 60–1, 65–6,
 72, 82–5
Donegal, 45
Dordogne, 60, 144
Dorset, 100
Douglas, Mary, 216–17
Draycott, 209
Dürer, Albrecht, plate 18
Dyffryn Cellwen, 210

East Anglia, 13, 61, 62, 73, 74–5,
 92, 95, 112, 113, 125, 211
Easter, 132–6
Edward VII, King, 74
Egan, William, 42–3, 44–5, 46, 83,
 89
Egypt, Ancient, 14–15, *59*, 118,
 127–8, *127*; plates 5, 11, 16, 20

Enniskillen, Lord, 74
Eskimos, 147–8
Estrange, General l', 87
Evans, George Ewart, 96, 146, 168, 174, 222, 226
Evans, Noah, 84
Ewen, C. L'Estrange, 155
eyesight, 48

Falmouth, 222
Farndale, 164
feet, used as charms, etc., 170, 234–5
Fianna, 159–60
fighting, 30, 47, 51–4
fire, and the hare, 121–6, 233
Flesher, Walter, 53–4
Foix, Count Gaston de, 61
food, hare as, 91–102, 210
food and feeding habits, 26–7, 35
forms, 22–4, 35, 43–4, 52, 63
Fortescue, Captain, 74
Four Branches, 15
Fowler, W. W., 216
foxes, 90, 231
France, 137, 144
Frazer, Sir James, 97, 133, 137
Freud, Sigmund, 109
Frost, A. B., 19
fur, 38–9, 41–3, 49, 50

Gabillou, Le, 59, 60, 144
Galloway, 137
Galway, 160
Gana, S., 150
Garrard, George, 113, 236
Gate of Horn, The, 18
Gately, John, 97
Gellia, 92
Georgia, 193
Gerish, W. B., 123
Germany, 133, 137
Gerson, J. H. C., 232
Gibbons, J. S., 177

Giffard, George, 155
Gill, W. Walter, 236
Giraldus Cambrensis, 41
Glamorgan, 78, 84, 206, 210, 229
Glanffrwd, 227
Glooskap, 179–81
Go forth, Wat! with Christ's curse!, 81
Godric, Saint, 223
Gomme, G. L., 123
Granard, 98
Graves, Robert, 97, 221
Great Bricett, 170
Great Hare, 130, 178–81, *181*, 198
Greece, Ancient, 15, 25, 60, 133–4, 216; plates 6, 13
Guerber, H. A., 133
Gwion, 226–7

Haig, Douglas, Earl, 74
Halkett, Norman, 34–6, 52, 53, 218
Hallaton, 135–6
hare, blue, 20, 33–40; plates 2, 24; brown, 20, 50–8; plate 3; common, 20, 50–8; plate 3; Irish, 20, 29, 41–9; plate 1; Jade, 117; mountain, 20, 33–40; plates 2, 24
Hare, hare, God send thee care, 146
Hare, to the Hunter, The, 250–2
hare-holes, 89
hare-lips, 20, 220–1
Hare-Pie Scramble, 134, 135–6
hare-pipes, 81–2
Harepath, 210
Harmer, Arthur Edward, 23, 62–68, 71, 230
Harris, Joel Chandler, 192
Harting, James Edmund, 208
Hastings, James, 130, 134, 148, 154, 213
hawking, 60, 209
Hazlitt, Carew, 220

heart, 19–20
Helmingham, 80, 92, 93
Hermes, 197–8
Herring, Colonel, 67
Hethel, 62
Hewson, Raymond, 38, 57
hieroglyphics, *127*; plates 11, 16
Hippocrates, 24
Hokkei, Totoya, plate 10
Hokusai, K., plate 9
Holford, Captain, 74
Holland, 137
Holland, Madelaine, 187
Home, 220
Horseman's Word, 147
Horstead, 67
Hottentots, 117
Howard, M. M., 222
Hoyle, Fred, 216–17
Hunt, Robert, 166
hunting, 33, 59–79
Hupton, Albert, 68–71, 230
Huxley, Julian, 237

I sall goe intill ane haire, 146, 149
Idriess, Ion L., 87
Ifan, Beti, 168–9
Inagh, Lough, 48
increase, hare as symbol of, 127–41
India, 14, 111, 114–15
Indians, American, 15, 118, 129–30
Inverness-shire, 176
Iona, 222
Iopassvs, 130
Ipswich, 75
Ireland, 85–90, 95, 97, 108, 137–41, 150, 181–2, 229, 231
Ireland, Emily, 67
Irish hare, 20, 29, 41–9; plate 1
Isturitz, *104*, 144
Italy, 137

Jade Hare, 117
Jameson, Mr., 74
Jamieson, J., 149
Japan, 190; plates 9, 10, 19
Jeffreys, Howell, 78, 210, 229–30
Jenkins, D. E., 168
Jenner, Harold, 75–6, 125, 234
Johnston, Patrick, 42, 44, 83–4, 85, 86, 89–90
Jones, Dan, 171
Jones, John Ellis, 170
Jones, Robin Gwyndaf, 170
Jubilate Agno, 207
Jung, Carl, 16, 109
Junod, H. A., 152, 188, 192, 194, 197

Kenny, John, 82, 90, 99
Kenyon, Lord, 74
Kilbeggan, 157
Kilcummins, 158
Killrodawn, 158
Kilmanock, 48
King of Liars, The, 138–41
Kozanji, plate 19
Kudian, Mischa, 229
Kurten, Björn, 18

Lacock Abbey, plate 21
Lang, Andrew, 118
Larousse, 198
La Touche, Mr., 74
Layard, John, 14, 119, 121–3, 128, 143
League Against Cruel Sports, 71
Leamonaghan, 158
Lefebre, Henri, 209
Leicestershire, 134–6
Leitrim, 98
Leland, C. G., 179, 180
leporids, 18–19
lepus capensis, 20, 50–8; plate 3
lepus Europaeus, 20, 50–8; plate 3
lepus Sinensis, 117

lepus terraerubra, 18
lepus timidus Hibernicus, 20, 29, 41–9; plate 1
lepus timidus Scoticus, 20, 33–40; plates 2, 24
Lethbridge, T. C., 15
leverets, 22–4, 27, 45, 51–2, 55, 63–4
Levy, Rachel, 18, 104–7, 108
Linn, Loch, 158–9
lip, split, 20, 220–1
Little Glemham, 97–8
Livy, 216
Llanfyrnach, 40
Llanwynno, 227
Lloyd, H. G., 19, 57, 207
Lockley, R. M., 21
Lockwood, Phoebe, 92
Londonderry, Lord, 74
Long Melford, 226
Lower Machen, 170
Luxuria, 133; plate 15
Lyman, Charles Peirson, 39
Lynch, Tommy, 221

Mabinogi, 15, 226
McCormick, Michael, 88
Maesgwyn, 170
Mair, Lucy, 175
Man, Isle of, 228, 236
Man who encounters the hare, The, 203
Manabozho, 153–4
Mannion, Ned, 44
March hare, 48, 57, 76, 113
Martial, 92
Master of the Game, The, 61
mating, 27, 53–4, 57–8
Matthews, Cornelius, 198
mawkin, 34, 211
Mayo, 139–40
Melangell, Saint, 223–4
Mettingham, 68
Metz Pontifical, plate 8

Mexico, 111
Michabo, 130
Minnigaff, 137
Mitrophanov, Igor, 115
Montagu, Ivor, 237
Montgomeryshire, 223–5
moon, and the hare, 14, 111–20
Moray, 57
Morda, 226
Morfran, 226
Morgan, Guto, 227–8
Morris, Desmond, 19
Morris, May, 98
moulting, 38–9
mountain hare, 20, 33–40; plates 2, 24
Murray, Margaret, 142, 145–6, 155
Muttit, Percy, 23, 29, 51–2, 54–6, 80, 123, 230
Myaldus, 92
mythology, 14–17, 103–10, 111–20, 121–3, 127–34

Nairn, 36
Namaquas, 97
names, of the hare, 34, 200–12
Names of the Hare in English, The, 203–5
Nanhyfer, 173
Nawton, 164
Nebo, 170
Needham, Joseph, 199
Nerthus, 118
Nevern, 173
Newport, 173
Newton, John, 242
Noah, 129
noise, hares and, 29–30
Norfolk, 20, 62–71, 166, 211, 215, 230
Northumberland, 211
Norway, 137
Nyakusa, 175

Ochotonids, 18–19
O'Connor, W. F., 186
Oisín, 159–60
Oliphant, Colonel, 74
Opie, Iona, 233
Opie, Peter, 233
Oran, Saint, 222
O Súilleabháin, Seán, 138, 139, 141, 160, 184
Ovid, 83
Owen, Dwalad, 170
Oxfordshire, 61

Page, John, 88, 158–9
Paine, R. T., 190
palaeolithic man, 18, 33, *59*, 60, 104–9
Parker, Eric, 22, 61
Parry, Thomas, 200
Parsons, W. C., 166
Payne-Gallwey, Sir Ralph, 209
Pembrokeshire, 77–8, 173, 208, 230
Pennant, 171
Pennant Melangell, 223–4
Pepys, Samuel, 234–5
Peredur, 228–9
pets, hares as, 27–8, 238, 242–7
pikas, 18–19
Pisanello, plate 15
Plas y Ffynnon, 173
Pliny, 24, 38
Potter, Beatrix, 21–2
Powell, Ned, 84, 85
Powys, 224
protection, 21
proverbs, 231–3
Purnell, 210
Pythagoras, 97

Quinn, Johnnie, 221

rabbits, and hares, 18–20, 26–7
Radford, E., 128, 214
Radford, M. A., 128, 214

Reepham, 168
Rees, Rhys, 79
Rhys, Sir John, 228
Richard II, King, 81
Richards, Ben, 77–8
rings, hares going round in, 47–8; hares sitting in, 53–4
Rink, Henry, 147
Rodgers, W. R., 108
Rome, Ancient, 15, 216, 218; plate 7
Rondelius, 25
Roscommon, 46, 88, 97, 137
Rosenfeld, 59
Ross, Alan S. C., 95, 200, 201
Runeckles, Cecil, 170
Russia, 181, 233

sacrificial hares, 222
Saga of Sassoun, 229
St. Alban's Cathedral, plate 22
St. Leger-Gordon, Ruth, 225
St. Olaves, 75–6
Salle, 166–7, 168
Salmon, Lefi, 173
Sandford, Lord Mount, 88
Saxon hare-headed goddess, 118–19, 144
Schoolcraft, H. R., 150, 154, 178
Scotland, 34–6, 47, 49, 52–3, 176, 211, 218
sea-hare, 210–11
Seal Common, 72
seats, *see* forms
Sennybridge, 78, 79
sex, 24–5
Shamans, *151*, 153
Shakespeare, William, 211
Shilluk, 185–6
Shottisham, 62
Shrewsbury, 224
Silimukha, 114–15
Smart, Christopher, 207
snares, 81–2, 85

Somerville, William, 207
Soper, A., 190
Spain, 144
spring, 127–36
Stevenson, Burton, 232
Stowlangtoft Hall, 73–4
Stowupland, 236
Strachey, William, 132
Strutt, Joseph, 15
stuffed hares, 42–3
Sturlason, Snorri, 198
Sudan, 184, 216, 217
Suffolk, 52, 57, 62, 75–6, 112, 113, 123, 211, 234, 236
Suir, river, 48
superfoetation, 24
superstitions, 96–9, 213–21
Swabia, 134
Sweden, 137
swimming, 48–9
symbolism, 127–41

taboos, on hare-flesh, 96–9
Tacitus, 118
tame hares, *see* pets, hares as,
Taoism, 117, 154
Tapero, 185–6
Tawney, G. H., 114
Tebble, Archibald, 13, 80, 93
Tegid Foel, 226
Tegner, Henry, 24, 29, 51
Tempest, Lord H. Vane, 74
Teyjat, 144
Thetford, 20
Thomas, Joseph, 173
Thomas, Samuel, 173–4
Thompson, Joe, 92
Thompson, Stith, 230
Thompson, William, 46, 48, 49
Thongas, 150
Thorndon, 92
Threadkell, Stanley, 75
Throsby, John, 135

throwing-sticks, hunting hares with, 86–8, 157
Tibet, 186–7
Tinners' Rabbits, The, 225–6,
Topsell, Edward, 22–3, 25, 28
Tornewton, 18
Trefdraeth, 173
Trelech, 40
trickster, hare as, 178–99
Trois Frères, Les, 144
Turberville, George, 82

Ucko, P. J., 59
Udal, J. S., 100
Uncle Remus, 19, 192–3
Ungava, 148
United States, 15, 111, 118, 129–30

Verey, David, 225
Vesey-Fitzgerald, Brian, 60, 81
Victoria, Queen, 33
Vijaya, 114–15
Vincent, S. F., 31

Waddell, Helen, 223
Wakefield, Edward, 41, 45
Wales, 40, 76–9, 84, 85, 95, 168, 212, 223–4, 229, 231
Waley, Arthur, 150, 197
Walker, Ernest C., 19
wall paintings, 18, 33, 59, 60, 104, 105–8, 144
Wasis, 180–1
Waugh, James L., 31
Welling, Charles, 20, 27, 51, 56–7
Welsh Folk Museum, 84, 170, 229
Westermann, Diedrich, 185
Westleton Estate, 52
Wheatley, Henry B., 234
White, Gilbert, 237
Whybrow, Charles, 210
Widecombe, 225, 226
Williams, C. A. S., 117

Williams, Ifor, 226
Williams, Robert, 229
Wiltshire, 61
witches, 15, 119, 142–77
Witchingham Wild Life Park, 28
Wolpe, Berthold, 235
woods, 56–7

Wright, E. M., 211
Wu Ch'êng-ên, 197
Wyatt, Thomas, 166

Xenophon, 60

Yorkshire, 75, 164, 211